VOCABULARY SUCCESS

Third Edition

Murray Bromberg
Principal Emeritus,
Andrew Jackson High School

Cedric Gale
New York University

BARRON'S

All inquiries should be addressed to:
Barron's Educational Series, Inc.
250 Wireless Boulevard
Hauppauge, New York 11788

Library of Congress Catalog Card No. 97-27775
International Standard Book No. 0-7641-0311-3

Library of Congress Cataloging-in-Publication Data
Bromberg, Murray.
Vocabulary success/by Murray Bromberg, Cedric Gale—3rd ed.
     p. cm.
   ISBN 0-7641-0311-3
   1. Vocabulary.   I. Gale, Cedric, 1905–   II. Title.
PE1449.B673 1998
428.1—dc21   97-27775
                                                          CIP

PRINTED IN THE UNITED STATES OF AMERICA
9 8 7 6 5 4

CONTENTS

PREFACE

Vocabulary Success has long been recognized as a classic in its field. Now it has been streamlined and edited to make it even more valuable for those students and adults who wish to gain mastery of our language—for those smart people who wish to become even smarter.

This book helps the reader to develop a large store of words, and provides the skills to use those words effectively. It offers methods of studying words, dictionary use, development of the English language, pronunciation, word building with roots, prefixes, and suffixes, and idiomatic and effective use of words. Newly included is a useful sampler of computer and Internet terms, a selected list of troublesome spelling words, and an Answer Key.

The vocabulary presented here for study is wide, varied, and challenging. In addition to terms drawn from literature, foreign languages, history, mythology, and the Bible, we include a story by Mark Twain and essays by Jonathan Swift, James Fenimore Cooper, and James Thurber that are interesting for their content, choice of vocabulary, and references to language.

Vocabulary Success may be studied as a course. Proceeding from section to section, the reader will be able to learn the words and principles in each and then practice them by doing the exercises. Those who are preparing for college entrance examinations and scholarships will find this book to be especially helpful. In short, *Vocabulary Success* can assist you in moving up to a new level of language mastery.

1. THE POWER AND GLORY OF WORDS

(The words that appear in boldface in this section are featured in the vocabulary test and exercises that follow.)

THE MAGIC AND LOGIC OF WORDS

Man has always had great faith in the power of words. **Primitive** man believed that to know the name of an object was to know it and to control it. Hence, primitive peoples concealed their true name from an enemy to prevent the enemy gaining power over them. A **remnant** of this belief **survives** in the custom among some people of renaming a child who has narrowly escaped death. The relationship between naming and knowing is shown by our word *name*. It comes from the Latin *nomen*, which means in its primitive sense the thing by which an object is known. And *nomen* comes from *nosco* or *gnosco*, which means *to know*.

Myths, **fables, folklore,** and religious writings contain ample testimony to our faith in words. The proper word would open the door to a treasure or **invoke** a **genie** to do one's bidding. The spirit of a place was believed to reside in its name, and place names have contributed to the development of folklore and religion. Words were woven into **charms** and **incantations** to **propitiate** the deity and **exorcise** the devil. Even today, *hocus-pocus* and *abracadabra* are words used, perhaps with tongue in cheek, for **conjuring** tricks and incantations.

More **rational** faith in the power and range of words is shown by the development of the Greek symbol *lógos*, meaning *word*. It comes from *légo*, which means, among other things, *to lay, to lay in order, to reckon* and *to say or speak*. To lay words in order is therefore to speak. Hence *lógos* also means *speech* and *inner speech* or *thought*. Indeed, many philosophers maintain that without speech we could not think.

WORDS IN THE ANCIENT WORLD

The Greeks were the greatest thinkers of the **ancient** world. They investigated man, nature, and the gods, and they recorded their observations and deductions in glorious language that has resounded through the ages. Homer's words have **immortalized** the heroic age of Greece. Aeschylus and Sophocles gave **lofty** expression to a tragic view of life that relates **finite** man to the infinite **cosmos.** And it is through the power and beauty of language that Plato's philosophy has helped to shape the thought of western people.

Because the Greeks treasured their language, they honored those who spoke it and wrote it with distinction. In the competitive games and **festivals** that the Greeks loved dearly, the **laurel** for **declamation,** poetry, and tragedy was as enthusiastically **coveted** and contested as the prize for victory in the athletic contests. Youths were nurtured on Homer's words and trained in **rhetoric** to prepare them for public life. Among the fruit of this nurture were the brilliant statesmen, like Draco, Solon, and Demosthenes, whose leadership was in large measure due to their skill in oratory.

The Romans, like the Greeks whom they **emulated,** also had great confidence in the power of words and speech. The education of a Roman youth was almost exclusively in rhetoric, for the **persuasive** use of language was thought to be the best preparation for the highest of callings, a

1

career in public service. Seneca wrote his plays, not as stage vehicles, but as school exercises in elocution. Julius Caesar was a statesman, general, orator, and historian who courted the multitude and wrote his account of the Gallic wars with as much care as he waged a campaign. And in his orations Cicero was as passionately concerned with the eloquence of expression as he was with the **advocacy** of a cause. From a rather clumsy and **intractable** popular language, Cicero, Ovid, Horace, Virgil, and others wrought a literary language, **refined,** eloquent, and subtle, that was the international medium of communication through the Dark and Middle Ages and into the Renaissance.

The Universal Concern for Words

Everywhere in every civilized era people have been deeply concerned with language. They have labored to preserve it from **contamination** and **corrosion,** to develop it, and to refine it. This concern for language is best **exemplified** by the French Academy, which was founded in 1635 by Cardinal Richelieu. Since its founding, one of its principal functions has been the **compilation** and the constant revision of a dictionary of the French language. The Academy also expresses its approval and disapproval of literary works, and a work that it approves is said to be "crowned." Membership in the Academy is made up of forty writers who are elected because they write the French language with distinction.

During the eighteenth century there were a number of attempts to found an English academy that would preserve and regulate the English language. Jonathan Swift, the **satirist,** put forth a vigorous proposal for an English academy, but it came to naught. Nevertheless, many **treatises** on the English language appeared in the eighteenth century, the foremost being Samuel Johnson's *Dictionary*, the first English dictionary to be compiled on modern principles of **lexicography**.

Words and Leadership

In every age forceful leadership has been exercised through forceful words; creative thought has been creatively expressed. **Random** examples come readily to mind. Jesus preached in **parables** and drew the multitude after him. The pulpit was the **fulcrum** on which Savonarola turned the moral life of Florence. Because of its powerful **exposition** of **statecraft,** Machiavelli's *The Prince* became the European handbook for political action. It is memorable language that molds and recommends the philosophy of Locke and Hume, Schopenhauer and Nietzsche, the scientific and mathematical thought of Newton and Darwin, and the psychology of Freud. In the more active realm of political conflict, words have determined the course of nations. Thomas Paine's *The Rights of Man* **precipitated** the American Revolution, and Harriet Beecher Stowe's *Uncle Tom's Cabin* hastened the Civil War, a conflict that **abolitionist** oratory had made inevitable.

In recent years we have seen how words can arouse nations. Italy and Germany were **seduced** and **perverted** by the oratory of **demagogues**. With ringing words, Franklin Delano Roosevelt rallied the American people from depression and won the presidency again and again and again. The most powerful weapon in the **ideological** warfare against Nazism was the eloquence of Thomas Mann's **indictment** of Hitler's savagery in a pamphlet titled *An Exchange of Letters*. And it was the voice of Winston Churchill that rallied the English to victory in the Battle of Britain.

The Dominance of Words Today

Although we no longer believe in the magical power of words, our faith in words has not otherwise diminished. On the contrary, it has increased. We use far more words than were ever used before and we use them in more ways and for more complex purposes. We are **inundated** and overwhelmed by words. We swim in a sea of **verbiage** streaming from the mass media of communication—the press, radio, films, and television. We are entertained by words, instructed and conditioned by words, **exhorted** and **cajoled** by them, depressed and damned by them, exalted and saved by them. Today we must therefore know a great many words, for words are the armory of contemporary life.

PRACTICAL REASONS FOR KNOWING WORDS

A few moments of reflection will reveal many practical reasons why we must know words. Education depends largely on them. Students must know words in order to understand their teachers and texts. They must also have a command of words in order to write clearly on examinations and reports. The outstanding students are the students who know a subject and who have the ability to express their knowledge in well-chosen, logically **articulated** words.

In business and the professions a knowledge of words is essential to success. To begin with, job seekers must be able to write persuasive letters of application in order to get an interview. And at the interview they must be able to speak correctly and confidently in order to get the job. With a good command of words, a business person and a professional person will be able to write impressive letters and reports and to speak forcefully and persuasively. As a rule, the leaders in business and the professions are educated people with a good command of words.

A knowledge of words is also necessary for enjoyment and personal fulfillment. The more words we understand, the more we enjoy conversation. We listen with pleasure to the play of words; we delight in the **badinage**; we understand and catch every **implication**. Moreover, we can join in the conversation with delight in our own wit and **erudition**.

Familiarity with words also increases our appreciation of other activities and pastimes. We can read with increased comprehension and extract from a book all the riches it has to yield, the deeper meanings, the **nuances** and subtleties of subject and language, and the artistry of composition that make reading a delight. In the same way we garner a full harvest of knowledge and pleasure from plays, films, and television programs. Indeed, as we improve our vocabulary we increase our understanding and enjoyment of every activity that is dependent upon words or accompanied by them.

THE INCREASING IMPORTANCE OF WORDS

At the present time the importance of knowing words and of speaking and writing with proficiency is being emphasized with increasing vigor. Schools, including graduate schools and technical institutes, are demanding that their applicants have more and better preparation in the language arts. Moreover, these schools are requiring students to take an increased amount of instruction in speaking and writing. A vocabulary test is a standard part of all qualifying examinations for colleges, for positions in civil service and many businesses, and for license to practice many professions. Spokesmen for business and industry are now declaring that the ability to speak and write is even more important to them than ability in technical matters. And finally, a number of vocabulary studies made in recent years have shown that there is a high degree of **correlation** between the size of one's vocabulary and success in life, regardless of how success is defined.

In the face of this evidence it is impossible for anyone to doubt the **efficacy** of a strong vocabulary. A knowledge of words and the ability to speak and write with proficiency are essential to one's intellectual development, achievement, and enjoyment. So equipped, people can face life, confident that they will make the most of their abilities.

VOCABULARY

PRELIMINARY TEST

Each of the numbered words appears in Chapter 1, "The Power and Glory of Words." Without consulting your dictionary, find the term that is most nearly synonymous with the numbered word and write the letter in the space to the right.

EXAMPLE

faith
a. confidence   b. obligation   c. fortune   d. hope

a

---

1. *primitive*
   a. crude   b. provincial   c. early   d. proper

2. *survives*
   a. lives on   b. belongs   c. clings   d. hovers

3. *myths*
   a. legendary stories   b. falsehoods   c. collective beliefs   d. proverbs

4. *fables*
   a. true stories   b. prayers   c. moral tales   d. recipes

5. *folklore*
   a. popular art   b. traditional beliefs   c. ballads   d. scrolls

6. *invoke*
   a. force   b. irritate   c. call forth   d. wake up

7. *genie*
   a. Mohammedan spirit   b. slave   c. magician   d. Greek athlete

8. *charms*
   a. trinkets   b. fascination   c. magic formulas   d. candies

9. *incantations*
   a. hymns   b. magical chanting   c. practices   d. descriptions

10. *propitiate*
    a. appease   b. anger   c. worship   d. instruct

11. *exorcise*
    a. physically exhaust   b. enslave   c. expel by ceremonies   d. annoy

12. *conjuring*
    a. harmful   b. verbal   c. magical   d. bodily

13. *rational*
    a. limited   b. reasonable   c. hasty   d. partial

14. *immortalized*
    a. thrilled   b. lauded   c. destroyed   d. perpetuated

15. *finite*
a. completed   b. limited   c. definite   d. curious

16. *cosmos*
a. a flower   b. universe   c. populace   d. atmosphere

17. *festivals*
a. races   b. religious fasts   c. holidays   d. religious feasts

18. *laurel*
a. emblem of victory   b. tree or shrub   c. praise   d. opportunity

19. *declamation*
a. exercise in oratory   b. discus throwing   c. refutation   d. choral music

20. *coveted*
a. regarded   b. witnessed   c. eagerly desired   d. donated

21. *rhetoric*
a. poetics   b. art of language   c. politics   d. philosophy

22. *emulated*
a. envied   b. despised   c. imitated   d. overcame

23. *advocacy*
a. advancement   b. espousal   c. explanation   d. preparation

24. *intractable*
a. impoverished   b. unrefined   c. unmanageable   d. irritating

25. *contamination*
a. disease   b. impurity   c. degeneration   d. weakness

26. *corrosion*
a. being torn apart   b. softening   c. being eaten away   d. stiffening

27. *exemplified*
a. shown by exception   b. explained   c. illustrated by example
d. pictured

28. *satirist*
a. believer in satyrs   b. pagan   c. writer of satires   d. a dandy

29. *lexicography*
a. law of words   b. movable type   c. writing of dictionaries
d. rules of pronunciation

30. *random*
a. obvious   b. haphazard   c. ready   d. numerous

31. *parables*
a. simple words   b. allegorical stories   c. puzzles   d. short prayers

32. *fulcrum*
a. pivot   b. subject   c. point of attack   d. support for a lever

33. *exposition*
a. exposure   b. explanation   c. recommendation   d. condemnation   _____

34. *statecraft*
a. art of government   b. politics   c. treason   d. despotic rule   _____

35. *precipitated*
a. hastened   b. caused   c. delayed   d. changed   _____

36. *abolitionist*
a. radical   b. destructive of slavery   c. justifying slavery
d. critical of slavery   _____

37. *seduced*
a. misled   b. confused   c. weakened   d. corrupted   _____

38. *perverted*
a. baffled   b. destroyed   c. led astray   d. inflamed   _____

39. *demagogues*
a. social democrats   b. unprincipled leaders   c. dictators   d. terrorists   _____

40. *ideological*
a. of a body of doctrines   b. speculative   c. of popular opinions
d. philosophical   _____

41. *indictment*
a. passionate rejection   b. legal brief   c. moral attack   d. formal charge   _____

42. *inundated*
a. flooded   b. swept away   c. made dizzy   d. covered   _____

43. *verbiage*
a tangled words   b. abundance of useless words   c. unusual words
d. misused words   _____

44. *exhorted*
a. urged   b. praised   c. taught   d. soothed   _____

45. *cajoled*
a. petted   b. flattered   c. coaxed   d. calmed   _____

46. *articulated*
a. clearly expressed   b. well chosen   c. distinct   d. related and joined   _____

47. *badinage*
a. argument   b. word games   c. banter   d. insults   _____

48. *erudition*
a. superiority   b. acquired knowledge   c. huge vocabulary   d. courtesy   _____

49. *nuances*
a. new meanings   b. shades of meaning   c. expressions of hope
d. verbal beauties   _____

50. *efficacy*
a. usefulness   b. desirability   c. effectiveness   d. power   _____

EXERCISE 1

USING WORDS IN CONTEXT

All of the words in this exercise appear in the essay you have just read. From the words in the box below find the one that can be properly substituted for the expression in parentheses in each of the following sentences. Write the word in the space to the right.

nuance	advocacy	ideological	contamination	correlation	immortalize
intractable	compilation	inundated	verbiage	efficacy	random
exorcise	lexicographer	articulate	cajole	survive	parables
covet	treatises	erudition	badinage	conjure	
emulate	demagogue				

1. Lacking (shades of expression), the performance was wooden. _____

2. The (putting together) of the data took weeks. _____

3. Be careful to (utter the syllables of the words) clearly. _____

4. Myra impressed all with a dazzling display of (wide and profound knowledge). _____

5. The (hit-and-miss) efforts were bound to fail. _____

6. Noah Webster was an American (editor of a dictionary). _____

7. Do you (desire to possess) that ring? _____

8. The idea is buried in a tangle of (many unnecessary words). _____

9. It is thought that few will (live on after) a nuclear war. _____

10. The climax of the play is the attempt to (drive out with prayers) the dybbuk. _____

11. This school is operated especially for (hard-to-manage) children. _____

12. Why don't you (try to be like) your uncle? _____

13. He is known for the (supporting and recommending) of unpopular causes. _____

14. The American (popular leader and agitator) Huey Long was assassinated. _____

15. The differences between America and the former Soviet Union were more than (of bodies of doctrines). _____

16. Buddy used all his skill in an attempt to (wheedle and flatter) his father into raising his allowance. _____

17. Ken took the (playfully teasing conversation) seriously. _____

18. Physicians doubt the (helpfulness) of chiropractic adjustments. _____

19. The library contains several (formal and methodical studies) on inflation and inflationary spirals. _____

20. In the spring the river rose and (spread over) the entire valley. _____

21. The preacher illustrated his message with (short, simple stories). _____

22. The reservoir is carefully guarded in order to keep the water safe from (being made impure). _____

23. We doubt that there is any (mutual relationship) between education and tolerance. _____

24. The gods sometimes tried to (bestow unending life on) a mortal. _____

25. The natives believed that their witch doctor could (raise and call) up evil spirits. _____

2. WAYS OF MASTERING WORDS

Words, both written and spoken, are arbitrary symbols, meaningless in themselves, that are used to name things. The things named are called referents. The meaning and referent of pear, for example, is the fruit itself. A referent may be a person, an object, a quality, an act, a sensation, or a relationship. The meaning of a word is always its referent, the object it names.

Children learn words by connecting them with their referents. Mother repeats the name nose while pointing to that organ, and baby soon learns the word. Similarly he learns the meaning of no by relating it to a stern voice and an admonitory gesture. Thus vocabulary grows from experience. In this way we have all acquired thousands of words without trying.

Unfortunately, this way of learning words has several defects. It restricts the vocabulary of many people to a narrow range of experience. It works rapidly in youth and the floodtime of experience, but tends to dry up as the mind becomes stocked with knowledge and the pace of learning slackens. It is far more effective for words meaning physical objects (concrete words) than for words meaning ideas, qualities, relationships, and the like (abstract words). Also, a vocabulary acquired in this way is likely to contain many words that are vaguely known or misunderstood.

To remedy these defects in a vocabulary randomly acquired, you should make a deliberate attempt to improve your command of words. The desired improvement is of two kinds: (1) a fuller, more precise understanding of words, and (2) the acquisition of new and useful words. The purpose of vocabulary study is to increase the understanding of the spoken and written word and to develop the ability to communicate effectively.

The conscious learning of words reverses the natural process of learning them, for when you learn a word, you learn a fact. Therefore, increasing your vocabulary develops your awareness of people and things. Vocabulary improvement leads to self-improvement and personal growth.

The deliberate learning of words is not easy. Words are arbitrary, capricious symbols; they are elusive, contradictory, and bewildering. Unbidden, they come to us naturally and easily, but they resist being forced. Nevertheless, words will yield to anyone who makes the effort to cultivate them.

WAYS OF STUDYING WORDS

There is no simple way of learning words. Vocabulary study must begin with an interest in words and must be diligently pursued in the following ways:

1. *A brief study of the origin, development, and nature of the English language.*

Knowledge of this kind provides helpful information about words themselves and especially about how they are related to form a system of communication.

2. *A study of the origins and development of words.*

English words have been acquired in different ways: (1) by borrowing from other languages, (2) by combining or shortening words already in the language, (3) by combining word elements in English or from other languages, and (4) by using the names of persons, places, and commercial products. Words also change in form, pronunciation, and meaning. A knowledge of the patterns of origin and change helps one to acquire words, to understand their meaning and behavior, and to avoid pitfalls in using them.

3. *A study of the use of words.*

Words are used literally, idiomatically, and figuratively. They exist on various levels of usage and are limited to various areas of meaning. In addition to knowing what words mean, one must know how they are used. To be correctly used, words must be appropriate, consistent, and idiomatic.

4. *A study of the pronunciation, spelling, and inflectional forms of words.*

One should, of course, learn to spell and pronounce words as they are acquired. Spelling and pronouncing words will help in remembering them. One must also learn how new words are inflected for number, case, and person.

In the following sections of this text, these ways of learning words are explained in logical order and are applied to words that every educated person should know. You should study the words and principles explained in each section. You should then do the accompanying exercises in order to apply your knowledge and fix it in your mind. In this way you will improve and enlarge your vocabulary. In this way, also, you will learn techniques of mastering words. The greatest benefit of a course in vocabulary study is not the number of words learned, but the ability to learn them and to use them effectively.

THE WORDS TO LEARN

Even in a lifetime it is impossible for anyone to learn more than a small number of the words in our language. Therefore you should learn the words you need to know in order to communicate with friends and acquaintances, to practice your trade or profession, to pursue a chosen course of study, and to develop the knowledge, taste, and appreciation of a cultured individual.

The choice of words to be learned should be governed by the following principles:

1. *Concentrate on words that are partially known.*

Everyone has an active vocabulary and a passive or recognition vocabulary. The active vocabulary consists of words that are known and used. The passive vocabulary consists of words that are recognized because they have been encountered before. One may even have a general notion of what they mean. However, they are not actually known and do not readily spring to the tongue or pen.

Students seeking to improve their vocabularies should concentrate on these passive words. They are words that they encounter and therefore need to know and use in order to express ideas. If passive words are already partially known, they can be learned quickly. Activating inactive words is the quickest and easiest way of improving vocabulary.

2. *Learn words useful now or in the near future.*

The purpose of learning words is to increase one's effectiveness in present activities. Words needed for the future should be learned then. Words learned before they can be used are quickly forgotten. Premedical students, for example, should master the vocabulary of their courses in biology rather than the vocabulary of an advanced medical course in pathology.

3. *College preparatory students should learn words that appear on qualifying tests.*

Language is a part of the college board examinations, the standard tests, and the qualifying tests for scholarships in various fields of study.

4. *Learn only those special and technical words that are in general use.*

Concentrate on learning medical, legal, nautical, and other specialized terms that are in general use. Examples: *tort, galley, cardiograph.*

LEARNING WORDS FROM LISTS

Word lists can be helpful. They present words students should know and they lead them gradually to higher levels of difficulty. Thus, students can save time by passing quickly from familiar words to unfamiliar ones and concentrating on them.

Nevertheless, studying word lists is not a satisfactory way of learning words. A list presents words out of context; each word has to be looked up in a dictionary and memorized. The task is slow, tedious, and dull, deadening rather than stimulating. Without a guiding context, students must study each word with extraordinary care and find examples of its use. A word list is helpful as a guide and a check, but it is otherwise of little use as a learning device.

THE IMPORTANCE OF STUDYING WORDS IN CONTEXT

Words should be studied in context. Consider the following sentences:

No one knows who made the *radical* error. [*Radical* means original or fundamental.]
The internist hopes to avoid *radical* surgery. [*Radical* means involving a vital organ.]
He proposed a number of *radical* changes in the sales department. [*Radical* means far-reaching or extreme.]
In his youth he joined two *radical* clubs. [*Radical* means revolutionary.]
The biography exposes the *radical* defects in his character. [*Radical* means existing inherently in a person.]

Besides these meanings in general use, *radical* has meanings in mathematics, chemistry, grammar, botany, and music. *Radical* may also be used as a noun with various general and special meanings.

Like *radical*, thousands of words have several meanings, and no word means precisely the same thing twice. Instead of asking, "What does this word mean?" we should ask, "What does this word mean in this passage?" Or better yet, "What does this word contribute to the meaning of this passage?" We know a word only when we know how it affects the meaning of a passage and how it helps to convey a thought. The way to learn words properly is to learn them in context.

The context illuminates the meaning of the word, shows its use, and impresses it on the mind. Consider the sentence:

> In its communiqué of December 16, the Pentagon released some details of the attack on the terrorists' stronghold.

As it is used here, communiqué means some sort of statement; it is official; and it pertains to the military; thus, the sentence almost explains the word.

From a study of context, we also learn the idiomatic use of words. We learn, for example, that the verb *differ* is used with the prepositions *from* and *with*.

> I *differ with* you about the reliability of these statistics. [*Differ with* expresses disagreement in opinion.]

> How does the new contract *differ from* the old one? [*Differ from* is used to contrast things.]

Context may also show that a word is applicable to one class of referents, but not to another. For example, *amoral* (without moral quality) may be applied to the universe, but never to a mountain. In some senses *mundane* and *worldly* are synonymous. However, a person can lose all of his *worldly* goods, but not his *mundane* goods.

THE ART OF DEFINITION

Definition is explaining a word in other words. It is a difficult art that requires care, skill, and practice. A definition must be precise, lucid, and illuminating. To possess these qualities a definition must observe the following principles:

A Definition Must Not Contain the Word Being Defined or a Cognate Form of It

UNSATISFACTORY: *Hospitable* means receiving guests in a *hospitable* manner.
IMPROVED: *Hospitable* means affording a generous welcome to guests or strangers.
UNSATISFACTORY: *Mendacity* is the quality of being *mendacious*.
IMPROVED: *Mendacity* is the quality of being false or untrue.

The Terms of a Definition Must Be Simpler, More Concrete, and More Familiar than the Word Being Defined

UNSATISFACTORY: *Sophistry* is *casuistical* reasoning. [What is *casuistical* reasoning?]
IMPROVED: *Sophistry* is sharp, tricky, false reasoning.
UNSATISFACTORY: To *scheme* is to engage in *intrigue*. [*Intrigue* is less common and more abstract than *scheme*.]
IMPROVED: To *scheme* is to take part in an underhand plot.

A Definition Must Be Developed Sufficiently to Explain the Term

A synonym or a brief phrase may be used if it does not omit essential qualities or qualifications of the term being defined. The following words are adequately defined:

> *Rapidly* means *quickly*.
> A *casket* is a *coffin*. [If this is the intended meaning of *casket*.]
> *Fatal* means causing death or destruction.
> *Pliant* means bending readily.

However, many words must be defined at some length so that they are completely and precisely explained. A definition must not omit important distinctions or qualifications.

INCOMPLETE:	*To halt* is *to stop.* [But *to stop* is not always *to halt.*]
IMPROVED:	*To halt* is to make a temporary stop, as in marching, etc.
INCOMPLETE:	A *platter* is a dish. [A *cup* is also a *dish*, but it is not a *platter*.]
IMPROVED:	A *platter* is a large, shallow dish, usually oval, for serving.
INCOMPLETE:	A *metamorphosis* is a *change.* [Not all *changes* are *metamorphoses.*]
IMPROVED:	A *metamorphosis* is a complete change in form, structure, substance, character, appearance, etc.

A Word Should Be Defined, Whenever Possible, as It Is Used in a Specific Context

| CONTEXT: | In question four of our theory test we were asked to find the *radical* in each of five chords. |
| DEFINITION: | In music *radical* is a noun meaning the root or base tone of a chord. |

Defining a word in context has the advantage of clarifying and reducing the task of definition. If a word is isolated, which of several general meanings should be given, or should all be given? Or should a special meaning be given? Should *effect*, for example, be defined as a noun, a verb, or both?

Tests may call for the definition of isolated words. If so, the examinee should state in what sense he or she is defining the word. The following illustrations show how a definition can be limited.

WORD	DEFINITION
effect	*Effect* (n.) is a result or a consequence. [*Effect* is designated and defined as a noun.]
chivalrous	In its original sense *chivalrous* (adj.) means having the ideal qualifications of a medieval knight such as courage, courtesy, generosity, etc. [The original meaning of *chivalrous* is specified.]
covenant	In Biblical usage *covenant* (n.) means the agreement of God with man as set forth in the Old and the New Testament. [The Biblical meaning is specified.]
or	In ecclesiastical use *covenant* (n.) means the solemn agreement between the members of a church, as that they will act together in harmony with the precepts of the gospel. [The ecclesiastical meaning is specified.]

A Definition Should Be Accompanied by an Illustrative Sentence

An illustrative sentence clarifies a definition. Care must be taken to see that the sentence really illustrates.

UNSATISFACTORY:	She could not bear to look at the *cadaver.* [A *cadaver* might be anything, an insect for example.]
IMPROVED:	When he was given the arm of a *cadaver* to dissect, the medical student nearly fainted. [The sentence implies that a *cadaver* is a dead human body.]
UNSATISFACTORY:	He told a *ribald* story. [*Ribald* might mean funny, short, or other qualities.]
IMPROVED:	He told a *ribald* story that made both the men and women present blush with shame and embarrassment. [*Ribald* must mean coarse and offensive.]

A Word Must Be Defined, Labelled, and Illustrated as the Same Part of Speech

That is, a word must not be defined as a noun, for example, but labelled and used as an adjective or a verb.

WRONG: *Provincial* (adj.) means showing the manners characteristic of inhabitants of a province.

ILLUSTRATION: When the *provincial* first saw Paris, he was dumb with amazement. [*Provincial* is labelled as adjective, defined as an adjective, but used a noun.]

RIGHT: *Provincial* (adj.) means showing the manners characteristic of inhabitants of a province.

ILLUSTRATION: By his *provincial* speech anyone could tell that he was not a Parisian. [*Provincial* is labelled, defined, and illustrated as an adjective.]

A Definition Should Begin by Assigning the Word to its Proper Group or Class

The first step in definition is to classify the term. For example, a *sonnet* is a poem. Thus, classifying *sonnet* separates it from all other kinds of objects and places it in the class of poems.

The next step is to explain how a *sonnet* differs from all other kinds of poems. The task of definition will be easier if the word *sonnet* is immediately placed in the narrowest possible group. For example: A *sonnet* is a short lyrical poem of fourteen lines. Now *sonnet* need be distinguished only from other short lyrical poems that happen to contain fourteen lines.

The initial step of classification applies to all definition. Properly classifying words at the outset simplifies the task of definition by starting it off correctly. Once properly started, a definition is likely to proceed accurately. The following examples will serve as illustrations:

NOUNS

A *sycophant* is *one who*, or *a person who* _____

Trepidation is the *emotion of* _____

Recrimination is the *act of* _____

Simony is the *practice of* _____

Magnitude is the *condition of* _____

Astonishment is the *state* or *condition of* _____

VERBS

Peregrinate means *to travel* _____

Bifurcate means *to divide* _____

ADJECTIVES

Multiple means *consisting of, having* _____

Dictatorial means *of or pertaining to* _____

Reverent means *characterized by* _____

Bovine means *like, having the qualities of* _____

Sorrowful means *sad.* [An adjective defined by another adjective.]

ADVERBS OF MANNER

Capably means *in an intelligent, competent manner* or *way.*

Patently means *openly, obviously.* [Defined by other adverbs.]

Sympathetically means *compassionately,* or *in a compassionate manner.*

KEEPING A VOCABULARY NOTEBOOK

Keeping a vocabulary notebook can be helpful to anyone who is conscientiously trying to improve his or her vocabulary. The act of entering, defining, and illustrating words is a formal, thoughtful discipline that aids the understanding and memory. The notebook is a record of study, an index to past learning, and a guide to future learning. A list of words drawn overwhelmingly from the arts, for example, reveals the desirability of rounding out the vocabulary with words from other fields.

The vocabulary notebook is useful for review. You can restudy words a few at a time. In this way you methodically refresh your memory and prevent words from slipping away.

To be useful, the entries in a vocabulary notebook should be full enough to be meaningful, but not so full as to be burdensome. The following form is suggested as one that avoids both extremes:

WORD protagonist	PART OF SPEECH n.	PRONUNCIATION prō tăg′ ō nĭst	
MEANING	(1) The principal character in a poem, play, or story. (2) One who espouses or champions a cause.		
SENTENCES	(1) Since Leopold Bloom is depicted as a modern hero, he is the *protagonist* of Joyce's *Ulysses*. (2) In the worldwide struggle against tyranny, Woodrow Wilson was the *protagonist* of freedom.		
SYNONYMS champion hero		**ANTONYMS** antagonist opponent	

A vocabulary list may be kept on index cards, preferably 4 x 6, for sufficient space. Index cards have the advantage of being more flexible than a notebook. The cards may be alphabetized or classified in any other way. For study, cards may be readily withdrawn from the file and returned. Blank cards may be carried in the pocket, available for posting an entry. Later the card can be completed and filed.

A good method of studying from cards is to write the word on one side and the full entry on the other. You can then take a group of cards and place them face down. If you can define and use the word, put the card aside and take the next. If you do not know the word, turn the card over, study the entry, and then put the card on the bottom of the group you are studying. You can continue to study in this way until you have learned and discarded all of the cards in the group.

The disadvantage of a file of cards is that it can become bulky and space consuming. The cards may become disarranged or scattered and lost. The notebook has the advantage of being confined and compact. Since there are advantages and disadvantages to both methods of keeping a vocabulary list, you should decide which method is most convenient for you.

EXERCISE 2

DEFINING WORDS IN CONTEXT

The following excerpts have been selected from the text of "Ways of Mastering Words." In the space provided write the part of speech and definition of each boldface word as it is used in the phrase. Then use the word in a sentence of your own.

Suggestion: if you cannot define the word even after seeing it in context, consult your dictionary for its meaning.

1. Words...are **arbitrary** symbols.

   Part of speech _____ Definition _____

   Sentence _____

2. A referent may be a person, an object, a **sensation**...

   Part of speech _____ Definition _____

   Sentence _____

3. Similarly he learns the meaning of *no* by relating it to...an **admonitory** gesture.

   Part of speech _____ Definition _____

   Sentence _____

4. Similarly he learns the meaning of *no* by relating it to ... an admonitory **gesture**.

   Part of speech _____ Definition _____

   Sentence _____

5. It is far more difficult for words meaning physical objects (**concrete** words)...

   Part of speech _____ Definition _____

   Sentence _____

6. It is far more effective for words meaning physical objects...than for words meaning ideas... (**abstract** words).

   Part of speech _____ Definition _____

   Sentence _____

7. To remedy these defects in a vocabulary **randomly** acquired...

   Part of speech _____ Definition _____

   Sentence _____

8. Words are arbitrary, capricious **symbols**...

   Part of speech _____ Definition _____

   Sentence _____

9. They [words] are **elusive**...

Part of speech _____ Definition _____

Sentence _____

10. Nevertheless, words will yield to anyone who will make the effort to **cultivate** them.

Part of speech _____ Definition _____

Sentence _____

11. Vocabulary study...must be **diligently** pursued...

Part of speech _____ Definition _____

Sentence _____

12. Words are used **literally**...

Part of speech _____ Definition _____

Sentence _____

13. Words are used...**idiomatically**.

Part of speech _____ Definition _____

Sentence _____

14. Words are used...**figuratively**.

Part of speech _____ Definition _____

Sentence _____

15. In this way, also, you will learn **techniques** of mastering words.

Part of speech _____ Definition _____

Sentence _____

16. Premedical students...should master the vocabulary of their courses in biology rather than the vocabulary of...**pathology**.

Part of speech _____ Definition _____

Sentence _____

17. In general use they (big words) often seem **ostentatious**.

Part of speech _____ Definition _____

Sentence _____

18. Everyone has...a **passive** or recognition vocabulary.

Part of speech _____ Definition _____

Sentence _____

19. The task is...deadening rather than **stimulating**.

Part of speech _____ Definition _____

Sentence _____

20. Without a guiding **context**, a student must study each word with...care.

Part of speech _____ Definition _____

Sentence _____

21. However, a person can lose all his worldly goods, but not his **mundane** goods.

Part of speech _____ Definition _____

Sentence _____

22. The notebook has the advantage of being ...**compact**.

Part of speech _____ Definition _____

Sentence _____

23. To scheme is to engage in **intrigue**.

Part of speech _____ Definition _____

Sentence _____

24. Language is a part of ... the standard **aptitude** tests.

Part of speech _____ Definition _____

Sentence _____

25. The task is slow, **tedious**, and dull.

Part of speech _____ Definition _____

Sentence _____

3. THE DICTIONARY

Because the dictionary is an indispensable tool for the study of language, everyone should be able to use it efficiently. Although schools teach the use of the dictionary and most people refer to it frequently, many of them use it haphazardly and ineptly. The purpose of this section is to explain what a dictionary is and how to use it efficiently.

THE DICTIONARY AND WHAT IT CONTAINS

The dictionary is an alphabetical reference list of words in the language. It is a record of how these words have been used and of the class of speakers and writers who have used them. In the main list of entries the dictionary records the following information about words:

- spelling
- pronunciation
- irregular forms
- meaning
- level of use
- etymology, such as the derivation and development of words
- synonyms and antonyms, of some words
- parts of speech

The main list may also include the following:

- prefixes, suffixes, and other elements in word formation
- abbreviations commonly used in writing
- the names of persons and places

The supplementary sections of the dictionary may contain the following kinds of information about words and language:

- rules of pronunciation and mechanics
- forms and conventions of letter writing
- rules for the preparation of manuscript, together with a list of proofreaders' marks
- lists of signs and symbols used in various fields of study
- a table of English spelling as related to the International Phonetic Alphabet
- a list of commonly used abbreviations, if they are not in the vocabulary list
- tables of weights and measures
- documentation of sources
- forms of address
- symbols for chemical elements
- a list of names of prominent people with brief biographical data (if these are not included in the vocabulary list)
- a list of geographical names with pronunciation and pertinent information (if these are not in the vocabulary list)
- astronomy signs and symbols
- Jewish and Islamic calendars
- foreign words and phrases
- list of foreign currencies
- signs of the Zodiac

HOW TO KNOW YOUR DICTIONARY

Although all dictionaries are generally similar, each has individual features and editorial practices. You should know the resources of your own dictionary and how it is arranged and edited. You should not take a strange dictionary for granted; consult the explanatory notes in order to learn about the material and its presentation.

The Explanatory Notes

The key to the dictionary is the section of explanatory notes in the preface. This section generally explains the following:

- how entries are arranged, whether in one or several lists
- how information within a vocabulary entry is arranged
- how a vocabulary entry is treated
- how pronunciation is indicated
- how parts of speech are indicated
- how inflected forms are given
- how restrictive labels are used
- how variant spellings are given
- how etymologies are given
- how and why run-on entries are used
- how synonyms and antonyms are treated

The Table of Abbreviations

The preface of almost every dictionary contains a table of abbreviations used in the dictionary. The meaning of every abbreviation used in presenting the material can be found here.

Explanatory Essays

For the information and guidance of its users, some dictionaries present explanatory essays on matters such as the following:

- the selection of entries and definitions
- the nature of English orthography and pronunciation
- the treatment of etymologies, antonyms, and synonyms
- an explanation of levels of use and dialect distribution
- a discussion of British and American usage

These sections should be consulted for information about the various aspects of language and for a detailed explanation of how the dictionary is compiled.

Each American publisher of a dictionary issues an explanatory guide or study outline. This guide, designed for use with the dictionary, explains its contents and the way it arranges material. The guide may also include (1) a sample page to illustrate the special features of the dictionary, (2) exercises designed to acquaint the user with the dictionary, and (3) tests on vocabulary and general information. For courses in language and vocabulary these study guides are available on request.

How to Use the Dictionary

To use the dictionary efficiently proceed as follows:

Read the Entry Carefully

Entries are compact with information and must be read with care. Be sure to note whether a word (1) has more than one meaning, (2) has alternate and irregular forms, and (3) is used as different parts of speech with different meanings.

Exercise special care with restrictive labels indicating (1) that a meaning applies to a specific subject or (2) that a word or meaning is limited to a specific level of use.

A careless or incomplete reading may yield only partial or incorrect information. The dictionary exercises great care in explaining the forms, uses, and meanings of words. Therefore, the reader must pay close attention in order to secure the necessary information and to benefit from it.

Take Care to Find the Appropriate Meaning of a Word, in Context

Consider the word *acquitted* in the sentence: John *acquitted* himself well during the trial. The dictionary states that *acquit* may mean the following:

- to relieve from a charge or fault
- to release (one) from an obligation
- to settle a debt, obligation, claim
- to behave

Obviously, only the last meaning fits the context. To seize on one of the other meanings would lead to misunderstanding and to the idea, perhaps, that John declared himself innocent.

Read the Etymology and Synonomy of the Word

Knowing the etymology of a word may clarify and intensify its meaning. For example, the meaning of *hysterical* (emotionally frenzied) is made more powerful by the knowledge that it has been adapted from a Greek word (*hysterikōs*), meaning suffering in the uterus.

Consider the word *companion*. Its connotations are warmer to those who know that the root *pan* comes ultimately from the Latin word for bread (*panis*) and that *companion* originally meant a messmate, one who shares another's bread.

Synonyms and antonyms also help to clarify the meaning of a word. Synonyms relate the word to others similar in meaning. Antonyms throw the word into sharp relief by expressing an opposite meaning. The synonym studies in the dictionary distinguish between the meaning and use of clusters of words with similar meanings.

Do not Overlook Run-on Entries

If you cannot find a word in the alphabetical list, look for it under a cognate form. Words that are derivatives of an entry word are frequently listed at the end of an entry. This kind of entry is called a run-on entry.

For example, in *The American College Dictionary*, the words *communicability, communicableness,* and *communicably* are listed as run-on entries at the end of the main entry, *communicable,*

How to Interpret a Word Entry

The following explanations apply to all dictionaries. Individual modes of arrangement and presentation are set forth in the explanatory notes of each dictionary.

Alternate and Irregular Forms

Most dictionaries give the irregular forms of verbs, the irregular plurals of nouns, and the irregular comparisons of adjectives. These irregular forms are usually listed immediately after the part of speech with accompanying explanatory notes, if necessary. Dictionaries also list regular forms if there can be any doubt about them.

Alternate spellings and pronunciations are also given. Usually the preferred or more frequently used form is given first. If the alternate form is British, it is so labelled. Sometimes there is a separate entry for each spelling. For example, *The American College Dictionary* lists *controller* and *comptroller* separately, labelling the latter a variant spelling.

If one spells or pronounces a word acceptably, one need not change to the preferred form unless there is a personal reason for doing so.

Parts of Speech

The part of speech is given immediately after the respelling of the word. A word used as more than one part of speech, for instance as a noun and a verb, is defined first as one and then as the other. The part of speech is preceded by a boldface dash, thus—*n.*, to indicate that the following meanings are nounal and to separate them from other meanings. The method of defining a word according to its parts of speech is illustrated by the following abstract entry:

> **con•cen•trate** (kŏn´sen•trāt). *v.* **—trated, —trating**, *n.*—*v.t.* **1.** to draw to a common center. **2.** to intensify.—*v.i.* **3.** to converge to a center. **—4.** a concentrated form of something; a product of concentration.

Note that verbs are identified and defined as transitive, intransitive, or both. The abbreviations of the parts of speech are explained in the table of abbreviations.

Pronunciation

Dictionaries give the pronunciation of a word by respelling it in parentheses immediately after the entry word. The respelling shows pronunciation by: (1) breaking the word into syllables, (2) using diacritical marks to give the vowel sound, and (3) using accent marks to show the distribution of stress over the syllables.

In most dictionaries the diacritical marks are explained in a brief key to pronunciation and etymological abbreviations printed across the bottom of every double page. In some dictionaries, the key is printed on the inside cover. A full key to pronunciation appears in the preface of most dictionaries.

In addition to the diacritical marks, some dictionaries use the *schwa* (ə) to indicate the indeterminate sound of *a* in the word *alone*. Examples: dĭs•pĕn´sə•rĭ, tĕl´ə•fōn. Besides illustrating the use of the *schwa* and the diacritical marks, these examples show the distribution of stress over the syllables of the words. Quite often, the primary or main accent mark (´) is in boldface type and the secondary in regular type. Some dictionaries use a double accent mark to indicate secondary stress; thus: tĕl´ə•fōn´´.

For a fuller explanation of pronunciation and the ways of indicating it see "Good Speech: Pronunciation," page 43.

Meanings

Dictionaries give the meanings of words in current use and of older words that readers are likely to encounter. Many words have more than one meaning; some, indeed, have a score or more. The order in which meanings are given varies among dictionaries. Dictionaries compiled on the historical principle (*The Oxford English Dictionary*) give them in the order of historical development. The Merriam-Webster dictionaries present meanings more or less in the order of development. *The American College Dictionary*, on the other hand, gives the central meaning of each part of speech first. The central meaning is usually the most common. After the central meaning the usual order is: figurative, specialized, obsolete, archaic, or rare. As usual, the preface of each dictionary explains the order in which meanings are arranged.

Dictionaries number definitions in single sequence. When two definitions are very closely related within the same area, they are marked in boldface letters under the definition number. The following abstract entry illustrates the numbering of definitions and the use of letters to indicate closely related definitions:

> **ad·den·dum** (ě děn′dəm), *n.* pl. da (—də). **I.** an added thing; an addition. **2.** an appendix to a book. **3.** *Mach.* a. part of a tooth that projects beyond the pitch circle or line of a toothed rack or wheel. **b.** also, **addendum circle**, an imaginary circle touching the ends of the teeth of a toothed wheel.

Subject Labels

When meanings are restricted to a specific field of information such as law, chemistry physics, etc., the fields are indicated by subject labels. The subject label, frequently abbreviated, appears immediately before the definition, thus for the word *abrupt:*

> **5.** *Bot.* truncate.

Some dictionaries print a table of subject label abbreviations in the front or back; others, like *The American College Dictionary*, explain the abbreviations in the regular word list.

Subject labels must be heeded because there may be wide differences between general and restricted meanings. For example, in general use the adjective *active* means in progress or motion; busy. But note the different restricted meanings of *active:*

GRAMMAR:	a voice of a verb inflection in which the subject performs the action expressed by the verb.
ACCOUNTING:	profitable; busy.
MEDICINE:	acting quickly; producing immediate results.

Usage Labels

Dictionaries label words and meanings according to their level of use, that is, according to the class of speakers and writers who employ them. It must be understood that words are not good or bad, right or wrong. Words simply exist because they are used by people. If they are used only by the ignorant and vulgar, they are not acceptable in refined speech. If they are used only by a small group of people in a limited area, they will not be widely known and accepted.

Dictionaries indicate the levels of usage so that we will know which words to select for the level of our own discourse. Dictionaries do not create meanings of words or judge them good or bad. What the dictionary does is to record words that have been used and explain how they have been used and by what class of speakers and writers.

Care must be exercised to note whether the usage label applies to the whole word or to specific meanings. If the usage label applies to the entire entry, it usually appears before the definition or before the first definition if there is more than one, thus:

whacko (wăk´ō). *adj., slang.* crazy.

If the usage label applies to only one definition, it usually appears between the definition number and the definition itself, thus:

last. 14. *Colloq.* the final mention or appearance: to hear the last of the rumor.

Dictionaries differ somewhat in the placement of usage labels. However, every dictionary is so careful to use the label clearly that there is seldom doubt. If there is, the user should consult the explanatory notes.

Each dictionary clearly explains the levels of use and its method of labelling them. However, there are several levels that are frequently misunderstood and that therefore require some explanation. They are: (1) formal or standard, (2) colloquial, (3) dialect, (4) slang, (5) archaic, and (6) obsolete.

1. *Formal or standard—no label*

This is the level of educated speakers and writers. It is accepted as correct everywhere by all classes of people. This level is not labelled in the dictionary; all other levels are labelled.

2. *Colloquial—Colloq.*

Colloquial is the level of informal writing and speaking, of friendly, personal, intimate conversation and writing. In this kind of discourse colloquial expressions are proper; however, they are inappropriate in formal discourse. Examples of colloquialisms are: *grouch, highbrow, jinks,* and *miff.* Note how inappropriate the word *crazy* is in this sentence: The Queen declared that in his last years the prime minister advocated a number of *crazy* policies. It should be noted that many of the words labeled *colloq.* in older dictionaries are quite acceptable now.

3. *Slang—Slang*

Slang often gets its start as the jargon of a particular profession or group of people. Most slang words are coined as substitutes for accepted words and hence serve no purpose except, perhaps, to make language somewhat shocking. Much slang is ephemeral; it comes and goes with fads. For these reasons slang is below the level of cultivated speech and should not be used except, perhaps, on rare occasions when a slang term might convey a meaning that is sharper than another. Examples of slang: *scram, screwy, nuts* (crazy), *pad* (living quarters), *pits, bummer, cool, bad* (meaning good), *gimme five, geek, nerd, chill out.*

4. *Dialect—Dial. or Dialect*

A dialect is a localized form of a language as distinguished from a standard language. Dialect, therefore, is the language of a class or district; or it is a special variety of language. *Merriam Webster's Collegiate Dictionary,* Tenth Edition, recognizes a number of U.S. dialects: New England, Southern, Northwest, Midland.

5. Archaic—Archaic

Archaic usage is usage of former times. An archaic word or meaning is one that was once used, but is no longer used except in certain fields of knowledge or for special effects. Examples: *Clomb* is the archaic participial form of *climb*. *Thou, thee, thy, thine* are archaic forms of personal pronouns. *Hast* and *wast* are archaic forms of the verb *to be*. *Grammercy* is an archaic interjection meaning many thanks. Because law, religion, and poetry are strongly bound by tradition and convention, they abound in archaic terms, as the following examples show:

RELIGION: The Lord is my shepherd; I shall not want.
He *maketh* me to lie down in green pastures;
He *leadeth* me beside the still waters.

POETRY: Little lamb, who made *thee*?
Dost thou know who made thee?

LAW: *misfeasance*—a wrong arising from or consisting of affirmative action
malfeasance—the wrongful performance of an act that the actor has
no right to do.

Outside of the fields in which archaisms are acceptable they should not be used except to give the flavor of fact to works of literature. When used for this purpose, they should be used sparingly.

UNABRIDGED DICTIONARIES

The Webster and Funk & Wagnall's dictionaries are the standard one-volume unabridged dictionaries available for reference use in schools and libraries. Unabridged dictionaries are the fullest dictionaries. They are designed for specialists, people who work closely with language and who are frequently seeking detailed information about words from many different periods of the language. Most libraries make unabridged dictionaries available for reference. They should be consulted for information not included in the shorter dictionaries. The best known unabridged dictionaries are

- *Oxford English Dictionary*, begun in 1858 and completed in 1928. Compiled on historic principles, it gives the history of every word presented and arranges meanings in the order of their appearance. It also illustrates words with dated quotations or excerpts from English writers. The most recent version, edited by Simpson & Weiner, was published by the Oxford University Press in 1994.
- Funk & Wagnall's *Comprehensive Standard International Dictionary*, Funk & Wagnall, 1995.
- Webster's Third *New International Dictionary*, unabridged, Merriam Co., 1989.
- Webster's *New Twentieth Century Dictionary*, unabridged, Collins-World, 1975.

ABRIDGED OR COLLEGIATE DICTIONARIES

Shorter dictionaries designed for general use are commonly called abridged or collegiate dictionaries. They are either reduced editions of the unabridged dictionary, or, like the *American College Dictionary*, they are edited specifically for this level of use. Besides containing fewer words than unabridged dictionaries, the one-volume or shortened dictionaries treat words in less detail, presenting fewer definitions, examples, and illustrations, and devoting less attention to etymology and synonomy. Every student should own a good collegiate dictionary; you can always consult the unabridged and special dictionaries in the library for information not included in your collegiate. The leading collegiate dictionaries are

- Webster's *New World Collegiate Dictionary*, Macmillan, 1989.
- *New College Standard Dictionary of the English Language*, Funk & Wagnall, 1990.
- *The American College Dictionary*, Random House, 1991.
- *Merriam-Webster's Collegiate Dictionary*, Tenth Edition, Merriam-Webster, Inc., 1993.

THE LIMITATIONS OF THE DICTIONARY

No dictionary contains every word of the past and present. Even unabridged dictionaries omit almost as many words as they include. A dictionary that listed all of these terms would exceed the resources of an editorial board and would be too cumbersome for practical use. Most of the omitted terms may be found in the special dictionaries and glossaries that abound as supplementary aids.

Since lexicographers are not infallible, dictionaries are sometimes wrong. Errors may result from overlooking the practice of certain writers and speakers. Omissions and errors may also occur because dictionaries cannot keep abreast of our changing language. New words and meanings may therefore be omitted, and changes in the level of use may not be indicated. If the dictionary is at variance with the established and accepted practice of cultivated writers and speakers, the latter must be regarded as right and appealed to as authority.

Since dictionaries are limited in space and deal with words in isolation, definitions are necessarily abstract, general, and brief. Many definitions are merely labels that identify a term but do not explain it. *Bridge,* for example, is defined as a game of cards, but the definition gives little information about how the game is played. For a satisfactory understanding of the game one must watch and play it or consult a manual. The same is true of *arbitrage* (a method of buying and selling money, securities, and commodities) and *cathedral.* To know what a cathedral really is, you must visit one.

Because they are general and brief, definitions do not express adequately the connotations and idiomatic use of words. These qualities could be satisfactorily indicated only by lengthy explanations, with several sentences to illustrate the use of the word. Consider the following:

impeach	to charge (a public officer) before a competent tribunal with misbehavior in office.
	The dictionary does not indicate that by usage we can impeach presidents, judges, and other high officials, but not lower-level office holders such as dogcatchers, probation officers, etc.
impeccable	of things, free from fault or error; for example, the costume she wore for her audience with the Pope was modish and expensive, but *impeccable* in taste.
	The dictionary does not show that *impeccable* may not be used as follows: To carve his statue of David, Michelangelo searched for a column of *impeccable* marble.
sweat	To excrete watery fluid through the pores of the skin, as from heat, exertion, and such.
	Nothing in this definition shows that *sweat,* because of its connotation, is never applied to a lady or gentleman. Athletes and laborers *sweat,* but ambassadors and debutantes *perspire.*
dichotomy	division into two parts or into twos; subdivision into halves or pairs. Idiomatic use: The joining of body and soul in man accounts for the *dichotomy* in human nature.
	Nothing in the dictionary indicates that *dichotomy* cannot be used as follows: Because of the *dichotomy* of the house, the two families dwelt there amicably.

We should be aware of these limitations of the dictionary and not expect more than it can provide. Entries should be studied carefully for whatever clues to usage they present. Whenever possible, however, words should be studied in context, and the guide to their meaning and use should be the current practice of cultivated speakers and writers.

Special Dictionaries

The dictionaries listed below are useful supplements to a general dictionary. Students of language may therefore wish to own them or to consult them in a library.

Burnam, Tom, *Dictionary of Misinformation*, Harper Collins, 1993.
Byrne, Joseph, *Dictionary of Unusual, Obscure and Preposterous Words*,
Carol Publishing Group, 1974.
Cassidy, Frederic, *Dictionary of American Regional English*, Belknap Press, 1985.
Elsevier's Dictionary of Medicine, French and European Publications, Inc. 1989.
Grosser, George, *Psychology Dictionary*, McGraw-Hill, 1994.
Kogan, Page. *A Dictionary of Classical and Foreign Words and Phrases*, Random House, 1991.
Morrison, Marvin. *Word Finder, The Phonic Key to the Dictionary*, Pilot Light, 1987.
New American Roget's College Thesaurus in Dictionary Form, NAL-Dutton, 1993.
Random House Dictionary of the English Language, Random House, 1987.

Webster's Dictionaries
Basic English Dictionary, Merriam-Webster, Inc., 1995.
Compact Dictionary of Quotations, Merriam-Webster, Inc., 1995.
Compact Rhyming Dictionary, Merriam-Webster, Inc., 1995.
Computer Dictionary, Pamco Publications, 1994.
Crossword Puzzle Dictionary, Paradise Miami, 1994.
Dictionary of Synonyms and Antonyms, Smithmark, 1996.

Oxford University Dictionaries
Desk Dictionary: American Edition, ed. L. Urdgang, OUP, 1995.
Dictionary and Usage Guide to the English Language, ed. A. Kenny, OUP, 1990.
Dictionary of Abbreviations, OUP, 1993.
Dictionary of English Proverbs, OUP, 1970.
Dictionary of Modern Quotations, ed. T. Augard, OUP, 1993.
Dictionary of Modern Slang, ed. Simpson & Ayto, OUP, 1994.
English Dictionary, 2 vols., ed. Simpson & Weiner, OUP, 1994.

ROGET'S THESAURUS

Roget's Thesaurus is a word finder. It presents a number of central ideas or concepts and under each it groups words and expressions in some way related to that concept. If you wished to find a word for a person who affects illness or pretends to be ill, you could not find it in the dictionary; before you can look up a word in the dictionary, you must know the word. In the *Thesaurus*, however, one can look under the heading **illness** or **disease** and there you will find the word **valetudinarian**. To make sure that this is the desired word, you must then look it up in the dictionary, for the *Thesaurus* merely lists words; it does not define them.

The *Thesaurus* may be helpful in finding words, but it must be used with care. The words grouped together are *not synonyms*; they differ widely in meaning, and their relationship to the central idea may be tenuous. Bearing these facts in mind, the user must discriminate among the words with care, select the one he wants, and then check it in the dictionary.

There are numerous editions of the *Thesaurus* available. A useful, inexpensive edition for students is *Roget's Pocket Thesaurus*, published by Pocket Books, Inc.

EXERCISE 3

SUBJECT LABELS

What does your dictionary tell you about the meaning of each of the following words in the designated field of knowledge?

WORD	DEFINITION
1. governor (*Mach.*)	
2. dip (*Geol.*)	
3. green (*Sports*)	
4. defeat (*Law*)	
5. dormant (*Biol.*)	
6. liaison (*Elect.*)	
7. negative (*Physiol.*)	
8. nucleus (*Astron.*)	
9. opaque (*Photog.*)	
10. pioneer (*Ecol.*)	
11. pneumatic (*Zool.*)	
12. rational (*Arith.*)	
13. regression (*Psychoanal.*)	
14. secondary (*Football*)	
15. tolerance (*Minting*)	

EXERCISE 4

INFLECTED AND VARIANT FORMS

Consult your dictionary for the following.

By consulting the dictionary give the comparative and superlative forms of each of the following adjectives and adverbs.

WORD	COMPARATIVE	SUPERLATIVE
1. ruddy	_____	_____
2. rural	_____	_____
3. shyly	_____	_____
4. sincere	_____	_____
5. sinister	_____	_____
6. thorny	_____	_____
7. comical	_____	_____
8. dewy	_____	_____
9. slowly	_____	_____
10. obscure	_____	_____

By consulting the dictionary, give the infinitive form of each of the following past participles.

PAST PARTICIPLE	INFINITIVE	PAST PARTICIPLE	INFINITIVE
11. bore	_____	16. slid	_____
12. agreed	_____	17. slunk	_____
13. lain	_____	18. set	_____
14. hanged	_____	19. flung	_____
15. fled	_____	20. blown	_____

By consulting the dictionary, give the plural or plurals of each of the following words.

WORD	PLURAL	WORD	PLURAL
21. leaf	_____	26. codex	_____
22. radius	_____	27. quiz	_____
23. stratum	_____	28. donkey	_____
24. tomato	_____	29. mongoose	_____
25. hero	_____	30. seraph	_____

How are the following words pronounced? Give the most widely used pronunciation first.

31. itinerant _____

32. abstract _____

33. anchovy _____

34. haphazard _____

35. lever _____

36. library _____

37. matricide _____

38. obligatory _____

39. plebiscite _____

40. calumny _____

What is the part of speech of each of the following words when the primary accent is on the first syllable?

41. perfect _____

42. increase _____

43. present _____

44. refuse _____

45. contest _____

Give the various pronunciations of the following words. Underline the pronunciation you use.

46. tomato _____

47. either _____

48. ration _____

49. advertisement _____

50. pumpkin _____

EXERCISE 5

LEVELS OF USE

Give the meaning of the following words on the level of usage indicated.

WORD	DEFINITION
1. fantastic (*Archaic*)	_____
2. fancy (*Obs.*)	_____
3. mystery (*Archaic*)	_____
4. object (*Obs. or Archaic*)	_____
5. perfect (*Obs.*)	_____
6. remember (*Archaic*)	_____
7. regard (*Archaic*)	_____
8. hood (*Slang*)	_____
9. bonnet (*British*)	_____
10. team (*Obs.*)	_____
11. temperament (*Obs.*)	_____
12. lull (*Archaic*)	_____
13. beak (*Slang*)	_____
14. conscience (*Archaic*)	_____
15. gentle (*Obs.*)	_____

Exercise 6

The Meaning of Words, Word Elements, and Abbreviations

Give the meaning of each of the following grammatical abbreviations.

Word	Definition
1. *v.t.*	
2. *pron.*	
3. *adv.*	
4. *adj.*	
5. *prep.*	

Give the meaning of each of the following initials or abbreviations.

6. Port. _____

7. obs. _____

8. dial. _____

9. A.P.O. _____

10. KKK _____

Give the meaning of each of the following word elements.

11. grapho- _____

12. -cule _____

13. -ette _____

14. ferri _____

15. -ana _____

Give the meaning and name the language of each of the following foreign terms.

16. *ora pro nobis* _____

17. *fiat lux* _____

18. *maison de santé* _____

19. *pied-à-terre* _____

20. *lied* _____

Give the meaning of each of the following terms.

21. nautical _____

22. metallic _____

23. biological _____

24. astronomy _____

25. musical _____

EXERCISE 7

SYNONYMS, ANTONYMS, AND ETYMOLOGY

Give three or more synonyms for each of the following words. Do as many as you can without consulting the dictionary.

1. pursue _____

2. complain _____

3. beat (v.) _____

4. fault _____

5. great _____

Write an antonym for each of the following words.

6. guess _____

7. honorable _____

8. imminent _____

9. luster _____

10. mere _____

Each of the following sentences offers a choice of synonyms. Underline the synonym that is most appropriate in the sentence.

11. He will be rewarded according to his (merit, deserts, worth).

12. She (covets, envies, begrudges) her sister-in-law's beauty.

13. We will (gladden, enliven, cheer) him with the good news.

14. To get their attention we must try a (new, fresh, novel) approach.

15. How delicious is the (perfume, odor, scent, aroma, fragrance) of a field of clover!

What language is the ultimate source from which English took each of the following terms?

16. tutelary _____

17. relief _____

18. diabetic _____

19. narcotic _____

20. kumquat _____

4. OUR LANGUAGE PAST AND PRESENT

(The words that appear in boldface in this section are featured in the exercises that follow this section.)

THE INDO-EUROPEAN FAMILY OF LANGUAGES

English belongs to the Indo-European family of languages. A family of languages consists of all of the languages that have descended from a common ancestor. Besides English, the Indo-European family includes almost all of the other European languages and some of the Eastern languages.

The **determination** of the family relationship among these languages resulted from the discovery and study of Sanskrit at the end of the eighteenth century and the beginning of the nineteenth. **Philologists** believe that Indo-European was a prehistoric language spoken by white races on the mainland of Europe and in far western Asia. Indo-European had already divided and scattered before the dawn of history. This **differentiation** of language was due to the separation of communities over a long period. Slight differences led to the growth of local **dialects**, and large differences led to full-fledged dialects.

The kinship leading to the **hypothesis** that these languages were at one time identical is easily demonstrated by the following **correspondences**:

English *mother*, German *mutter*, Swedish *moder*, Spanish *madre*, French *mére*, Latin *mater*.

English *brother*, Dutch *broeder*, German *bruder*, Greek *phrater*, Latin *frater*, Sanskrit *bhrater*, Irish *braither*.

Indo-European consists of nine principal groups. These groups, together with their subdivisions, are shown on the chart opposite.

English was first spoken in Britain in the middle of the fifth century. Therefore, English has a history of only 1,500 years. The first known language spoken in Britain was Celtic, an Indo-European tongue still spoken by some people. After Caesar's unsuccessful invasion of Britain during the Celtic period in 55 B.C., the Romans finally conquered Britain in 43 A.D. and began to Romanize the province. Christianity was introduced in 597 A.D. and by the end of the next century had made considerable progress.

During the Roman occupation Latin did not replace Celtic. Latin was spoken only by the Romans and by Celts of the upper class. It was not spoken enough to survive the Germanic invasions of Britain, which began in 449 A.D.

English has its origins in the dialects of the invading Germanic tribes of Jutes, Picts, Scots, Saxons, and Angles. Among these dialects there were only slight differences, about which very little is known.

There are three periods in the history of English:

- Old English, 450–1150 A.D., the period of full inflection
- Middle English, 1150–1500, the period of level inflection
- Modern English, 1500—the period of lost inflection

Indo-European

- Indian
  - Sanskrit
- Iranian
- Armenian
- Celtic
  - Irish
  - Welsh
- Albanian
- Balto-Slavic
  - Russian
  - Polish
  - Lithuanian
  - Czech
  - Bulgarian
- Hellenic
  - Greek
- Italic
  - Latin
    - French
    - Spanish
    - Italian
    - Portuguese
- Teutonic
  - Norse
    - Danish
    - Swedish
    - Norwegian
  - Gothic
  - High
    - German
  - Low
    - Anglo-Saxon (English)
    - Dutch

The Old English Period, 450–1150 A.D.

Old English was a period of full inflection; that is, nouns, adjectives, verbs, and pronouns were divided into **categories** or **declensions** and assumed different forms to indicate case, number, gender, tense, and mood. Any language, such as Old English, that uses inflections to show the relationship between words is called a **synthetic** language. Old English was more fully inflected than most modern languages and about as fully inflected as Latin.

The vocabulary of Old English was small. However, it readily formed new words by combining old ones and it was rich in prefixes and suffixes with which old words could be changed for new uses. The words were almost entirely native. Aside from a small number of place names, the number of Celtic words in Old English was negligible. Some Old English words were borrowed from Latin. Of these the greater number came through Christianity, which was introduced in 597 A.D. Among the religious loan words from this early period are *abbot, altar, candle, martyr,* and *relic.* Among the Latin loan words used in domestic life we have *cap, silk, mat, beet, radish, box,* and *school.*

Old English was also influenced by Danish. The Danes began a series of attacks upon Britain about 787 A.D. and increased their power until they were finally checked by King Alfred in 878 A.D. A later Danish invasion under Olaf Trygvasson in 991 A.D. established Danish rule over Britain from about 1014 to 1040 A.D. Then the Angles, Saxons, and Danes **amalgamated**.

From the language of the Danes Old English acquired many words now in common use. For example, English words with *sk* are likely to be Danish in origin: *sky, bask, skirt, skill, scrape.* Among the other common words borrowed from Danish are *band, bank, egg, dirt, race, call, dip, raise, give.* British place names from Danish include *Grimsby, Whitby, Derby,* and *Lowestoft.*

The Middle English Period, 1150–1500 A.D.

The greatest influence on our language was the conquest and occupation of England by the Normans from 1066–1200 A.D. During this period when the rulers, the officials, and the nobility were Norman, French was the language of the court and the upper classes. Only the uncultured classes spoke English. Even after 1200, when the ruling classes lost their holdings on the continent and were forced to become English, French remained the **dominant** language, because the ties with the continent were still close and French literature and French culture remained in favor.

In time, however, the growth of national feeling and the rise of the middle class led to a **resurgence** of English. In the fourteenth century English was again generally spoken and became the language of the nobility, the law courts, and the schools.

The most important **linguistic** influence of the Norman occupation was the breaking up of the inflectional system. Adjectives and pronouns decayed. Nouns lost most of their inflectional endings. The strong conjugations of verbs all but disappeared, and new verbs were **conjugated** as weak. Today less than one hundred strong verbs remain in the language. Strong verbs are those with irregular forms: *sing, sang, sung; blow, blew, blown,* etc. The past and past participles of all weak verbs are formed by the addition of *ed: talk, talked, talked; want, wanted, wanted.* Therefore the shift from strong to weak verbs was a great simplification.

The influence of French on the English vocabulary was great, but not sudden or overwhelming. From French came government and administrative words (*crown, state, empire, realm*); ecclesiastical words (*religion, theology, sermon, hermit*); legal words (*bar, plea, plaintiff, bail*); military words (*army, navy, defend, lieutenant*); words from social life (*apparel, gown, robe, attire*); and words from art and learning (*music, poet, art, medicine*).

When English and French words were duplicated, their meanings frequently differentiated. Today we have the following words that were originally the same in meaning.

Of English Origin	Of French Origin
doom	judgment
hearty	cordial
sheep	mutton
swine	pork
calf	veal
house	mansion
ask	demand

Toward the end of the fourteenth century a written language began to **emerge**. It became recognized during the following century and developed into standard English. Standard English is based largely on the dialect of the East Midlands district and especially on the dialect of London. This dialect **prevailed** because it was the language of Chaucer and because the East Midlands was the largest and most populous of the dialect areas and contained the universities and the capital city.

MODERN ENGLISH, 1500–

The most important influences on the development of modern English were the introduction of the printing press, the growth of popular education, the increase in commercialism, and the growth of social consciousness. During the Renaissance in England, English had to struggle against Latin for recognition. At first the revival of learning strengthened the position of Latin. Soon, however, English was vigorously championed by schoolmen like Elyot, Ascham, and Mulcaster. English was ultimately victorious because people in all walks of life wanted to enjoy the fruits of the **Renaissance** and they created the climate in which Bacon, Marlowe, Shakespeare, Hobbes, and the other **eminent** figures of the Elizabethan and Jacobean age could **flourish**.

In the fifteenth century great changes began in the pronunciation of English. During Chaucer's age the long vowels were pronounced in the continental manner. Now they were being raised and given the sounds they receive today.

As modern English developed, its vocabulary had to be enriched in order to meet the demands placed upon it by new knowledge and new activities. To meet these demands English borrowed heavily from Latin, French, and Spanish. Borrowing was easier than in former eras because of the prevalence of books.

Modern English also had to develop a grammar and a standard practice of spelling. By the middle of the sixteenth century a uniform practice in spelling began to develop. The most intense efforts to standardize, refine, and fix the language were made in the eighteenth century. Grammarians attempted to reduce the language to rules and to settle disputed points of use. Several attempts were made to establish a British academy, modeled on the French, which would be the arbiter of language. Although an academy was not established, the work of grammarians and **lexicogaphers** did much to establish rules and to set standards. Samuel Johnson's *Dictionary* (1755), the first to be **compiled** on modern principles of lexicography, helped to show the riches and variety of the language and to standardize its spelling and pronunciation.

In the eighteenth and nineteenth centuries the expansion of the British Empire and the growth of science greatly affected the language. The vocabulary was increased by words borrowed from American Indians (*caribou, hominy, moose*), from Spain and Portugal (*chili, chocolate*), India (*bandana, bungalow, calico*), Africa (*boorish, gorilla, palaver*), and from other areas. From science were added words like *acidosis, appendicitis, alkali,* and *electron*. Similarly, the continued development of science and the international upheavals of our own century have extended the vocabulary of English and affected its grammar and use.

THE NATURE AND IMPORTANCE OF ENGLISH TODAY

English is one of the largest and richest of modern languages. It is spoken by more than 500,000,000 people, and the number of speakers will increase. English plays a large political and cultural role because English-speaking people are leaders in art, science, politics, and practical affairs. People everywhere learn English in order to keep abreast of the major trends and developments in the world.

Our language has many assets. It has a large, flexible vocabulary, is rich in synonyms and idiomatic expressions, and is capable of expressing a wide range of ideas and **subtle** refinements of thought. Of all European languages English is the simplest in grammar. From a synthetic language (an inflected language) it has developed into an analytic language, that is, one that indicates the relationship of words by position and by the use of prepositions. All modern languages have simplified, but no other is as simple as English.

Nevertheless, English suffers from two serious liabilities. In the absence of inflections it is largely dependent upon idioms. As a result, English idioms are more numerous, more illogical, and thornier than those in most other languages. English spelling is irregular and nearly chaotic. We use several different symbols for the same sound and one symbol for several different sounds. Note how the long e sound is represented in *believe, machine, receive, leave, be, rapidly, dream,* and *see.* Another example is the *sh* sound in *shin, sugar, tissue, expansion, fission, motion, suspicion, ocean, nauseous, conscious, chaperon, schist,* and *fuschia.*

The difficulties of English spelling and idiom largely negate the essential simplicity of the language. Our own students must struggle to speak and write English correctly, and foreigners often find the task extremely hard.

EXERCISE 8

DEFINING WORDS IN CONTEXT

Written below is a number of phrases from "Our Language Past and Present." Consult your dictionary and find the appropriate definition for each of the boldface words. Write the part of speech and the definition in the spaces provided.

1. The **determination** of the family relationship between the languages…

   Part of speech _____ Definition _____

2. **Philologists** believe that Indo-European was…

   Part of speech _____ Definition _____

3. The **differentiation** of language was due to…

   Part of speech _____ Definition _____

4. Slight differences lead to the growth of local **dialects**…

   Part of speech _____ Definition _____

5. The kinship led to the **hypothesis**…

   Part of speech _____ Definition _____

6. The hypothesis … is easily demonstrated by the following **correspondences**…

   Part of speech _____ Definition _____

7. It was not spoken enough to **survive**…

   Part of speech _____ Definition _____

8. Old English was a period of full **inflection**.

   Part of speech _____ Definition _____

9. That is, nouns, adjectives … were divided into **categories**…

   Part of speech _____ Definition _____

10. That is, nouns, adjectives … were divided into categories or **declensions**…

    Part of speech _____ Definition _____

11. Any language that uses inflection … is called a **synthetic** language.

    Part of speech _____ Definition _____

12. Then the Angles, Saxons, and Danes **amalgamated**.

    Part of speech _____ Definition _____

13. French remained the **dominant** language.

Part of speech _____ Definition _____

14. ...the rise of the middle class led to the **resurgence** of English.

Part of speech _____ Definition _____

15. The most important **linguistic** influence...

Part of speech _____ Definition _____

16. ...new verbs were **conjugated** as weak...

Part of speech _____ Definition _____

17. From French came **ecclesiastical** words...

Part of speech _____ Definition _____

18. ...a written language began to **emerge**.

Part of speech _____ Definition _____

19. This dialect **prevailed** because...

Part of speech _____ Definition _____

20. ... to enjoy the fruits of the **Renaissance**...

Part of speech _____ Definition _____

21. ...and other **eminent** figures...

Part of speech _____ Definition _____

22. ...the climate in which...eminent figures could **flourish**.

Part of speech _____ Definition _____

23. ...was the work of grammarians and **lexicographers**...

Part of speech _____ Definition _____

24. ... the first dictionary to be **compiled**...

Part of speech _____ Definition _____

25. ...**subtle** refinements of thought...

Part of speech _____ Definition _____

EXERCISE 9

WORDS AND THEIR COGNATES

The words below have been selected from "Our Language Past and Present." Each word is followed by a number of incomplete statements. Complete each statement by using either the appropriate cognate of the word or the other information called for. Consult your dictionary for help where needed.

ECCLESIASTIC

1. A clergyman is an _____
2. The practice of the principles of the church is _____
3. The worship of the church is _____
4. A book of the Old Testament traditionally assigned to Solomon is _____

RENAISSANCE

5. The noun meaning revival or rebirth is _____
6. The adjective meaning being reborn or springing up again is _____
7. When and where did Renaissance architecture originate? _____

EMINENT

8. The noun meaning high station or repute is _____
9. The title of honor of a cardinal is _____
10. Synonyms of *eminent* are _____

CORRESPONDENCE

11. To be in agreement or conformity is to _____
12. A thing that corresponds to something else is _____
13. One who writes to another or for a newspaper is _____
14. The adjective meaning responsive or answering is _____

SURVIVE

15. One who remains alive is a _____
16. The noun meaning the act of remaining alive is _____
17. The term in biology for the principle of the survival of forms of life best suited for the existing conditions is the _____

EMERGE

    18. The act of rising or coming forth is _____

    19. A sudden, urgent occasion for action is an _____

    20. The adjective meaning rising up or coming into view is _____

PREVAILED

    21. The adjective meaning predominant or generally current is_____

    22. The adjective meaning widespread, of wide extent or occurrence is _____

    23. The condition of being widespread is _____

COMPILED

    24. The act of putting together a book is _____

    25. One who puts a book together is a _____

5. GOOD SPEECH: PRONUNCIATION

To be effective a speaker must pronounce words distinctly and correctly. The proper articulation of words is everywhere admired as a mark of cultivation. On the other hand, the speaker who slurs and mispronounces words is regarded as uneducated.

Today the spoken word is as important as the written word. We are obliged to listen to a large volume of speech and we have learned to enjoy it. Whether we are being instructed or entertained, however, we expect to be addressed clearly and correctly. We insist upon a standard of correctness that we ourselves are therefore obliged to comply with in speaking to others. These occasions are numerous; in a world that admires talk we must talk often and well.

Correct speech is reputable, national, and contemporary. It is the standard of speech established by cultivated speakers. Broadcast by radio and television, it is heard everywhere and is everywhere accepted as correct. As a result, the demand for conformity to this standard is increasing. More than ever before correct pronunciation is important.

GOOD SPEECH IS DISTINCT SPEECH

Good speech is distinct. It is crisp and clear; all of the voiced letters and syllables are distinctly sounded. To speak distinctly one must obey the following rules:

Pronounce Final Consonants Clearly

Sound the final *ng* in words ending in *ing: saying, running;* not sayin', runnin'.
Sound the final consonant in words ending in two consonants.

SAY	DO NOT SAY
worlD	worl'
nighT	nigh'
builD, builT	buil'
direcT	direc'
rafT	raf'
demanD	deman'
clamP	clam'
amounT	amoun
assisT	assis'

Pronounce the *ed* of the Past Participle

walkED	*not* walk'
askED	*not* ask'

Sound the Voiced Letters and Syllables within a Word

SAY	DO NOT SAY
enTertaiNment	en'ertai'ment
goverNment	gover'ment or gov'ment
inTeresting	in'erestin' or in'ertes'in
physIcal	phys'cal
exERcise	ex'cise
agOny	ag'ny
alTer	al'er
amenDment	amen'ment
attenTive	atten'ive
bAlloon	b'loon
banDage	ban'age
breaKfast	brea'fast
breaDth	brea'th
capItal	cap'ta
cenTer	cen'er
cerTainly	cer'nly
certifIcate	certif'cate
compAny	comp'ny
cOrrect	c'rect
counTer	coun'er
crimInal	crim'nal
diffIcult	dif'cult
genTleman	gen'lman
gEography	g'ograph
regUlar	reg'lar
moVement	moo'ment
mulTiply	mul'iply
numBer	num'er
onLy	on'y
particUlar	partic'lar

Note: Do not, on the other hand, add syllables to words.

athlete	*not* athUHlete
elm	*not* elUM
film	*not* filUm

In addition to slurring sounds and running words together, many faulty speakers distort the sounds of some consonants and vowels in various ways. People who cannot place and pronounce various sounds correctly should not rely on pronunciation lists and their own efforts to improve their speech. They should seek the aid of a good speech teacher or therapist.

GOOD SPEECH IS CORRECTLY PRONOUNCED

English spelling and pronunciation are phonetic. In order to understand and to indicate the pronunciation of words one must therefore know the sounds our language employs. These sounds are listed below in a reduced and convenient form that is adequate for all general use.

Simplified International Phonetic Alphabet

b ch (chief) d f g (get) h j k l m n p r s sh (shoe) t th (thin) ᴛʜ (then) v w y x zh (vision) z
exactly—ĕg•zăkt´lĭ

ā ē ī ō ū (exactly as pronounced when reading the alphabet)

ă	ĕ	ĭ	ŏ	ô	ŭ	o͝o	o͞o	ou	ä—ah	ə (schwa)	oi
sat	set	sit	shot	draw	shut	shook	food	out	park	pə•rād´	oil

Anyone working with language should be familiar with this alphabet of sound. It is the standard method used by dictionaries and other authorities to show pronunciation. Since this alphabet is consistent and reasonably precise, it is more reliable than various forms of respelling and is therefore used in this text. Students are also required to use it so that they will learn it and be more proficient in showing pronunciation and using the dictionary.

Since the consonants cause little difficulty, there are only two essentials of pronunciation:

1. *The sound of the vowels*

For example, is *penal* pronounced *pē´nal* or *pĕn´al*? Is *penalty* pronounced *pē´nal ty* or *pĕn´al ty*?

2. *The distribution of stress or accent over the syllables of words*

Syllables receive either a primary or heavy stress (´) or a secondary stress (´) or no stress. Note that the primary stress is shown by a boldface accent mark and the secondary stress by an accent mark in regular type.

Penalty receives one primary stress: *pĕn´al ty.*
Penalize receives a primary and a secondary stress: *pē´na līz´.*
Indefatigable receives a primary and a secondary stress: *in´də fă´tĭ gə bl.*

Although English is spelled phonetically, there are so many exceptions and contradictions that spelling is an unreliable guide to pronunciation. Note the difference between the spelling and the pronunciation of the following common words:

awry (ə rī´)	comptroller (kŏn trōl´lər)
breeches (brĭch´iz)	trough (trŏf)
colonel (kər´nəl)	rheumatism (ro͞o´mə tĭz´əm)

For the same reason analogy is also an unreliable guide to pronunciation. It might be assumed that *breech* (the posterior of the human body) rhymes with the first syllable of *breeches*. But *breech* is pronounced phonetically and rhymes with *screech*. The dangers of pronouncing by analogy are apparent in the pronunciation of the following common words: cough (kôf, kŏf), tough (tŭf); though (thō), and *bough* (bow). Consider also the following pairs of words:

flour (flour)	flourish (flər´ĭsh)
fantastic (făn tăs´ tĭk)	phantom (făn´təm)
predict (prĭ dĭkt´)	indict (ĭn dīt´)
ear (ēr)	earnest (ər´nĭst)
comptroller (kŏn trō´ler)	comptometer (kŏmp tom´e ter)

The authority to consult about pronunciation is the dictionary. Lexicographers strive to show contemporary pronunciation as accurately as possible. In addition to giving the spelling and pronunciation of each entry, every dictionary contains a preface explaining the sounds and symbols of the language, a table of spellings, and a key to pronunciation. For a fuller treatment of pronunciation, a dictionary of pronunciation should be consulted.

The lexicographers are the first to admit the limitations and inadequacies of the dictionary in giving pronunciation. It is impossible for any dictionary to keep abreast of contemporary practice or to indicate individual and regional pronunciations and discriminate among them. Furthermore, the signs and symbols used by the dictionary can at best only approximate the sound of a word.

NOTE: Unusual care must be exercised in the pronunciation of the names of persons and places, especially if they are of foreign origin (see page 56). The safest practice is always to consult the dictionary. Remember that if the name is not listed in the main vocabulary section, it may appear in a separate section in the appendix.

First Aid for Faulty Pronunciation

The following list of words is limited to common words that are mispronounced because the wrong syllable is stressed or the sounds distorted. Words that are mispronounced in other ways have, for the most part, been excluded. A supplementary list of words often mispronounced appears in the appendix.

WORD	CORRECT PRONUNCIATION	
alias	(ā´lĭəs)	A li us
arctic	(ärk´tĭk)	ARK tic
athletic	(ăth lĕt´ĭk)	ath LET ic
attacked	(ə tăkt´)	a TAKT
bade	(băd)	Bad
bayou	(bī´oo)	BY oo
burglar	(bər´glər)	BER gler
children	(chĭl´drən)	CHIL dren
column	(cōl´əm)	COL um
comparable	(kŏm´pə rə bəl)	COM pa ra b'l
corps	(kōr, sing.	CORE
	kōrz, pl.)	CORES

b ch (chief) d f g (get) h j k l m n p r s sh (shoe) t th (thin) ‍th (then) v w y x zh (vision) z
exactly—ĕg•zăkt´lĭ

ā ē ī ō ū (exactly as pronounced when reading the alphabet)

ă ĕ ĭ ŏ ô ŭ o͝o o͞o ou ä—ah ə (schwa) oi
sat set sit shot draw shut shook food out park pə•rād´ oil

WORD	CORRECT PRONUNCIATION	
despicable	(dĕs´pi kə bəl)	DES pic a b'l
elm	(ĕlm)	ELM
faucet	(fô´sĭt)	FAW sit
fellow	(fĕl´ō)	FEL lo
February	(Fĕb´ro͞o ər´ĭ)	FEB ru a ry
film	(fĭlm)	FILM
formidable	(fôr´mĭ də bəl)	FOR mi da b'l
genuine	(jĕn´yo͝o ĭn)	JEN yu in
gondola	(gŏn´də lə)	GON do la
height	(hīt)	HITE
hundred	(hŭn´drəd)	HUN dred
hungry	(hŭn´grĭ)	HUNG gry
idea	(i dē´ə)	i DEE uh
incidentally	(ĭn sə dĕn´tə lĭ)	in ci DEN tal ly
incomparable	(ĭn cŏm´pə rə bəl)	in COM pa ra b'l
indict	(ĭn dīt´)	in DITE
infinite	(ĭn´fə nĭt)	IN fi nit
length	(lĕngth)	LENKTH
library	(lī´brər ĭ)	LIE brer y
mischievous	(mĭs´chə vəs)	MIS chi vus
modern	(mŏd´ərn)	MOD ern

b ch (chief) d f g (get) h j k l m n p r s sh (shoe) t th (thin) ‍th (then) v w y x zh (vision) z
exactly—ĕg•zăkt´lĭ

ā ē ī ō ū (exactly as pronounced when reading the alphabet)

ă ĕ ĭ ŏ ô ŭ o͝o o͞o ou ä—ah ə (schwa) oi
sat set sit shot draw shut shook food out park pə•rād´ oil

WORD	CORRECT PRONUNCIATION	
municipal	(mū nĭs´ə pəl)	mu NIS i p'l
orchestra	(ôr´kĕs trə)	OR ches tra
perspiration	(pər´spə rā´shən)	per spi RA tion
positively	(pŏs´ə tĭv lĭ)	POS i tiv ly
potato	(pə tā´tō)	po TA to
qualm	(kwäm)	KWOM
quay	(kē)	KEY
recipe	(rĕs´ə pē)	RES i pee
roof	(ro͞of, ro͝of)	ROOF
secretive	(sə crē´tĭv)	se KREE tiv
strength	(strĕngth)	STRENGTH
theater	(thē´ə tər)	THEE a ter
tragedy	(tră´jə dĭ)	TRA ge dy
width	(wĭdth)	WIDTH
yellow	(yĕl´o)	YEL lo

b ch (chief) d f g (get) h j k l m n p r s sh (shoe) t th (thin) t͟h (then) v w y x zh (vision) z

exactly—ĕg•zăkt´lĭ

ā ē ī ō ū (exactly as pronounced when reading the alphabet)

ă	ĕ	ĭ	ŏ	ô	ŭ	o͝o	o͞o	ou	ä—ah	ə (schwa)	oi
sat	set	sit	shot	draw	shut	shook	food	out	park	pə•rād´	oil

EXERCISE 10

THE ACCENTED SYLLABLE OF A WORD

Each word in the first column is syllabified in the second column. In the last column write in capital letters the accented syllable of each word.

WORD	SYLLABIFICATION	ACCENTED SYLLABLE
1. gondola	gon do la	_____
2. plethora	pleth o ra	_____
3. perforate	per fo rate	_____
4. formidable	for mi da ble	_____
5. impotent	im po tent	_____
6. vagary	va gar y	_____
7. mischievous	mis chie vous	_____
8. demoniacal	de mo ni a cal	_____
9. municipal	mu nic i pal	_____
10. exigent	ex i gent	_____
11. applicable	ap pli ca ble	_____
12. lamentable	la men ta ble	_____
13. precept	pre cept	_____
14. irremediable	ir re me di a ble	_____
15. condolence	con do lence	_____
16. preferable	pref er a ble	_____
17. irrevocable	ir rev o ca ble	_____
18. positively	pos i tiv ly	_____
19. intricacy	in tri ca cy	_____
20. combatant	com bat ant	_____
21. irreparable	ir rep a ra ble	_____
22. hospitable	hos pi ta ble	_____
23. impious	im pi ous	_____
24. comparable	com pa ra ble	_____
25. indefatigable	in de fa ti ga ble	_____

EXERCISE 11

THE PRONUNCIATION AND MEANING OF WORDS

Using the symbols employed in this text, indicate the pronunciation of each of the following words. Then define the word. You will need your dictionary for help with this exercise.

WORD	PRONUNCIATION	DEFINITION
1. scion	_____	_____
2. onerous	_____	_____
3. naive	_____	_____
4. desultory	_____	_____
5. heinous	_____	_____
6. incognito	_____	_____
7. machinations	_____	_____
8. covert	_____	_____
9. equitable	_____	_____
10. ultimatum	_____	_____
11. ribald	_____	_____
12. respite	_____	_____
13. posthumous	_____	_____
14. qualm	_____	_____
15. apropos	_____	_____

EXERCISE 12

THE PRONUNCIATION AND MEANING OF WORDS

Using the symbols employed in this text, indicate the pronunciation of each of the following words and then define each word.

WORD	PRONUNCIATION	DEFINITION
1. archipelago (*n.*)		
2. august (*adj.*)		
3. coup (*n.*)		
4. exponent (*n.*)		
5. impotent (*adj.*)		
6. irrelevant (*adj.*)		
7. lamentable (*adj.*)		
8. schism (*n.*)		
9. topography (*n.*)		
10. bestial (*adj.*)		
11. clandestine (*adj.*)		
12. chasm (*n.*)		
13. desultory (*adj.*)		
14. maniacal (*adj.*)		
15. plethora (*n.*)		
16. vagary (*n.*)		
17. disastrous (*adj.*)		
18. acumen (*n.*)		
19. automation (*n.*)		
20. autopsy (*n.*)		

VOCABULARY TEST 1

UNDERSTANDING WORDS IN CONTEXT

We have already studied the following words. How many of them do you know? For each of the boldface words select the word or expression that means most nearly the same and write the letter in the space to the right.

1. The belief **survives**…
   a. belongs   b. clings   c. lives on   d. hovers

2. To **invoke** a genie…
   a. wake up   b. call forth   c. irritate   d. insult

3. To **exorcise** evil spirits…
   a. expel by ceremonies   b. physically exhaust   c. summon   d. create

4. The **coveted** prize…
   a. donated   b. desired   c. rejected   d. admired

5. The **ideological** differences between them…
   a. philosophical   b. of popular opinions   c. of a body of doctrines
   d. abstract

6. **Advocacy** of strict discipline…
   a. abandonment   b. espousal   c. advancement   d. application

7. **Precipitated** a crisis…
   a. avoided   b. encouraged   c. caused   d. hastened

8. The rule of a **demagogue**…
   a. terrorist   b. illegitimate ruler   c. dictator   d. unprincipled leader

9. **Inundated** with verbiage…
   a. inflated   b. flooded   c. swollen   d. covered

10. We pleaded and **cajoled**…
    a. threatened   b. coaxed   c. flattered   d. punished

11. A woman of vast **erudition**…
    a. rudeness   b. technical skill   c. inherited wealth   d. acquired knowledge

12. I was shocked by his **mendacity**.
    a. falseness   b. ignorance   c. indifference   d. gluttony

13. Arguments of sheer **sophistry**…
    a. brilliance   b. wisdom   c. tricky reasoning   d. deep prejudice

14. The **metamorphosis** of the caterpillar…
    a. habitat   b. destructive effect   c. complete change   d. physical structure

15. God's **covenant** with Abraham…
    a. solemn agreement   b. discourse   c. rendezvous   d. brief sojourn

16. A **ribald** story...
    a. plagiarized   b. exaggerated   c. coarse and offensive   d. short and satirical   _____

17. One of the king's **sycophants**...
    a. adverse critics   b. admirers   c. servile flatterers   d. loyal supporters   _____

18. Words are **arbitrary** symbols...
    a. uncertain   b. concrete   c. written   d. unreasonable   _____

19. Words are often **elusive**...
    a. hard to grasp   b. winged   c. harsh   d. quickly learned   _____

20. A student of **pathology**...
    a. science of the mind   b. science of the planets   c. science of space
    d. science of disease   _____

21. An **ostentatious** display of riches...
    a. showy   b. huge   c. reluctant   d. impressive   _____

22. A man of **mundane** interests only...
    a. practical   b. worldly   c. physical   d. vulgar   _____

23. His **capricious** behavior...
    a. whimsical   b. jaunty   c. jovial   d. moody   _____

24. Engaged in **intrigue**...
    a. crime   b. underhand plots   c. family problems   d. philandering   _____

25. An **insipid** novel...
    a. tedious   b. divinely inspired   c. exciting
    d. lacking attractive qualities   _____

26. He made an **incendiary** speech.
    a. extemporaneous   b. politically conservative   c. turgid
    d. tending to arouse strife   _____

27. This is a **dormant** shrub.
    a. flowering   b. temporarily inactive   c. deciduous   d. rapidly growing   _____

28. An **itinerant** preacher...
    a. journeying   b. Protestant   c. evangelical   d. uncouth   _____

29. He was guilty of **matricide**.
    a. incest   b. treason   c. killing his mother   d. betraying his brother   _____

30. She proposed a clever **hypothesis**.
    a. scheme   b. explanatory proposition   c. mathematical analysis
    d. logical solution   _____

31. The statement is a **calumny**.
    a. exaggeration   b. falsehood   c. recommendation   d. slander   _____

32. The several **categories** of animals...
    a. classes   b. sizes   c. protective organs   d. functions   _____

33. Several provinces **amalgamated**.
a. rebelled   b. seceded   c. yielded   d. combined

34. We are not bound by **ecclesiastical** law.
a. of the ancient world   b. of the common people   c. of the church
d. of legislative committees

35. Here children **flourish**.
a. play   b. learn   c. sicken   d. thrive

36. I dislike **synthetic** materials.
a. rough-textured   b. chemically manufactured   c. hand-printed
d. hand-loomed

37. Suspected of a **heinous** crime...
a. wilful   b. hateful   c. political   d. sexual

38. Engaged in political **machinations**...
a. party politics   b. controversies   c. intrigues   d. primary elections

39. Their **covert** participation in the business.
a. inactive   b. concealed   c. desultory   d. profitable

40. His **lamentable** record in office...
a. regrettable   b. mediocre   c. meritorious   d. inconclusive

VOCABULARY TEST 2

USING WORDS IN ILLUSTRATIVE SENTENCES

The following words have been used in the text or exercises. Show that you know these words by using each in an illustrative sentence—a sentence that throws some light on the meaning of the word.

WORD	SENTENCE
1. incognito	_____
2. schism	_____
3. bestial	_____
4. clandestine	_____
5. vagary	_____
6. maniacal	_____
7. incantation	_____
8. conjure	_____
9. intractable	_____
10. random	_____
11. perverted	_____
12. exhort	_____
13. articulated	_____
14. chivalrous	_____
15. trepidation	_____
16. peregrination	_____
17. tedious	_____
18. eminent	_____
19. onerous	_____
20. apropos	_____

6. WORDS BORROWED FROM OTHER LANGUAGES

Our language has acquired words from every people with whom English-speaking people have had any political, economic, or cultural contact; thus the English vocabulary is a mixture of native words and words borrowed from about fifty other languages. An estimated thirteen percent of our words has been derived from Greek, and a far larger percentage has come from Latin and the Romance languages, French, Italian, and Spanish. In all, a total of about seventy-five percent of the words in English are borrowed words. Nevertheless, English retains its linguistic integrity because its grammar, syntax, and a large stock of common words are essentially native.

Some of the languages from which English has borrowed are listed below with a few of the borrowings from each.

French	depot, chute, hangar, dime, camouflage
Spanish	alligator, banana, barbecue, lariat, stevedore
Dutch	boss, cruller, scow, waffle, stoop
Italian	bulletin, fascism, cavalry, dome, miniature
Persian	orange, lemon, damson, sugar, veranda
Latin	devil, hospital, vespers, alms, chalk
Danish	law, sister, scold, dairy, cake
Arabic	admiral, cotton, zenith, apricot, magazine
East Indian	pajama, cashmere, thug, shampoo, dungaree
German	drill, waltz, poodle, nickel, veneer
Greek	hypocrite, enthusiasm, hoi polloi, Bible, phlegmatic
Russian	troika, tzar, samovar, vodka, caracul
Hebrew	cherub, seraph, amen, matzo, kosher

The ease with which English has absorbed words has made it a leader among world languages, but it has also made English a difficult language to speak and write correctly. Although our language has been persistent in borrowing words, it has been inconsistent in adapting them to English usage. Some borrowed words have been completely adapted, some have been partially adapted, and some remain unchanged despite their use in English. As a result our language contains many words that are inflected, spelled, and pronounced in strange and irregular ways. Moreover, since usage constantly changes, it is difficult to know what stage of absorption a word is in. The only way of making sure is to consult the latest edition of a standard dictionary.

ANGLICIZED WORDS

Many borrowed words have been so completely absorbed that we are not aware of their foreign origin. They seem to be native words because they correspond to the English practice of pronunciation, spelling, and inflection, or the lack of it. These words have been completely Anglicized.

For example, the old French word *tūr* has been completely Anglicized to *tower* by the changes in spelling and pronunciation. Like all English names of objects, *tower* is a neuter noun that forms its plural with a final *s* and has no possessive form, the possessive being indicated by the prepositional phrase *of the tower*. Similarly, the Italian word *novella* has been completely Anglicized to *novel*.

PARTLY ANGLICIZED WORDS

Words that correspond only in part to the English practice of spelling, pronunciation, and inflection are *partly Anglicized words*. Although the plural of *garage* is *garages,* we accent the second syllable and give the word a French pronunciation: *gə·räzh´*. The British, however, have Anglicized *garage* completely, pronouncing it like an English word with the accent on the first syllable: *gă´rĭj*.

The plural of *concerto* from the Italian is either *concertos* (the Anglicized form) or *concerti* (the Italian form). Also we pronounce the *c* of the second syllable in the Italian manner, *ch*. The plural of *antenna* is either *antennae* (the regular Latin form) or *antennas* (the regular English form). Note that *antennas* refers to *radio* and *television*, whereas *antennae* refers to zoology. Other words with two acceptable plurals, both the foreign and the English forms, are *curriculum* (*curricula, curriculums*), *gymnasium* (*gymnasia, gymnasiums*), and *appendix* (*appendices, appendixes*).

WORDS THAT REMAIN FOREIGN

Many borrowed terms remain un-Anglicized in accepted English usage. An example is the commonly used word *alumnus,* which forms its plural according to the Latin rule and also retains its Latin endings to indicate gender:

masculine singular	alumnus	He is an *alumnus* of Cornell.
masculine plural	alumni	The *alumni* have protested the dropping of football.
feminine singular	alumna	She is an *alumna* of Harvard.
feminine plural	alumnae	Vassar has just appealed to its *alumnae* for funds.

The following commonly used terms are also un-Anglicized:

de facto (dē făc´tō)	a Latin term meaning *functioning;* in fact, in reality:
	Germany will recognize the *de facto* government.
sine die (sīn ē dī´ē)	a Latin term meaning without a day being set for a meeting again:
	Because of the chairman's illness, the committee adjourned *sine die*.
per diem (pər dī´əm)	a Latin term meaning by or for the day; daily:
	The *per diem* workers receive no pension.
mélange (mā länzh´)	a French word meaning mixture, blend, medley:
	His music is a *mélange* of different styles.
tour de force (to͞or də fôrs´)	French term meaning a feat of unusual strength, skill, or ability:
	Since Ravel's *Bolero* still appeals, it is more than a *tour de force*.

ā ē ī ō ū (exactly as pronounced when reading the alphabet)

ă	ĕ	ĭ	ŏ	ô	ú	o͝o	o͞o	ou	ä—ah	ə—(schwa)	oi
sat	set	sit	shot	draw	shut	shook	food	out	park	pə • rād´	oil

57

THE PRONUNCIATION OF FORMAL PROPER NAMES

The pronunciation of proper names of foreign origin is particularly troublesome, as the following examples show:

Los Angeles	(Spanish for the angels)—completely Anglicized and pronounced Lŏs An´gələs—Spanish—Lōs Än´hä läs
San Juan	Partly Anglicized and pronounced Săn Hwän´—Spanish—Sän Hwän´
Don Juan	Completely Anglicized to Dŏn Jōō´ən—Spanish—Dōn Hōō´än
Louis	Louis may be Anglicized to Lōō'ĭs, Lōō ĭ´, or given the French pronunciation Lwē. When the name refers to a Frenchman or to one of the French kings, it is always given the French pronunciation. The American city *St. Louis* is Anglicized as St. Lōō'ĭs or St. Lōō´ĭ.
Handel	The name of this German composer has been Anglicized to Hăn´dəl (German Hĕn´dəl).
Wagner	Although this family name has been Anglicized to Wăg´nər, the name of the German composer is un-Anglicized: Väg´nər.
Mozart	This composer's name is pronounced in the Viennese manner: Mō´tsärt.

FOREIGN TERMS USED IN ENGLISH

English employs a rather large number of foreign terms. Below is a list of those most commonly used and useful to know. An additional list appears on pages 182 to 186 in the appendix. The words are accompanied by their pronunciation in English. Anyone who prefers to give the Latin terms their Latin pronunciation may do so.

Latin Expressions

ad nauseam	(ăd nô´zē əm) To a disgusting or sickening degree: He talked about his sickness *ad nauseam*.
ante bellum	(ăn´tĭ bĕl´əm) Before the war; referring especially to the American Civil War: This novel depicts the *ante bellum* South in realistic terms.
a priori	(ā prī ōr´ī, ä prĭ ōr´ĭ) Reasoning based on assumption, unsupported by factual examination: His conclusion is invalid because it is based on *a priori* reasoning.
bona fide	(bōn´ə fī´dĭ) In good faith; without fraud: If the offer is *bona fide*, I shall consider it.
caveat emptor	(kā´vē ăt ĕmp´tôr) "Let the buyer beware." This is a legal phrase meaning that the purchaser buys at his or her own risk: Since no agency has the power to regulate this class of merchandise, *caveat emptor*.

ā ē ī ō ū (exactly as pronounced when reading the alphabet)

ă	ĕ	ĭ	ŏ	ô	ŭ	ŏŏ	ōō	ou	ä—ah	ə—(schwa)	oi
sat	set	sit	shot	draw	shut	shook	food	out	park	pə•răd´	oil

deus ex machina	(dē´əs ĕks măk´ə nə) "A God from a machine." In ancient drama a hopelessly tangled plot was sometimes untangled by a god who was lowered onto the stage by a hoisting device. Any unreal or illogical solution is called a *deus ex machina*: He appeared like a *deus ex machina* and put an end to all of their troubles.
ergo	(ər´gō) Therefore; hence: He had the motive; he had the opportunity; he had the strength: *ergo* he is the culprit.
ex officio	(ēks´ə fĭsh´ ĭō´) "By virtue of one's office": An officer whose position includes his being a member of a committee is a member *ex officio*.
ex post facto	(ēks´pōst´ făc´tō) After the event or deed; retroactive. This term is applied to a law passed after the commission of the offense with which it is concerned: This law will be declared unconstitutional because it is *ex post facto*.
in medias res	(ĭn mē´dĭ ăs´rēz´) "Into the middle of things"; starting in the middle of an action or a story: Since Conrad's novel *Lord Jim* begins in *medias res*, we do not at first know the cause of Jim's disgrace.
in toto	(ĭn tō´tō) In full; entirety: He made a generous offer and purchased the inventory *in toto*.
magnum opus	(măg´nəm ōp´əs) A great work; masterpiece; greatest achievement: *Paradise Lost* is Milton's *magnum opus*.
non sequitur	(nŏn sĕk´wətər) "It does not follow." Applied to remarks or conclusions that are not logically related to what has gone before: This last remark is a *non sequitur* and will have to be deleted for the sake of logic and coherence.
per se	(pər sē´) By itself; by one's self; essentially: There is nothing wrong with the proposed regulation *per se*, but the bill is too loosely drawn.
quid pro quo	(kwĭd´ prō kwō´) Something for something; an equivalent exchange: The commissioner was naive, to say the least, if he really thought that his wealthy benefactor would not exact his *quid pro quo*.
status quo	(stā´təs kwō) Things as they are; present conditions. A conservative is one who wishes to preserve the *status quo*.

Greek Expressions

eureka	(yo͞o rē´kə) "I have found it." A cry of triumph: "*Eureka!*" he cried when he succeeded in making a magic square.
hoi polloi	(hoi pə loi´) The masses; the common people. *The* is not used with this term because *hoi* means *the*: Expressing contempt for *hoi polloi*, he stepped forward on the gallows and spat.

ā ē ī ō ū (exactly as pronounced when reading the alphabet)

ă	ĕ	ĭ	ŏ	ô	ŭ	o͝o	o͞o	ou	ä—ah	ə—(schwa)	oi
sat	set	sit	shot	draw	shut	shook	food	out	park	pə • rād´	oil

French Expressions

avant-garde (ă′vä[n] gärd′) Pioneers; vanguard: In music Schönberg is a modernist or what newspaper critics call an *avant-garde* composer.

bistro (bĭs′trō) A tavern or small wine shop: Every evening on his way home from work he stops off at his favorite *bistro* for a glass of wine.

carte blanche (kärt′ blänsh′) "A white paper"; blanket permission; unlimited authority: Since the board would not give him *carte blanche* in dealing with the union, he resigned as plant manager.

cause célèbre (kōz sĕ lĕb′r) A celebrated legal case; a cause or a criminal case that arouses wide interest: The trial and conviction of the Rosenbergs was a *cause célèbre* of international proportions.

coup d'état (kōō′ dĕ tä′) A sudden stroke of state policy; a sudden stroke that overthrows a government: I expect that the insurgent generals will attempt a *coup d'état* within the year.

cul-de-sac (kŭl′də săk′) A blind alley; a dead end street: Caught in a *cul-de-sac,* the gangster was killed, trying to shoot his way out.

double entendre (dōō′blä[n] tä[n]′dr) An expression with two interpretations, one of which is indelicate: The truly innocent will not catch the *double entendre* and will therefore not be embarrassed.

esprit de corps (ĕs prē′də kôr′) A common spirit of pride in a group: He vainly tried to develop e*sprit de corps* among the disgruntled reservists.

fait accompli (fĕ tă kô[m] plē′) An accomplished and irrevocable act; a completed action that must be accepted: My son's marriage is a *fait accompli,* but I will never receive his wife.

faux pas (fō pä′) "A false step"; a social error: He was so afraid of making a *faux pas* that he refused to take tea.

laissez-faire (lĕs′ā fār′) "Let them do what they wish"; a policy of noninterference; the economic doctrine that government should not interfere in business: In periods of boom they advocate *laissez-faire,* but in depression they clamor for government assistance.

nom de plume (nŏm′də plōōm′) Pen name. In English the pseudonym of an author; in French any pseudonym: Mark Twain is the *nom de plume* of Samuel Langhorne Clemens.

petit bourgeois (pətē′ bŏŏrzhwä′) "The little man"; one of the lower middle class: Hitler was a *petit bourgeois* who became the dictator of Germany.

ā ē ī ō ū (exactly as pronounced when reading the alphabet)

ă	ĕ	ĭ	ŏ	ô	ŭ	ŏŏ	ōō	ou	ä—ah	ə—(schwa)	oi
sat	set	sit	shot	draw	shut	shook	food	out	park	pə • răd′	oil

60

sans	(sănz or Fr. sä[n]) Without; deprived of: I was stranded in a foreign city *sans* money, *sans* health, and *sans* friends.
savoir-faire	(săv′wär fār′) "To know how to do" something; tact; polish: Only a man with *savoir faire* could entertain his ex-wife and her new husband for a weekend.
tête-à-tête	(tāt′ə tāt′) "Head to head"; a confidential conversation; a face-to-face talk: By correspondence we could accomplish nothing, but in an hour's *tête-à-tête* we settled our differences and agreed on a course of action.

Spanish Expressions

aficionado	(ä fĭs ĭ ō nä′dō) A fan; a devoted follower of a sport: Hemingway was an *aficionado* of bullfighting and big game hunting.
bonanza	(bō năn′zə) A mine with a rich yield of gold or silver; a source of unusually large income: The slum property he purchased during the depression became a *bonanza* and made him a multimillionaire.

Italian Expressions

al fresco	(ăl frĕs′kō) "In the fresh air"; out of doors; I dislike picnics and every other kind of *al fresco* dining.
chiaroscuro	(kĭ är ′ōs kūr ′ō) "Light and dark"; a sketch in black and white; dramatic interplay of light and shade in a painting: When he became more interested in *chiaroscuro* than in rendering a likeness, Rembrandt lost his popularity as a portrait painter.
dilettante	(dĭl′ə tănt′) An amateur; a dabbler in the fine arts: He remained a *dilettante* in music because he never had to earn his living or a position of respect.
presto	(prĕs′tō) A direction in music calling for a fast tempo; quickly; rapidly: He played the second movement *presto* although it is clearly marked "with movement, but not fast."
sotto voce	(sot′to vo′chi) "Under the voice"; in a whisper or undertone: Michelle spoke *sotto voce* so that only those seated on either side of her could hear.
virtuoso	(vər′choo ō′sō) One who is technically excellent in the practice of an art; especially a musician: His music is seldom heard because it is so difficult that only a *virtuoso* can play it.

ā ē ī ō ū (exactly as pronounced when reading the alphabet)

ă	ě	ĭ	ŏ	ô	ŭ	oŏ	ōō	ou	ä—ah	ə—(schwa)	oi
sat	set	sit	shot	draw	shut	shook	food	out	park	pə • rād′	oil

German Expressions

ersatz   (ĕr zäts´) Substitute material; therefore shoddy and inferior: There is so much *ersatz* in our automobiles today that they fall apart after 20,000 miles.

hinterland   (hĭn´tər lănd) Remote regions; frontiers; the "sticks": The people in the *hinterland* of the United States seldom see a play.

weltschmerz   (vĕlt´shmĕrts) Sorrow about life or the condition of the world; sentimental, pessimistic longing: Youth and spring are the times for *weltschmerz* and the times to read German romantic poetry, which is awash in tears of *weltschmerz*.

zeitgeist   (tsīt gīst) Spirit or soul of the times: Factually these studies are not always reliable; but they are excellent in conveying the *zeitgeist* of the eighteenth century.

ā ē ī ō ū (exactly as pronounced when reading the alphabet)

ă	ĕ	ĭ	ŏ	ô	ŭ	o͝o	o͞o	ou	ä—ah	ə—(schwa)	oi
sat	set	sit	shot	draw	shut	shook	food	out	park	pə•rād´	oil

Exercise 13

The Origin of Borrowed Words

By consulting the dictionary give the language of ultimate origin and the meaning of each of the following words.

Word	Original Language	Meaning
1. corpse (n.)		
2. cosmetic (adj.)		
3. banal (adj.)		
4. scepter (n.)		
5. tyrant (n.)		
6. quintessence (n.)		
7. portage (n.)		
8. plebeian (adj.)		
9. litany (n.)		
10. knave (n.)		
11. huckster (n.)		
12. gourmet (n.)		
13. fortuitous (adj.)		
14. dogma (n.)		
15. debacle (n.)		
16. kleptomania (n.)		
17. chronicle (n.)		
18. blaspheme (v.)		
19. adamant (adj.)		
20. aesthetic (adj.)		

Exercise 14

Using Terms of Foreign Origin

By consulting the dictionary and the list of foreign terms in this text, give the meaning of each of the following terms and use each in an illustrative sentence of your own.

FOREIGN TERM	MEANING	SENTENCE
1. alter ego		
2. per diem		
3. a priori		
4. bona fide		
5. in toto		
6. ersatz		
7. per se		
8. quid pro quo		
9. cul-de-sac		
10. fait accompli		
11. tête-à-tête		
12. hinterland		
13. annus mirabilis		
14. au courant		
15. raison d'être		
16. vis-à-vis		
17. hors de combat		
18. homo sapiens		
19. ad nauseam		
20. caveat emptor		

EXERCISE 15

USING TERMS OF FOREIGN ORIGIN

Each of the following sentences contains an expression in parentheses. Write the foreign term for this expression in the space to the right.

1. Some critics believe that his novel is an amazing (feat of unusual skill).

   _____

2. This orchestral suite is a charming (mixture or medley) spoofing the Viennese composers.

   _____

3. There are not many places to dine (out of doors) in New York.

   _____

4. This used car is a (without fraud) bargain.

   _____

5. Shakespeare's practice of beginning plays (in the middle of things) annoys me.

   _____

6. She has decided to publish her mystery stories under a (pen name).

   _____

7. This novel by Balzac is about a French (one of the lower middle class).

   _____

8. When Phil realized that he had made a (social error), he blushed with embarrassment.

   _____

9. You may regard him as an (vanguard) painter, but he is quite academic.

   _____

10. The only way to solve our school problems is to hire a strong superintendent and give him (blanket permission) to reorganize the system.

    _____

11. More than any other twentieth-century novelist, Mann expresses the (soul of the times) of the century.

    _____

12. His plot is so hopelessly tangled that it can be untangled only by some (unreal and illogical) solution.

    _____

13. In my opinion *An American Tragedy* is Theodore Dreiser's (greatest work or achievement).

    _____

14. Anyone satisfied with the (things as they are at present) should not be a member of this organization.

    _____

15. Adam Smith is the foremost exponent of the doctrine of (let them do as they wish) in economics.

    _____

16. The instructor wrote (it does not follow) all over my composition.

    _____

17. Some politicians are trying to make a (celebrated cause arousing wide interest) of the FBI scandal. _____

18. The director said, "You must seem to be speaking these lines (in a whisper or undertone)." _____

19. Despite all of his experience and talent, Roger remains a (amateur and dabbler) in sculpture. _____

20. I like most sports, but I am really an (devoted follower) of hockey. _____

7. WORDS DERIVED FROM NAMES

Many English words have been derived from names. Processes, discoveries, and inventions are frequently named for the persons who made them or were otherwise connected with them. *Pasteurization,* for example, is a treatment devised by Louis Pasteur, the French bacteriologist, to destroy microorganisms in milk. The *guillotine,* a device for beheading people, is named for J. I. Guillotin, the French physician who urged its use. *Amperes, ohms,* and *watts* are electrical terms taken from A. M. Ampere, G. S. Ohm, and James Watt, respectively. The word *benedict,* meaning a newly married man, is derived from the scornful bachelor in Shakespeare's *Much Ado About Nothing,* who is tricked into courting and marrying Beatrice.

By association English words have also been derived from the names of places. People associate a product with its place of origin, a custom with its place of practice, and name the product or custom accordingly. For example *hamburger* is named for Hamburg, Germany where it originated or was popular. One who makes hats is called a *milliner* because Milan, Italy, was a famous center of hat making.

Many English words have also been derived from Biblical names, from names in the mythology and history of ancient Greece and Rome, and from the names of fictional characters. The Biblical Jezebel was so iniquitous that she became a prototype, and all shameless women are called *Jezebels.* So impressive was the strict discipline of ancient Sparta that we call any rigorously simple life *Spartan.* A person is *tantalized* when he is tormented like Tantalus, the son of Zeus. Words like these establish a frame of reference to the early experiences of humans and these show how deeply we have studied the past and been influenced by it.

In former years when the Bible was more thoroughly read than it is now and when schoolchildren were immersed in the language and history of the classical past, the words drawn from these sources were more meaningful than they are in our age of self-absorption. To many of our students today they are either entirely known or without association. And yet they are words that are frequently encountered in the writing and speaking of cultivated individuals and that should therefore be known by all.

It is always interesting and sometimes astounding to discover that a common word comes from a name in our fictive or historical past. The word leads us to something we may not have known, and the knowledge, in turn, makes the word vivid and memorable. Below are classified lists of name words, together with their derivations, that everyone should know.

WORDS FROM THE NAMES OF PERSONS

WORD	MEANING	ORIGIN
boycott (*v.t.*)	to combine in abstaining, or preventing dealings with, as a means of intimidation or coercion	Captain Boycott, the agent of an Irish landlord, was the first victim (1880) of such action because of his rapacity.
byronic (*adj.*)	equivocal in nature and characterized by melodramatic energy, melancholy, etc.	From the British romantic poet George Gordon, Lord Byron (1788–1824) whose poetry is characterized by such qualities.

WORD	MEANING	ORIGIN
bowdlerize (v.t.)	to expurgate a book by eliminating or changing passages that may be considered indelicate or offensive	Dr. Thomas Bowdler published *The Family Shakespeare* (1812) from which was omitted words and expressions "which cannot with propriety be read aloud in a family."
chauvinism (n.)	blind enthusiasm for military glory; zealous and belligerent patriotism or devotion to a cause	From Nicholas Chauvin, an old soldier and enthusiastic admirer of Napoleon I. A play written in 1831, *La Cocarde Tricolore,* presented a young soldier named Chauvin who sang patriotic songs. The word was probably taken from the character in the play.
gargantuan (adj.)	gigantic; enormous; prodigious	From Gargantua, the amiable giant and king of enormous capacity for eating and drinking, in the satirical romance *Gargantua and Pantagruel* by François Rabelais (1535).
gerrymander (n.)	an arbitrary arrangement of the political divisions of a state, county, etc., made so as to give one party an unfair advantage in elections	From Elbridge Gerry, governor of Massachusetts, whose party in 1812 redistricted Essex County. *Gerry* and *(sala) mander,* from a fancied resemblance of the map of the districted county to the animal, led to the word *gerrymander.*
lothario (n.)	a jaunty libertine; a rake	From the heartless libertine and rake in Nicholas Rowe's play *The Fair Penitent* (1703). A character of the same name and similar type appears also in Cervantes' *Don Quixote* and in Goethe's *Wilhelm Meister.*
Machiavellian (adj.)	characterized by craft, cunning, and deceit	Niccolò Machiavelli (1469–1527) was an Italian statesman and writer on government. His famous book, *The Prince,* was a guide for the rulers of his day. It set down the principles of acquiring power and leadership as he observed them.
malapropism (n.)	act or habit of ridiculously misusing words; a word so misused	From Mrs. Malaprop, a character in Sheridan's play, *The Rivals* (1775), who ludicrously misapplies long words.
martinet (n.)	a rigid disciplinarian, esp. military or naval	From General Martinet, an infamous drillmaster in the army of Louis XIV.
maudlin (adj.)	tearfully or weakly emotional or sentimental, esp. from drink	From Mary Magdalene, frequently identified with the repentant woman in Luke 7:37-50, whose tearful countenance as represented in medieval art was irreverently attributed to excessive drinking.

WORD	MEANING	ORIGIN
masochism (n.)	self-torture; in psychiatry, a condition in which sexual gratification depends on suffering and humiliation	From an Austrian novelist, Leopold von Sacher Masoch (1836–1895), who vividly described such a condition.
maverick (n.)	a dissenter; an unpredictable politician	Probably from Samuel A. Maverick, a Texas rancher of the 1840s, who did not brand his calves. The word was first applied to an unbranded calf and was extended to anyone who avoids the herd.
Pecksniffian (adj.)	making a hypocritical display of benevolence and high principles	From Mrs. Pecksniff, a vivid and ludicrous character in Dickens' *Martin Chuzzlewit.*
quixotic (adj.)	extravagantly chivalrous and romantic; visionary, impractical	From Don Quixote in Cervantes' famous satire of the same name. Don Quixote, the hero of the novel, was inspired by lofty and chivalrous ideals that led him to impractical and ludicrous deeds.
sadistic (adj.)	characterized by morbid enjoyment in being cruel	From Count de Sade (1740–1814) who was notorious for the characters of his book who took pleasure in tormenting others.
sandwich (n.)	a layer of meat, cheese, etc., between two slices of bread	From the Earl of Sandwich (1718–1792) whose passion for gaming was so great that he was reluctant to leave the gaming table for dinner. He is said to have ordered meat between slices of bread and thus to have created the sandwich.
spoonerism (n.)	a slip of the tongue whereby initial or other sounds are transposed	From the Rev. William A. Spooner (1844–1930) famous for the habit of transposing the initial sounds of words and phrases: "our queer old dean" for "our dear old queen."
thespian (n.)	an actor	Thespis (fl.534 B.C.) was a Greek dramatist who contributed to the development of tragedy, which then consisted solely of choruses, by introducing an individual actor.
titian (adj.)	a yellowish, reddish, or golden-brown color; auburn	The color was made famous by the great Italian painter Titian (Tiziano Veccillio, c.1477–1576) who liked to use it for hair.

WORDS FROM THE NAMES OF PLACES

WORD	MEANING	ORIGIN
billingsgate (n.)	foul or abusive language	From Billingsgate, a game and fish market in London where abusive language was heard.
buncombe (n.) (also bunkum and the abbreviation bunk)	insincere speechmaking or talk; claptrap; humbug	From a congressional representative's phrases "talking for Buncombe." Buncombe is a county of North Carolina whose residents and virtues the congressman eulogized in flowing speech.
canter (n.)	an easy gallop; the gait of a horse between a trot and a gallop	From the speed at which pilgrims, anxious to end their onerous journey, entered Canterbury, England, where they would visit the Cathedral and the shrine of St. Thomas à Becket. Becket (1118–70) was the archbishop of Canterbury who was murdered because of his opposition to King Henry II's policies toward the church.
mecca (n.)	a center or goal for many people	From Mecca, the birthplace of Mohammed, and spiritual center of Islam.
meander (v.t.)	to proceed by a wandering course; wander aimlessly	The Mendere (Greek Maiandros) is a river in Asia Minor noted in ancient times for its winding course.
sardonic (adj.)	bitterly ironic; sarcastic	From a poisonous Sardinian plant, known to the Romas as herba Sardonia, which contorted a victim's face into a grim, fixed laugh.
shanghai (v.t.)	to render insensible, as by drugs, in order to ship forcibly on a vessel needing sailors; to effect by force or compulsion	Apparently a shortened form of "to ship to Shanghai," a port to which sailors were reluctant to go; or from the method used to get sailors at Shanghai for ships whose crew had run off.
solecism (n.)	a substandard intrusion into standard speech; any error, impropriety, or inconsistence	From the city of Soloi in Cilicia where the Athenian colonists spoke a corrupt form of the Attic dialect.
utopia (n.)	a place or state of ideal perfection	From Utopia, an imaginary island described in Sir Thomas More's Utopia (1516) as enjoying the utmost perfection in law, politics, etc.

WORDS FROM THE NAMES OF BIBLICAL PERSONS AND PLACES

WORD	MEANING	ORIGIN
Armageddon (n.)	any great, crucial armed conflict	Armageddon is the place where the final battle will be fought between the forces of good and evil. Rev. 16:6
babel (n.)	a confused mixture of sounds; a scene of noise and confusion	An ancient city (Babylon) where the building of a tower intended to reach heaven was begun and a confounding of the people took place. Gen. 11:4-9
bedlam (n.)	any lunatic asylum; a madhouse; a scene of wild uproar and confusion	An alteration of *Bethlehem* as used in the name of a London lunatic asylum called the Hospital of St. Mary of Bethlehem.
behemoth (n.)	a huge and powerful man, beast, etc.	An animal, perhaps the hippopotamus, mentioned in Job 40:15.
jeremiad (n.)	a prolonged lamentation; a lugubrious complaint	From the prophet Jeremiah whose lament for Jerusalem and Zion is contained in the "Lamentations of Jeremiah."
Jezebel (n.)	a shameless, abandoned woman	The wife of Ahab, King of Israel, who was notorious for introducing the worship of the god Baal, persecuting Elijah the prophet, and instigating the murder of Naboth. I Kings 16:31,21,25, II Kings 9:30-37
mammon (n.)	riches or material wealth	Mammon was a personification of riches as an evil spirit or deity. Mat. 6:24, Luke 16:9,11,13
philistine (adj.)	lacking in culture; commonplace	The Philistines were a non-Semitic people with whom the history of Israel is intimately connected. They were reviled as smug people who lacked culture.
samaritan (n.)	one who is compassionate and helpful to people in distress	A Samaritan was an inhabitant of the ancient kingdom of Samaria in North Palestine. See Luke 10:30-37 for the story of the good Samaritan.
satanic (adj.)	extremely wicked; diabolical	In the Bible Satan is the chief evil spirit; the great adversary of man; the devil.

WORDS AND EXPRESSIONS FROM THE HISTORY OF GREECE AND ROME

WORD	MEANING	ORIGIN
Augustan (*adj.*)	pertaining to the Augustan Age in Roman literature or to the highest point in the literature of any country; having some of the characteristics of Augustan literature, as classicism, correctness, brilliance, etc.	Augustus Caesar (63 B.C.–A.D. 14) was the first emperor of Rome. His reign, known as the Augustan Age, was the golden age of Latin literature.
cesarean (*adj.*)	a surgical operation to remove a fetus from the uterus	Such an operation was supposedly performed at the birth of Julius Caesar (102 or 104–44 B.C.), the Roman general, statesman, historian, and conqueror of Gaul, Britain, etc.
Croesus (*n.*)	a very rich man	From Croesus (died 546 B.C.), King of Lydia, noted for his great wealth.
crossing the Rubicon	to take a final, irrevocable step that may be dangerous	The Rubicon is a small river separating ancient Italy from Cisalpine Gaul crossed by Julius Caesar in 49 B.C. in defiance of the Senate's order to disband his troops. As he made his decision, he said, "The die is cast."
cutting the Gordian knot	attacking and solving a problem directly and boldly	Gordius, a legendary King of Phrygia, fastened the pole of his chariot, dedicated to Jupiter, with an inextricable knot that was to be undone only by one who should rule Asia. Instead of trying to untie the knot, Alexander the Great summarily cut it with his sword.
cynical (*adj.*)	of a sneering, fault-finding nature; distrusting the motives of others	The Cynics were a sect of Greek philosophers who taught the value of self-control and independence. They were contemptuous of wealth, ease, and the motives of men. *Cynic* is related to the word for dog and was applied to these philosophers because of their snarling manner.
dionysian (*adj.*)	wild, orgiastic	Dionysius was the Greek god of wine and drama. He is identified with the Roman god Bacchus. *Dionysia* were the orgiastic and dramatic festivals in honor of Dionysius, celebrated periodically in various parts of Greece.

WORD	MEANING	ORIGIN
draconian (*adj.*)	rigorous; severe; cruel	Draco (fl. seventh cent. B.C.) was an Athenian statesman and lawgiver noted for his code of laws, so severe that they were said to be written in blood.
epicurean (*adj.*)	given or adopted to luxury or indulgence in sensual pleasures; of luxurious tastes or habits, esp. in eating and drinking	From Epicurus (342?–270 B.C.) the Greek philosopher whose chief doctrines were that the world came into being by accident and that the highest good in life is pleasure, which consists of freedom from disturbance or pain.
hedonism (*adj.*)	the doctrine that pleasure or happiness is the highest good; devotion to pleasure	*Hedonism,* from a Greek word meaning pleasure or sweetness, is the name of a philosophical doctrine. See *epicureanism.*
Lucullan (*adj.*)	rich; sumptuous; lavish, esp. pertaining to food	Lucius Licinius Lucullus (c.110–57? B.C.) was a Roman consul and general famous for his great wealth and luxury, and esp. for diverse and elaborate cookery.
Maecenas (*n.*)	a generous patron, esp. of the arts	Gaius Cilnius Maecenas, was bet. 73 and 63 B.C. a Roman statesman and a friend and generous patron of the great Latin poets, Virgil and Horace.
philippic (*n.*)	any discourse or speech of bitter denunciation	When King Philip II of Macedonia invaded Greece, Demosthenes, the greatest orator of his times, attacked him bitterly in a number of celebrated speeches known as *Philippics.*
solon (*n.*)	a wise lawgiver	Solon (c.638–c.558 B.C.) was an Athenian statesman noted for his political reforms and his great wisdom.
Spartan (*adj.*)	rigorously simple, frugal, or austere; sternly disciplined; brave	The ancient Greek city of Sparta was famous for its strict discipline and training of soldiers.
stoicism (*n.*)	conduct conforming to the precepts of the Stoics; repression of emotion and indifference to pleasure and pain	Stoic was the name of a school of philosophy founded by Zeno (about 308 B.C.). The philosophy was named after the Stoa, a colonnade in Athens, where the school was established. One of the doctrines was that men should be free from passions, unmoved by joy or grief, and should submit without complaint to unavoidable necessity.

WORD	MEANING	ORIGIN
the sword of Damocles (*n.*)	imminent danger; impending doom	Damocles was a companion and flatterer of Dionysius, the ruler of Syracuse. Weary of Damocles' remarks about the happy lot of a king, Dionysius decided to teach him a lesson. He placed Damocles at a magnificent banquet, with a sword suspended over his head by a single horsehair, to show him the perilous nature of that happiness.

WORDS AND EXPRESSIONS FROM CLASSICAL MYTHOLOGY

WORD	MEANING	ORIGIN
Achilles heel (*n.*)	a vulnerable spot	Achilles, the hero of the *Iliad*, was dipped in the River Styx to make him invulnerable. Achilles' only veak spot was his heel, by which his mother had held him. He was killed at Troy by Paris, who shot him in the heel with a poisoned arrow.
Adonis (*n.*)	a very handsome young man	In Greek mythology Adonis, a favorite of Aphrodite, was slain by a wild boar, but was permitted by Zeus to spend part of the time on earth with Aphrodite.
aegis (*n.*)	protection or sponsorship	Aegis was the shield of Zeus lent by Zeus to other deities: The contest will be held under the *aegis* of the First Baptist Church.
aphrodisiac (*n.*)	a preparation for the purpose of arousing physical desire	From Aphrodite, the Greek goddess of love.
argonaut (*n.*)	a voyager; a person who emigrated to California in 1848 when gold was discovered there	From Greek legend, a member of the band that sailed to Colchis in the ship *Argo* in search of the golden fleece.
bacchanalian (*adj.*)	like a Roman festival in honor of Bacchus; like drunken orgies	Bacchus was the Roman god of wine who was honored by feasts known as Bacchanalia.
calliope (*n.*)	a musical instrument consisting of a set of steam whistles played from a keyboard	In Greek myth Calliope was the muse of heroic poetry.

Word	Meaning	Origin
Cassandra (*n.*)	a prophet of doom and destruction	Cassandra, the daughter of King Priam of Troy, was a prophetess. Apollo gave her the gift of prophecy, but when she did not fulfill her promise to love him, he decreed that no one should believe her although she spoke the truth.
chimera (*n.*)	a horrible or unreal creature of the imagination; a vain or odd fancy	The Chimera was a mythological, fire-breathing monster commonly represented with a goat's head, a lion's body, and a serpent's tail. (for example: Many doctors oppose any plan for public medical care because of the *chimeras* of socialized medicine.)
cornucopia (*n.*)	an overflowing supply; a horn-shaped or conical receptacle or ornament	Zeus was suckled by a goat Amalthaea whose fabulous horn was overflowing with anything the god wanted.
Cyclopean (*adj.*)	gigantic, vast; in architecture representing an early style of masonry employing massive stones	The Cyclops were a race of one-eyed giants. They made buildings of large stones piled one upon another without cement.
erotic (*adj.*)	pertaining to sexual desire	Eros was the Greek god of love. His Roman name was Cupid.
gorgon (*n.*)	a terrible or repulsive woman	In Greek legend the Gorgons were three sisters whose heads were covered with snakes and who turned to stone anyone who gazed upon them.
herculean (*adj.*)	prodigious in strength, courage, or size	Hercules, the celebrated Greek hero, performed twelve extraordinary feats, known as the labors of Hercules.
hydra-headed (*adj.*)	difficult to destroy, esp. pertaining to an evil that when apparently eliminated in one place, springs up in another	Hydra was a monstrous serpent represented as having nine heads, each of which was replaced by two when cut off, unless the wound was cauterized. It was slain by Hercules.
iridescent (*adj.*)	displaying colors like those of the rainbow	Iris, a lovely maiden, was a messenger of the Greek gods and the goddess of the rainbow. As she carried messages from the gods to the earth, she left a trail of lovely colors.
Janus-faced (*adj.*)	two-faced; deceitful	Janus was an ancient Italian deity, commonly represented as having two faces, who presided over doors and gates and over the beginnings and endings of ceremonies. January derived its name from him.

WORD	MEANING	ORIGIN
jovial (adj.)	hearty, joyous; pertaining to good fellowship	Jove or Jupiter was the supreme god of the ancient Roman deities. In astrology the planet Jupiter is regarded as exerting a happy influence.
martial (adj.)	inclined or disposed to war; war-like; pertaining to war; pertaining to the army or navy	Mars was the ancient Roman god of war.
mentor (n.)	a wise counsellor or teacher	Mentor, a friend of Odysseus, was appointed to teach Odysseus' son Telemachus.
mercurial (adj.)	sprightly; volatile; changeable; having the qualities of mercury	Mercury was the swift messenger of the gods.
narcissism (n.)	self-love; admiration of one's own physical or mental attributes	In Greek legend Narcissus was a beautiful youth who fell in love with his own image in water, pined away, and was metamorphosed into the narcissus.
nemesis (n.)	an agent of doom or retribution	Nemesis was the Greek goddess of retribution or doom.
odyssey (n.)	a long voyage; a dangerous journey	In the ten years that Odysseus, the hero of Homer's *Odyssey* took to get home from Troy, he experienced many marvelous adventures.
Olympian (adj.)	grand, imposing; awe-inspiring; aloof	The Greek gods dwelt on Mount Olympus and were known as Olympians.
palladium (n.)	anything believed to afford effectual protection or safety	From the name Pallas Athena, a palladium was a statue of her, and especially the one in the citadel of Troy on which the safety of the city was supposed to depend.
Pandora's box (n.)	see story of origin	Zeus gave Pandora a box, which she was not to open. Yielding to curiosity, she opened it and out came all the ills of the world. In another version of the myth, the box contained all the hopes of the world, which escaped and were lost when she opened it.
protean (adj.)	readily assuming different forms or characters; exceedingly variable	Proteus was the sea god of classical mythology who could change his form and appearance at will.

Word	Meaning	Origin
saturnine (*adj.*)	of heavy, sluggish, gloomy temperament; taciturn	Saturn (the Greek Cronus) was the father of Jupiter. Saturn was jovial and the feasts (Saturnalia) celebrating his worship were gay. The gloomy aspect of *saturnine* comes from astrology; persons born under the influence of the planet Saturn are supposed to be gloomy and taciturn.
stentorian (*adj.*)	very loud or powerful in sound	Stentor, the herald of the Greeks in the Trojan War, was noted for his loud and powerful voice.
stygian (*adj.*)	dark, gloomy; infernal, hellish	In Greek mythology the Styx was the river of the underworld over which the souls of the dead were ferried by Charon.
tantalize (*v.*)	to tease by arousing expectations that are repeatedly disappointed	For revealing secrets of the gods, Tantalus, son of Zeus, was condemned to stand, hungry and thirsty, in water up to his chin and under a tree laden with fruit, neither of which he could reach.
terpsichorean (*adj.*)	pertaining to dancing	Terpsichore, one of the nine Muses of the arts, was the Muse of the dance.

Exercise 16

Learning Words Derived from Names

From each name in the column on the left a word has been derived to express the meaning given in the next column. Write this word in the space on the right.

EXAMPLE		
NAME	**MEANING**	**WORD**
J. J. Guillotin	a device for beheading people	guillotine

	NAME	MEANING	WORD
1.	Nicholas Chauvin	blind enthusiasm for military glory	_____
2.	Elbridge Gerry	an arbitrary arrangement of political divisions to give a political party an unfair advantage	_____
3.	Count de Sade	characterized by morbid enjoyment in being cruel	_____
4.	Thespis	an actor	_____
5.	Captain Boycott	to combine in abstaining, or preventing dealings with, as a means of intimidation	_____
6.	Sardonia	bitterly ironic	_____
7.	Louis Pasteur	process for destroying the majority of microorganisms in liquid foods, esp. milk	_____
8.	Lord Byron	characterized by melodramatic energy, melancholy, etc.	_____
9.	Thomas Bowdler	to expurgate by eliminating indelicate passages	_____
10.	Mrs. Malaprop	the ridiculous use of a word	_____
11.	Don Quixote	extravagantly chivalrous, romantic, and visionary	_____
12.	William A. Spooner	the transposition of sounds in an expression	_____
13.	Canterbury	an easy gallop	_____
14.	Mecca	a center or goal for many people	_____
15.	Bethlehem	a madhouse; a wild uproar	_____
16.	Jeremiah	a prolonged lamentation or complaint	_____
17.	Lothario	lover, rake	_____
18.	Caesar	a surgical operation to remove a fetus from the uterus	_____
19.	Draco	rigorous; severe; cruel	_____
20.	King Philip	a denunciatory speech	_____

EXERCISE 17

RELATING NAME WORDS AND OTHER WORDS

In each of the following groups of words there is one word that does not belong. Find the word that does not belong and write it in the space to the right.

EXAMPLE

ohms, watts, radii, amperes   radii

---

1. solon, sage, skeptic, genius _____

2. Spartan, stoical, austere, hedonistic _____

3. martial, belligerent, pugnacious, herculean _____

4. counsellor, mentor, Maecenas, pedagogue _____

5. philippic, jeremiad, eulogy, tirade _____

6. patron, Maecenas, Croesus, benefactor _____

7. Cyclopean, epicurean, herculean, massive _____

8. euphemism, spoonerism, malapropism, solecism _____

9. volatile, mercurial, protean, adamant _____

10. paean, philippic, panegyric, eulogy _____

11. behemoth, chimera, gargantuan, colossus _____

12. Eden, babel, pandemonium, bedlam _____

13. astronaut, charioteer, odyssey, stoic _____

14. saturnine, jovial, sardonic, lugubrious _____

15. demonic, satanic, fiendish, cryptic _____

16. Mammon, Croesus, Dionysius, Draco _____

17. abundance, cornucopia, paucity, plethora _____

18. infernal, martial, stygian, Plutonian _____

19. hypocritical, philistine, sycophantic, philippic _____

20. jeremiad, behemoth, philistine, Augustan _____

Exercise 18

The Meaning and Origin of Name Words

For each numbered word select a word from line a. below it that means most nearly the same thing and write it in the space to the right. From line b. select the name from which the numbered word is derived and place it in the space to the right.

Example

maudlin
a. meddlesome, cheerful, audible, tearfully sentimental   _tearfully sentimental_
b. Medea, Athene, Mary Magdalene, Pandora   _Mary Magdalene_

---

1. iridescent
   a. shining, sprightly, joyous, rainbowlike   _____
   b. Mercury, Eros, Iris, Jove   _____

2. jovial
   a. volatile, noisy, gay, warlike   _____
   b. Mars, Jove, Bacchus, Jehovah   _____

3. martial
   a. marriageable, infernal, warlike, wise   _____
   b. Mercury, Saturn, Mars, Ares   _____

4. mercurial
   a. volatile, variable, hearty, strong   _____
   b. Proteus, Tantalus, Mercury, Hercules   _____

5. narcissism
   a. narcotic, conceit, pride, nervousness   _____
   b. Eros, Aphrodite, Narcissus, Nazarene   _____

6. saturnine
   a. sanguine, surly, benign, smiling   _____
   b. Atreus, Saturn, Tantalus, Satan   _____

7. stentorian
   a. soft, infernal, loud, stern   _____
   b. Tenebrae, Mentor, Stentor, Styx   _____

8. tantalize
   a. tease, spoil, tempt, increase   _____
   b. Atalanta, Circe, Tantalus, Theseus   _____

9. erotic

    a. neurotic, erratic, amorous, erosive   _____

    b. Erebus, Cupid, Eros, Venus   _____

10. Bacchanalian

    a. orgiastic, merry, festive, epicurean   _____

    b. Dionysius, Bach, Epicurus, Bacchus   _____

11. cynical

    a. distrustful, harsh, swanlike, hopeful   _____

    b. Cygnus, Seneca, Ceres, Cynics   _____

12. jeremiad

    a. eulogy, panegyric, a jeer, tirade   _____

    b. Jericho, Hermione, Tiresias, Jeremiah   _____

13. satanic

    a. saintly, sardonic, diabolical, sinful   _____

    b. Mephistopheles, Samson, Satan, Titania   _____

14. draconian

    a. gentle, devilish, tyrannical, puritanical   _____

    b. Drake, Racine, Tiberius, Draco   _____

15. philippic

    a. hippodrome, ellipse, filibuster, denunciation   _____

    b. Philip, Philomena, Hippocrates, Hippolytus   _____

EXERCISE 19

USING WORDS DERIVED FROM NAMES

A word derived from a name can be substituted for the expression in parentheses in each of the following sentences. Place the correct word in the space provided at the right.

> **EXAMPLE**
>
> The baseball game was played between the bachelors
> and (the newly married men).   benedicts

1. The mob branded her a (shameless, abandoned woman). _____

2. Our large selection of ballet music will delight the heart of any (one devoted to the dance). _____

3. The reign of Queen Anne is sometimes called the (highest point in literature) age of English literature. _____

4. *Dorian Gray* is regarded by some as an expression of Oscar Wilde's (doctrine that pleasure or happiness is the highest good). _____

5. Her salon is celebrated for its artists and wits, but certainly not for its (sumptuous and lavish) food. _____

6. Mrs. Jack Gardner wanted to be known as the female (generous patron of the arts) of her day. _____

7. Our stepmother instituted a (rigorous, sternly disciplined) regimen, which caused all three of us to run away from home. _____

8. What you call his (repression of emotion and indifference to pleasure and pain), I call stupidity and apathy. _____

9. When Daniel Webster supported the Compromise of 1850, the antislavery factions no longer regarded him as the American (wise lawgiver). _____

10. She wrote several of television's most (excessively, tearfully sentimental) soap operas. _____

11. Whenever I ride on the carousel, the (musical instrument operated by steam) gives me a headache. _____

12. Judging by the sounds from my upstairs neighbor's apartment, I would say that his parties are (like drunken orgies). _____

13. We always welcomed Uncle Ned, for he brought a (overflowing supply) of presents for everybody. _____

14. Uncle Ned was an (person who migrated to California in 1848 in search of gold) who struck it rich. _____

82

8. MARK TWAIN'S VOCABULARY

Anyone who is trying to improve his or her vocabulary and, at the same time, develop a feel for language would do well to read Samuel Clemens, better known as Mark Twain. Although he specialized in accurate reporting of dialect, idioms, and American colloquialisms, Clemens was a master of crisp, clear English. In this colorful story of Buck Fanshaw's funeral, Clemens shows how difficult it is to communicate when the speakers are using different levels of language.

BUCK FANSHAW'S FUNERAL
—MARK TWAIN (1835–1910)

Somebody has said that in order to know a community, one must observe the style of its funerals and know what manner of men they bury with most ceremony. I cannot say which class we buried with most **eclat** in our "flush times," the distinguished public benefactor or the distinguished rough—possibly the two chief grades or grand divisions of society honored their illustrious dead about equally; and hence, no doubt the philosopher I have quoted from would have needed to see two representative funerals in Virginia before forming his estimate of the people.

There was a grand time over Buck Fanshaw when he died. He was a representative citizen. He had "killed his man"—not in his own quarrel, it is true, but in defence of a stranger unfairly beset by numbers. He had kept a **sumptuous** saloon. He had been the proprietor of a dashing helpmeet whom he could have discarded without the formality of a divorce. He had held a high position in the first department and been a very Warwick in politics. When he died there was great **lamentation** throughout the town, but especially in the vast bottom-stratum of society.

On the inquest it was shown that Buck Fanshaw, in the delirium of a wasting typhoid fever, had taken arsenic, shot himself through the body, cut his throat, and jumped out of a four-story window and broken his neck—and after due deliberation, the jury, sad and tearful, but with intelligence unblinded by its sorrow, brought in a verdict of death "by the visitation of God." What could the world do without juries?

Prodigious preparations were made for the funeral. All the vehicles in town were hired, all the saloons put in mourning, all the municipal and fire-company flags hung at half-mast, and all the firemen ordered to muster in uniform and bring their machines duly draped in black. Now—let us remark in parenthesis—as all the peoples of the earth had representative adventurers in the Silverland, and as each adventurer had brought the slang of his nation or his locality with him, the combination made slang of Nevada the richest and the most infinitely varied and **copious** that had ever existed anywhere in the world, perhaps, except in the mines of California in the "early days." Slang was the language of Nevada. It was hard to preach a sermon without it, and be understood. Such phrases as "You bet!" "Oh, no, I reckon not!" "No Irish need apply," and a hundred others, became so common as to fall from the lips of a speaker unconsciously—and very often when they did not touch the subject under discussion and consequently failed to mean anything.

After Buck Fanshaw's inquest, a meeting of the short-haired brotherhood was held, for nothing can be done on the Pacific coast without a public meeting and an expression of sentiment. Regretful resolutions were passed and various committees appointed; among others, a committee of one was deputed to call on the minister, a fragile, gentle, spiritual new **fledgling** from an Eastern theological seminary, and as yet unacquainted with the ways of the mines. The committeeman, "Scotty" Briggs, made his visit; and in after days it was worth something to hear the minister tell about it. Scotty was a **stalwart** rough, whose customary suit, when on weighty official business, like committee work, was a fire helmet, flaming red flannel shirt, patent leather belt with spanner and revolver attached, coat hung over arm, and pants stuffed into boot tops. He formed something of a contrast to the pale theological student. It is fair to say of Scotty, however, in passing, that he had a warm heart, and a strong love for his friends, and never entered into a quarrel when he could reasonably keep out of it. Indeed, it was commonly said that whenever one of Scotty's fights was investigated, it always turned out that it had originally been no affair of his, but that out of native goodheartedness he had dropped in of his own accord to help the man who was getting the worst of it. He and Buck Fanshaw were bosom friends, for years, and had often taken adventurous "pot-luck" together. On one occasion, they had thrown off their coats and taken the weaker side in a fight among strangers, and after gaining a hard-earned victory, turned and found that the men they were helping had deserted early, and not only that, but had stolen their coats and made off with them! But to return to Scotty's visit to the minister. He was on a sorrowful mission, now, and his face was the picture of woe. Being admitted to the presence he sat down before the clergyman, placed his fire-hat on an unfinished manuscript sermon under the minister's nose, took from it a red silk handkerchief, wiped his brow and heaved a sigh of dismal impressiveness, explanatory of his business. He choked, and even shed tears; but with an effort he mastered his voice and said in **lugubrious** tones:

"Are you the duck that runs the gospel-mill next door?"

"Am I the—pardon me, I believe I do not understand?"

With another sigh and a half-sob, Scotty rejoined:

"Why you see we are in a bit of trouble, and the boys thought maybe you would give us a lift, if we'd tackle you—that is, if I've got the rights of it and you are the head clerk of the doxology- works next door."

"I am the shepherd in charge of the flock whose fold is next door."

"The which?"

"The spiritual adviser of the little company of believers whose **sanctuary** adjoins these premises."

Scotty scratched his head, reflected a moment, and then said:

"You ruther hold over me, pard. I reckon I can't call that hand. Ante and pass the buck."

"How? I beg pardon. What did I understand you to say?"

"Well, you've ruther got the bulge on me. Or maybe we've both got the bulge, somehow. You don't smoke me and I don't smoke you. You see, one of the boys has passed in his checks and we want to give him a good sendoff, and so the thing I'm on now is to roust out somebody to jerk a little chin-music for us and waltz him through handsome."

"My friend, I seem to grow more and more bewildered. Your observations are wholly incomprehensible to me. Cannot you simplify them in some way? At first I thought perhaps I understood you, but I grope now. Would it not **expedite** matters if you restricted yourself to categorical statements of fact unencumbered with obstructing accumulations of **metaphor** and **allegory**?"

Another pause, and more reflection. Then, said Scotty,

"I'll have to pass, I judge."

"How?"

"You've raised me out, pard."

"I still fail to catch your meaning."

"Why, that last lead of yourn is too many for me—that's the idea. I can't neither trump nor follow suit."

The clergyman sank back in his chair perplexed. Scotty leaned his head on his hand and gave himself up to thought. Presently his face came up, sorrowful but confident.

"Gospel-sharp. Parson."

"Oh! Why did you not say so before? I am a clergyman—a parson."

"Now you talk! You see my blind and straddle it like a man. Put it there!"—extending a brawny paw, which closed over the minister's small hand gave it a shake indicative of **fraternal** sympathy and **fervent** gratification.

"Now we're all right, pard. Let's start fresh. Don't you mind my snuffling a little—becuz we're in a power of trouble. You see, one of the boys has gone up the flume—"

"Gone where?"

"Up the flume—throwed up the sponge, you understand."

"Thrown up the sponge?"

"Yes—kicked the bucket—"

"Ah—has departed to that mysterious country from whose bourne no traveler returns."

"Return! I reckon not. Why pard, he's *dead*!"

"Yes, I understand."

"Oh, you do? Well I thought maybe you might be getting tangled some more. Yes, you see he's dead again—"

"*Again?* Why, has he ever been dead before?"

"Dead before? No! Do you reckon a man has got as many lives as a cat? But you bet you he's awful dead now, poor old boy, and I wish I'd never seen this day. I don't want no better friend than Buck Fanshaw. I knowed him by the back; and when I know a man and like him, I freeze to him—you hear *me*. Take him all round, pard, there never was a burlier man in the mines. No man ever knowed Buck Fanshaw to go back on a friend. But it's all up, you know, it's all up. It ain't no use. They've scooped him."

"Scooped him?"

"Yes—death has. Well, well, well, we've got to give him up. Yes indeed. It's a kind of a hard world, after all, *aint* it? But pard, he was a rustler! You ought to see him get started once. He was a bully boy with a glass eye! Just spit in his face and give him room according to his strength, and it was just beautiful to see him peel and go in. He was the worst son of a thief that ever drawed breath. Pard, he was *on* it! He was on it bigger than an Injun!"

"On it? On what?"

"On the shoot. On the shoulder. On the fight, you understand. *He* didn't give a continental for *anybody. Beg* your pardon, friend, for coming so near saying a cuss-word—but you see I'm on an awful strain, in this palaver, on account of having to cramp down and draw everything so mild. But we've got to give him up. There ain't any getting around that, I don't reckon. Now if we can get you to help plant him—"

"Preach the funeral discourse? Assist at the **obsequies**?"

"Obs'quies is good. Yes. That's it—that's our little game. We are going to get the thing up regardless, you know. He was always nifty himself, and so you bet you his funeral ain't going to be no slouch—solid silver doorplate on his coffin, six plumes on the hearse, and a boy on the box in a biled shirt and a plug hat—how's that for high? And we'll take care of *you,* pard. We'll fix you all right. There'll be a kerridge for you; and whatever you want, you just 'scape out and we'll 'tend to it. We've got a shebang fixed up for you to stand behind, in No. 1's house, and don't you be afraid. Just go in and toot your horn, if you don't sell a clam. Put Buck through as bully as you can, pard, for anybody that knowed him will tell you that he was one of the whitest men that was ever in the mines. You can't draw it too strong. He never could stand it to see things going wrong. He's done more to make this town quiet and peaceable than any man in it. I've seen him lick four Greasers in eleven minutes, myself. If a thing wanted regulating, *he* warn't a man to go browsing around after somebody to do it, but he would prance in and regulate it himself. He warn't a Catholic. Scasely. He was down on 'em. His word was, 'No Irish need apply!' but it didn't make no difference about that when it came down to what a man's rights was—and so, when some roughs jumped the Catholic bone-yard and started in to stake out town-lots in it he *went* for 'em! And he *cleaned* 'em, too! I was there, pard, and I seen it myself."

"That was very well indeed—at least the impulse was—whether the act was strictly defensible or not. Had deceased any religious convictions? That is to say, did he feel a dependence upon, or acknowledge allegiance to a higher power?"

More reflection.

"I reckon you've stumped me again, pard. Could you say it over once more, and say it slow?"

"Well, to simplify it somewhat, was he, or rather had he ever been connected with any organization sequestered from **secular** concerns and devoted to self-sacrifice in the interests of morality?"

"All down but nine—set 'em up on the other alley, pard."

"What did I understand you to say?"

"Why, you're most too many for me, you know. When you get in with your left I hunt grass every time. Every time you draw, you fill; but I don't seem to have any luck. Let's have a new deal."

"How? Begin again?"

"That's it."

"Very well. Was he a good man, and—"

"There—I see that; don't put up another chip till I look at my hand. A good man, says you? Pard, it ain't no name for it. He was the best man that ever—pard, you would have doted on that man. He could lam any galoot of his inches in America. It was him that put down the riot last election before it got a start; and everybody said he was the only man that could have done it. He waltzed in with a spanner in one hand and a trumpet in the other, and sent fourteen men home on a shutter in less than three minutes, He had that riot all broke up and prevented nice before anybody ever got a chance to strike a blow. He was always for peace, and he would *have* peace—he could not stand disturbances. Pard, he was a great loss to this town. It would please the boys if you could chip in something like that and do him justice. Here once when the Micks got to throwing stones through the Methodis' Sunday school windows, Buck Fanshaw, all of his own notion, shut up his saloon and took a couple of six-shooters and mounted guard over the Sunday school. Says he, 'No Irish need apply!' And they didn't. He was the bulliest man in the mountains, pard! He could run faster, jump higher, hit harder, and hold more tangle-foot whisky without spilling it than any man in seventeen countries. Put that in, pard—it'll please the boys more than anything you could say. And you can say, pard, that he never shook his mother."

"Never shook his mother?"

"That's it—any of the boys will tell you so."

"Well, but why *should* he shake her?"

"That's what *I* say—but some people does."

"Not people of any repute?"

"Well, some that averages pretty so-so."

"In my opinion the man that would offer personal violence to his own mother, ought to—"

"Cheese it, pard; you've banked your ball clean outside the string. What I was a drivin' at, was, that he never *throwed off* on his mother—don't you see? No indeedy. He give her a house to live in, and town lots, and plenty of money; and he looked after her and took care of her all the time; and when she was down with the small-pox I'm d—d if he didn't set up nights and nuss her himself! *Beg* your pardon for saying it, but it hopped out too quick for yours truly. You've treated me like a gentleman, pard, and I ain't the man to hurt your feelings intentional. I think you're white. I think you're a square man, pard. I like you, and I'll lick any man that don't. I'll lick him till he can't tell himself from a last year's corpse! Put it *there*!" [Another fraternal handshake—and exit.]

The obsequies were all that "the boys" could desire. Such a marvel of funeral pomp had never been seen in Virginia. The plumed hearse, the dirge-breathing brass bands, the closed marts of business, the flags drooping at half mast, the long, plodding procession of uniformed secret societies, military battalions and fire companies, draped engines, carriages of officials, and citizens in vehicles and on foot, attracted **multitudes** of spectators to the sidewalks, roofs and windows; and for years afterward, the degree of grandeur attained by any civic display in Virginia was determined by comparison with Buck Fanshaw's funeral.

Scotty Briggs, as a pall-bearer and a mourner, occupied a prominent place at the funeral, and when the sermon was finished and the last sentence of the prayer for the dead man's soul ascended, he responded, in a low voice, but with feeling:

"Amen. No Irish need apply."

As the bulk of the response was without apparent **relevancy,** it was probably nothing more than a humble tribute to the memory of the friend that was gone; for, as Scotty had once said, it was "his word."

Scotty Briggs, in after days, achieved the distinction of becoming the only convert to religion that was ever gathered from the Virginia roughs; and it transpired that the man who had it in him to **espouse** the quarrel of the weak out of inborn nobility of spirit was no mean timber whereof to construct a Christian. The making him one did not **warp** his generosity or diminish his courage; on the contrary it gave intelligent direction to the one and a broader field to the other. If his Sunday-school class progressed faster than the other classes, was it matter for wonder? I think not. He talked to his pioneer small-fry in a language they understood! It was my large privilege, a month before he died, to hear him tell the beautiful story of Joseph and his brethren to his class "without looking at the book." I leave it to the reader to fancy what it was like, as it fell, riddled with slang, from the lips of that grave, earnest teacher, and was listened to by his little learners with a consuming interest that showed that they were as unconscious as he was that any violence was being done to the sacred proprieties!

EXERCISE 20

MARK TWAIN'S WORDS

The words and expressions in this exercise are bold in the article you have just read. After carefully studying each word in context and looking it up in the dictionary, write the part of speech and the definition of the word in the space provided.

1. eclat

Part of speech _____ Definition _____

2. sumptuous

Part of speech _____ Definition _____

3. lamentation

Part of speech _____ Definition _____

4. inquest

Part of speech _____ Definition _____

5. copious

Part of speech _____ Definition _____

6. fledgling

Part of speech _____ Definition _____

7. stalwart

Part of speech _____ Definition _____

8. lugubrious

Part of speech _____ Definition _____

9. sanctuary

Part of speech _____ Definition _____

10. expedite

Part of speech _____ Definition _____

EXERCISE 21

MORE OF TWAIN

The terms in this exercise are bold in the article you have just read. After carefully studying each term in context and looking it up in the dictionary, write the definition of the term in the space provided.

1. metaphor

   Part of speech _____ Definition _____

2. allegory

   Part of speech _____ Definition _____

3. fraternal

   Part of speech _____ Definition _____

4. fervent

   Part of speech _____ Definition _____

5. obsequies

   Part of speech _____ Definition _____

6. secular

   Part of speech _____ Definition _____

7. multitude

   Part of speech _____ Definition _____

8. relevancy

   Part of speech _____ Definition _____

9. espouse

   Part of speech _____ Definition _____

10. warp

   Part of speech _____ Definition _____

EXERCISE 22

NEVER THE TWAIN...

The vocabulary words from Exercises 20 and 21 appear in the box below. Select the proper words to fit into the blanks in these sentences.

eclat	inquest	lugubrious	metaphor	fervent
sumptuous	copious	sanctuary	allegory	multitude
lamentation	fledgling	expedite	fraternal	relevancy

1. The president's car was surrounded by a vast _____ of people, all eager to see the head of our government.

2. A _____ appeal for a reprieve was made to the governor by the condemned man's wife.

3. When I saw Ellen's _____ face, I knew that she had lost the tennis match.

4. Although it was her first year as a professional, the _____ golfer earned $50,000.

5. "The rowboat husband followed his battleship wife into the room" is an example of a_____.

6. When Uncle Ben was ill, many visitors from his _____ organization came to the hospital.

7. All term long I took _____ notes in my chemistry class but I failed the final exam anyway.

8. The television chef prepared a _____ feast that was low in calories.

9. A sound of _____ arose in the village when the wounded soldiers were brought in from the battlefield.

10. The automobile company hired my aunt to _____ the many claims that had been filed against them.

Exercise 23

Twain, Continued

Using the vocabulary found in "Buck Fanshaw's Funeral," answer the following questions by selecting the correct term from the box below.

eclat	fledgling	lugubrious	expedite	relevancy
sumptuous	stalwart	sanctuary	allegory	warp

1. Which word is used to describe a beginner? _____
2. Which word means brilliance of reputation; fame? _____
3. Which word is a synonym for pertinence or appropriateness? _____
4. Which word describes a holy place or shelter? _____
5. Which word means bend or reform? _____
6. Which word might describe a fable by Aesop? _____
7. Which word is a synonym for strong, sturdy, or robust? _____
8. Which adjective describes many tearful soap operas? _____
9. Which word may be substituted for speed up or facilitate? _____
10. Which word might describe a magnificent, splendid palace? _____

EXERCISE 24

TWAIN, CONCLUDED

Do the same as you did in Exercise 23. Select the correct term from the box below.

lamentation	copious	fraternal	obsequies	multitude
inquest	metaphor	fervent	secular	espouse

1. Which word describes funeral rites? _____
2. Which word is a synonym for plentiful? _____
3. Which word serves as a figure of speech? _____
4. Which word describes a judicial inquiry? _____
5. Which word stands for worldly things rather than religious ones? _____
6. Which word usually precedes the expression "...of sins"? _____
7. Which word means to be in favor of? _____
8. Which word describes a brotherly relationship? _____
9. Which word is related to heat? _____
10. Which noun is an outward expression of grief? _____

VOCABULARY TEST 3

SELECTING THE BEST DEFINITION

We have already studied the following words. How many of them do you know? For each of the boldface words select the word or expression that means most nearly the same and write the letter in the space to the right.

1. We should recognize the **de facto** government.
   a. people's   b. democratic   c. in fact   d. military

2. A **mélange** of musical styles…
   a. symphony   b. medley   c. suite   d. chorus

3. In poetry he was an inspired **dilettante**.
   a. writer of poetic drama   b. writer of light verse   c. amateur writer
   d. occasional writer

4. They recited the **litany**.
   a. martial ode   b. oath of loyalty   c. apostle's creed   d. liturgical prayer

5. A **fortuitous** meeting…
   a. daring   b. produced by chance   c. ill-starred   d. secretly arranged

6. In search of freedom from **dogma**…
   a. system of principles   b. oppressive rule   c. religious ceremonies
   d. civic restrictions

7. About grades the teacher was **adamant**.
   a. liberal   b. hardhearted   c. flexible   d. unfair

8. The old man warned them not to **blaspheme**.
   a. break fast   b. speak profanely   c. speak irreverently   d. worship idols

9. Do not confuse patriotism and **chauvinism**.
   a. belligerent patriotism   b. political enthusiasm   c. race prejudice
   d. religious zeal

10. The lieutenant is a **martinet**.
    a. dandy   b. self-seeker   c. rigid disciplinarian   d. shirker of responsibility

11. A **maudlin** story of human frailty…
    a. tearfully sentimental   b. excessively long   c. sordid   d. sympathetic

12. Grandfather's **quixotic** behavior…
    a. queer   b. senile   c. unpredictable   d. impracticable and visionary

13. To **meander** in the garden…
    a. walk slowly   b. sit quietly   c. wander aimlessly   d. ponder deeply

14. His mournful sermon was a **jeremiad**.
    a. moral tale   b. modern parable   c. lugubrious complaint   d. sad farewell

15. Of brilliant mind, but **saturnine** temperament…
a. capricious   b. temperamental   c. taciturn   d. violent _____

16. He made a short, **sardonic** speech.
a. quietly apologetic   b. bitterly ironic   c. slightly contemptuous
d. abusive _____

17. It was her **fervent** wish…
a. passionate   b. sentimental   c. excited   d. confused _____

18. To **espouse** the cause of freedom…
a. attack   b. advocate   c. thwart   d. amend _____

19. The state is a **utopia**…
a. monarchy   b. matriarchy   c. oligarchy   d. ideal state _____

20. The **sadistic** punishment of the boys…
a. prolonged   b. characterized by morbid enjoyment
c. pertaining to a thonged whip   d. righteous _____

21. The attempt to **gerrymander** the county…
a. deprive of representation   b. deprive of courts
c. provide with inferior schools   d. arrange districts for political advantage _____

22. A(n) **solecism** in the essay…
a. error in expression   b. factual error   c. personal reference
d. general plea _____

23. The **philippic** delivered by the senator from the South…
a. eulogy   b. denunciatory address   c. prayerful appeal
d. patriotic oration _____

24. Under the **aegis** of the YMCA…
a. opprobrium   b. by-laws   c. sponsorship   d. sustained assault _____

25. The band played **martial** music.
a. pertaining to war   b. for marching   c. pertaining to marriage
d. pertaining to dictators _____

26. Words are **protean** symbols.
a. exceedingly variable   b. effectively expressive   c. arbitrary
d. both concrete and abstract _____

27. The **stentorian** call of the bugle…
a. unmusical   b. warlike   c. shrill   d. very loud _____

28. The **per diem** workers lacked security.
a. unskilled   b. daily   c. unprofessional   d. lazy _____

29. **Banal** criticism of the poetry…
a. aesthetic   b. adverse   c. technical   d. hackneyed _____

30. A **virtuoso** of the violin…
a. expert player   b. manufacturer and restorer   c. connoisseur
d. delighted listener _____

31. The **aesthetic** principles of architecture…
a. pertaining to the science of engineering
b. pertaining to the science of beauty
c. pertaining to zoning regulations
d. pertaining to structural supports

32. Niobe shed **copious** tears.
a. bitter   b. plentiful   c. salty   d. false

33. The **stalwart** knights of the Round Table…
a. amorous   b. religious   c. belligerent   d. valiant

34. Richard III's nephews sought **sanctuary** in the church.
a. compensation   b. shelter   c. assistance   d. counsel

35. The lack of **relevancy**…
a. truth   b. appropriateness   c. nourishment   d. protest

36. To live a **Spartan** existence…
a. warlike   b. strenuously physical   c. secluded   d. rigorously simple

37. A **bowdlerized** edition of Shakespeare…
a. expurgated   b. edited with critical notes   c. edited for the stage
d. edited by the author

38. The **boycott** of the butchers in our neighborhood…
a. prosecution   b. sanitary regulation   c. forced closing on holidays
d. abstention from trading with

39. Her **titian** hair…
a. auburn   b. frizzed   c. elaborately curled   d. short-cropped

40. The **bedlam** of visiting day in camp…
a. extreme happiness   b. tiresome routine   c. noise and confusion
d. tearful outbursts

VOCABULARY TEST 4

USING WORDS IN ILLUSTRATIVE SENTENCES

The following words and expressions have been used in the text and exercises. How many of them do you know? Use each in an illustrative sentence that throws some light on the meaning of the expression.

EXAMPLE

WORD	SENTENCE
bivouac	The soldiers on <u>bivouac</u> slept in tents.

WORD	SENTENCE
1. status quo	
2. double entendre	
3. fait accompli	
4. laissez-faire	
5. al fresco	
6. sotto voce	
7. virtuoso	
8. fledgling	
9. banal	
10. quintessence	
11. litany	
12. gourmet	
13. fortuitous	
14. dogma	
15. debacle	
16. blaspheme	
17. bowdlerize	
18. gerrymander	
19. chauvinism	
20. martinet	

VOCABULARY TEST 5

USING WORDS IN ILLUSTRATIVE SENTENCES

The following words and expressions have been used in the text and exercises. How many of them do you know? Use each in an illustrative sentence that throws some light on the meaning of the word.

WORD	SENTENCE
1. malapropism	
2. Machiavellian	
3. sadistic	
4. spoonerism	
5. thespian	
6. meander	
7. sardonic	
8. solecism	
9. utopia	
10. babel	
11. jeremiad	
12. philistine	
13. samaritan	
14. philippic	
15. aegis	
16. copious	
17. mercurial	
18. eclat	
19. allegory	
20. espouse	

9. WORDS FROM PART TO WHOLE

WORD ELEMENTS

Many English words are a combination of word elements. For example, the word *conduction* consists of *con + duc + tion*. The root or stem of this combination is *duct*, meaning *to lead*. This root can be combined with other elements to form other words, for example:

> induction
> production
> reduction
> deduction
> seduction

Roots

A root, therefore, is a word element, frequently of Latin or Greek origin, from which English words are formed by the addition of other elements to modify the meaning of the root itself.

Prefixes

A prefix is a word element that is placed at the beginning of a root to modify its meaning and form a word. Like most roots, prefixes are not words in themselves. Note how the meaning of the root *duce, to lead,* is changed by different prefixes:

reduce	*produce*
seduce	*adduce*
induce	*introduce*

Suffixes

A suffix is a word element attached to the end of a root or a word to modify its meaning and establish its part of speech. For example, by the addition of suffixes the verb *protect* can be changed to *protection* (n.), *protective* (adj.), and *protectively* (adv.).

THE VALUE OF KNOWING WORD ELEMENTS

Roots, prefixes, and suffixes are clues to the meaning of thousands of words. The root of the word expresses its area of meaning, and the prefix and suffix give it shape and definition. Therefore, a knowledge of word elements provides a methodical and economical technique of analyzing words, of working out their meaning, and of remembering them by relating them to words already known. With this technique words can also be organized meaningfully and learned in groups rather than individually.

A WORD OF CAUTION: the meaning of a word is frequently not the sum of its parts. *Prediction* cannot be construed as an equation: *before + speak + the act of = the act of speaking before.* *Prediction* means *prophesying* or *foretelling.* Similarly *transgression* does not mean *the act of walking across.* *Transgression* means *the violation of a law.*

Some Common Latin Roots

Root	Meaning	Examples
cede, cess	yield, move, go	recede, procession
cred	believe	credence, credulous
dict	say	predict, dictator
duce, duct	lead	produce, reduction
fac, fee, fic	make, do	facsimile, effect, efficient
fer	bring, bear, carry	infer, refer
gress	wander, go	transgress, congress
jac, jec	throw	ejaculate, rejection
mit, miss	send	transmit, permission
port	carry	report, export
scribe, script	rite	inscribe, scripture
specs, spic	look, see	spectator, conspicuous
string, strict	tighten	stringent, restriction
tend, tent, tens	tighten	attend, retention, tensile
tort	twist	torture, retort
tract	draw	retract, distract
ven, vent	come	convene, invention
vers, vert	turn	reverse, divert
vid, vis	see	evident, invisible
voc	call	vocal, vocation

Some Common Greek Roots

Root	Meaning	Examples
anthropo	man	anthropoid, anthropology
auto	self	automatic, autograph
bio	life	biology, biography
chron	time	chronic, chronology
ge, geo	earth	geology, geography
gen	race, birth	generation, genetics
hydr	water	hydrant, hydraulic
log, ology	thought, science	logic, astrology

ROOT	MEANING	EXAMPLES
meter, metr	measure	diameter, symmetry
pan	all	panacea, panorama
path	feeling	apathy, pathos
phil	friend, lover	philosopher, bibliophile
phob	fear	hydrophobia, Russophobe
phon	sound	phonetics, symphony
soph	wisdom	sophistry, sophisticated

Some Common Prefixes

Note: For ease of pronunciation the spelling of a prefix sometimes changes slightly when it is added to a root: ex + ject = eject, sub + fer = suffer, ad + scribe = ascribe.

PREFIX	MEANING	EXAMPLES
ab	away from	abnormal, abject
ad	to, toward	admit, adhesive
bene	well, good	benefit, benefactor
com, con	together with	complement, contain
de	down, from	describe, defer
dis	apart from	dismiss, disappoint
ex	out, former	expect, ex-wife
homo	same, man	homogeneous, Homo sapiens
in	in, into, not	invade, insincere, inadequate
inter	between	intermediate, intercollegiate
mal	bad, evil	malevolent, malpractice
mis	wrong	misbehave, misstatement
per	through	percolate, perforate
post	after	posterior, posthumous
pre	before	prevent, preamble
pro	forward, in favor of, in place of	protagonist, protest, pronoun
re	back, again	repeat, retreat
sub	under	submerge, substitute
syn, sym	together	synthetic, symphony
trans	across	transmit, transgress

Some Common Suffixes
NOUN SUFFIXES

Suffix	Meaning	Examples
ance, ence, ancy, ency	act of, state of, condition of	attendance, precedence, hesitancy, presidency
dom	state or condition of	kingdom, martyrdom
er, or, ar, eer, ess (feminine), ist	one who	painter, governor, bursar, profiteer, actress, segregationist
hood	state of	childhood, falsehood
ism	doctrine of, practice of	pragmatism, mannerism
ment	state, quality, act of	treatment, wonderment, statement
ness	state of	fondness, shyness

ADJECTIVE SUFFIXES

Suffix	Meaning	Examples
able, ible	capable of	capable, visible
ful	full of	hopeful, meaningful
ish, y, ic, ac, al	like, pertaining to	childish, chalky, rustic, cardiac, practical
less	without	hopeless, careless
ory, ary	relating	sensory, auditory, stationary
ous, ose	full of, like	marvelous, perilous, treacherous, verbose
ward	in the direction of	homeward, downward

Word Elements Meaning Number

Word Element	Meaning	Examples
uni	one	unit, universe
du, bi, di	two	duet, biped, dichotomy
tri	three	tricycle, trinity
quadr, quart	four	quadrangle, quadroon, quartet
quint, penta	five	quintuplet, pentagon, Pentateuch
ses, sext, hexa	six	sestet, sextet, sextuple hexagon, hexameter
sept	seven	septennial, septuple
oct	eight	octagon, octavo, octet
non, nov	nine	nonagon, nonagenarian, November
deca	ten	decade, decathlon

COMPOUND WORDS

In addition to words composed of roots, prefixes, and suffixes, English contains many words that were made by joining two words already in accepted use. The following list of compound words illustrates the process and shows that words are still being formed in this way to express new meanings.

airport	earthquake	income
battleship	fallout	rowboat
blastoff	football	windshield
bombproof	gearshift	
countdown	household	

BLENDS

Words are also formed by blending or fusing the elements of two words into a single word. Words formed in this way are known as blends or portmanteau words. Here are some blends that have been accepted into the language:

Amerind	from American and Indian
Eurasian	from European and Asian
Interpol	from international and police
motel	from motor and hotel
motorcade	from motor and cavalcade
paratroop	from parachute and troop
smog	from smoke and fog
travelog	travel and log

EXERCISE 25

THE MEANING OF ROOTS

Write the literal meaning of each boldface root in the blank space in each of the following sentences and also in the blank space to the right.

EXAMPLE

If water re**ced**es, it <u>moves</u> back.   moves

---

1. If we im**port** merchandise, we _____ it into the country. _____

2. To di**gress** is to _____ away from the subject. _____

3. Since this computer is **port**able, you can _____ it home. _____

4. A **spec**tator can _____ well from this section of the arena. _____

5. Although labor has made several con**cess**ions, management refuses to _____ an inch. _____

6. You may think that his statement is **cred**ible, but I cannot _____ it. _____

7. If you re**ject** this offer, you will _____ away a good opportunity. _____

8. His suf**fer**ing is too great to _____. _____

9. Such con**duct** will _____ grief. _____

10. After contra**dict**ing the charge, he refused to _____ anything more. _____

11. I will in**spect** the installation to _____ if it is satisfactory. _____

12. No matter what is done to pre**vent** me, I will _____. _____

13. Destroy the old con**tract** and _____ up another. _____

14. A con**tort**ionist can _____ himself into any shape. _____

15. A **ten**acious man will _____ to his course no matter what the difficulties. _____

16. The doctor who gave you this pre**script**ion should learn how to _____. _____

17. He is so **cred**ulous that he will _____ anything. _____

18. We tried several things to di**vert** the child's attention, but we could not _____ it aside. _____

19. Many writers of **fict**ion do not _____ up their plots. _____

20. If they seek ad**miss**ion, _____ them away. _____

EXERCISE 26

THE MEANING AND USE OF PREFIXES

For each of the following roots list three words that have been formed by the addition of different prefixes. Give the meaning of each prefix and briefy define each word.

EXAMPLE

TORT, meaning *twist*

Prefix _____ dis _____ Word _____ distort _____ Meaning _____ to twist out of shape _____

JECT, meaning *throw*

1. Prefix _____ Word _____ Meaning _____
2. Prefix _____ Word _____ Meaning _____
3. Prefix _____ Word _____ Meaning _____

SCRIBE, meaning *write*

4. Prefix _____ Word _____ Meaning _____
5. Prefix _____ Word _____ Meaning _____
6. Prefix _____ Word _____ Meaning _____

TRACT, meaning *draw*

7. Prefix _____ Word _____ Meaning _____
8. Prefix _____ Word _____ Meaning _____
9. Prefix _____ Word _____ Meaning _____

DICT, meaning *say*

10. Prefix _____ Word _____ Meaning _____
11. Prefix _____ Word _____ Meaning _____
12. Prefix _____ Word _____ Meaning _____

FER, meaning *bear or carry*

13. Prefix _____ Word _____ Meaning _____
14. Prefix _____ Word _____ Meaning _____
15. Prefix _____ Word _____ Meaning _____

EXERCISE 27

PREFIXES AND ROOTS

In the first blank space, write the prefix and root of the preceding word. Then write the meaning of the prefix and the root in the proper columns and briefly define the word.

EXAMPLE	MEANING OF PREFIX	MEANING OF ROOT	MEANING OF WORD
The reporter distorted dis-tort my remarks.	away from	twist	to twist out of shape

	MEANING OF PREFIX	MEANING OF ROOT	MEANING OF WORD
1. The procession _____ moved slowly past the tomb.	_____	_____	_____
2. The prologue _____ tells what to expect.	_____	_____	_____
3. The malefactor _____ was apprehended.	_____	_____	_____
4. We extended our sympathy _____ to the bereaved.	_____	_____	_____
5. He is cynical enough to be a misanthrope _____.	_____	_____	_____
6. Will the grand jury indict _____ the inspector?	_____	_____	_____
7. We believe in the progress _____and perfectibility of man.	_____	_____	_____
8. The miscreants were restricted _____ to quarters.	_____	_____	_____
9. The minister delivered the invocation _____in a squeaky voice.	_____	_____	_____
10. The senator interceded _____ for us to no avail.	_____	_____	_____
11. He fears that even the Boy Scouts will subvert _____ the nation.	_____	_____	_____
12. If I have omitted any information from the letter, I will add a postscript _____.	_____	_____	_____

	MEANING OF PREFIX	MEANING OF ROOT	MEANING OF WORD

13. We transport _____ goods by air and rail.

14. Synchronize _____ your watches at five o'clock.

15. Under dictators people suffer _____ a loss of freedom.

16. The president will not attend _____ the conference.

17. The cost of repairing the transmission _____ is high.

18. Young people like to drive convertible_____ cars.

19. His reputation is too great to be discredited _____ by a rumor.

20. Many people were disturbed by Dr. Johnson's grunts and noises _____.

21. Being a coward, the count made a retraction _____ and avoided a duel.

22. Some Latin American countries profess to fear intervention _____ by the United States.

23. The student read a proscribed _____ book and was expelled.

24. After various deductions _____ my salary is inadequate.

25. This assignment takes precedence _____ over all other work.

Exercise 28

Words with Greek Roots

Complete each of the following statements with a word composed of one or more Greek roots. Write the word in the space to the right. If necessary, consult your dictionary.

1. The branch of mathematics that is literally named "The measurement of the earth" is ___.

   _____

2. The disease marked by a revulsion to water is ___.

   _____

3. Systematized, rational thought is ___.

   _____

4. A student who has been in school long enough to know its customs is ___.

   _____

5. Because they are biologically similar to man, apes are called ___.

   _____

6. A single initial embossed on an article is called a ___.

   _____

7. The type of literature in which a person writes about himself or herself is called ___.

   _____

8. A disease prevalent throughout all of a country is said to be ___.

   _____

9. The word describing the theory that puts the earth at the center of the universe is ___.

   _____

10. The extermination of a racial or national group is called ___.

    _____

11. The instrument that uses wires to transmit sound across a distance is a ___.

    _____

12. A mechanical man is an ___.

    _____

13. A short, quotable inscription or statement is an ___.

    _____

14. The study of the descendants of a common progenitor is ___.

    _____

15. The arrangement of events in time is ___.

    _____

16. A man who has a bad reputation for deceptive wisdom is called a ___.

    _____

17. The name for the science of or study of disease is ___.

    _____

18. The method of teaching reading by the sound of letters is ___.

    _____

19. A brake operated by water or another liquid is ___.

    _____

20. A speech commending someone is a ___.

    _____

10. DEVELOPMENT AND CHANGE IN THE MEANING OF WORDS

WORDS WITH SEVERAL MEANINGS

Many words have more than one meaning. In general use the adjective *high* may mean *tall, intensified, expensive, exalted, chief, elated, remote,* and about thirteen other ranks and qualities. In addition, the adjective *high* has restricted meaning in music, biology, automobiling, and phonetics.

The noun *fire* expresses at least seventeen different meanings, some of which are illustrated in the following sentences:

- Marsha's face has the look of one who has been through *fire*. [severe trial or trouble]
- Juan's clothes show that he has been fighting *fire*. [physical fire; a conflagration]
- Bob's face and manner are full of *fire*. [passion; ardor]
- The patient's whole body is on *fire*. [fever; inflammation]
- The lieutenant gave the command to *fire* on the enemy. [discharge guns]

Since there are a great many words like *fire* and *high,* the specific meaning of a word depends on its context. In looking up a word in the dictionary one must carefully study the several definitions and select the one that fits the context in which the word appears. Otherwise the passage may be misinterpreted.

Care must also be taken in defining words. [See "The Art of Definition," page 12] A definition must include at least the common meanings of the word, or it must be limited to a specific field or context. A synonym or short phrase is seldom a satisfactory definition.

INADEQUATE DEFINITION: *Desolate* means dreary or dismal.
SATISFACTORY DEFINITION: *Desolate* means devastated, deserted, lonely as applied to places; applied to persons, it means dismal, or feeling abandoned by friends or hope.
LIMITED DEFINITION: As applied to people, *desolate* means dismal or feeling abandoned by friends or hope.

MEANING AND PART OF SPEECH

One reason why words have more than one meaning is that they are used as more than one part of speech. For example, *fire* is used as a noun and a verb; *high* is used as an adjective, an adverb, and a noun. Like *fire* and *high,* a great many other words are used as two or more parts of speech and therefore have two or more meanings. How the meaning of a word differs with each part of speech can be illustrated with *record,* a word that is a noun, verb, or adjective.

Jane's *record* in school was good. [Noun meaning achievement]

The clerks *record* these figures. [Verb meaning to write down, enter into a book. Note that the pronunciation has also changed.]

Our *record* year for sales was 1997. [Adjective denoting extraordinary performance]

Here are some additional examples of how the meaning of a word depends upon its part of speech:

effect (*n.*)	The *effect* of this policy will be disastrous. [result]
effect (*v.*)	We were unable to *effect* any change in the plans. [produce, bring about]
sentence (*n.*)	The *sentence* was death. [decree of a court]
sentence (*v.*)	The murderer was *sentenced* to death. [doomed, condemned]
defile (*n.*)	It will take hours for the enemy to pass through the *defile*. [narrow passage or gorge]
defile (*v.*)	At this point the troops will halt and then *defile*. [march off in a line, file by file]

Frequently the pronunciation of a word changes with the part of speech. The following words are pronounced differently as nouns, adjectives, and verbs. There are, however, many words that remain unchanged in pronunciation despite a change in the part of speech.

per´fect (*adj.*)	per•fect´ (*v.*)
prog´ress (*n.*)	pro•gress´ (*v.*)
an´nex (*n.*)	an•nex´ (*v.*)
con´vict (*n.*)	con•vict´ (*v.*)
per´mit (*n.*)	per•mit´ (*v.*)
ob´ject (*n.*)	ob•ject´ (*v.*)

CHANGES IN THE MEANING OF WORDS

Words are dynamic, fluid symbols. They are continually changing to express the interests and ideas of different times and different people. Words grow and decay; they shed old meanings and acquire new ones. They wax and wane in strength and stature. *Silly* once meant *happy*. A *deer* was originally any wild beast; *queen* simply meant wife; and a *minister* was a menial servant.

Words are therefore too mercurial to be trusted. They must be checked constantly if misunderstanding or bafflement is to be avoided. Consider, for example, the early English morality play called *Nice Wanton*. The title poses the question, "How can a *wanton* (a lascivious person) be *nice*?" However, the title becomes meaningful when, upon consulting an etymological dictionary, we learn that *nice* once meant *ignorant* and *wanton* once meant *undisciplined* or *unruly*. Translated literally, then, the title would read *The Ignorant, Undisciplined One*.

This illustration shows that words can never be taken for granted. It must never be assumed that a word meant the same thing to Shakespeare and Shelley or that a word means to us what it meant to our grandparents. Whenever a familiar word seems odd or meaningless in context, it should be checked. The chances are that the meaning of the word has changed.

The task of frequently consulting the dictionary for the meaning of words in current and older literature can be irksome, but it has its rewards. In addition to assuring accuracy, it reveals fascinating information about words and their users, information that makes the word meaningful and unforgettable. Anyone who traces the word *fetish* (any object of blind reverence) to its original meaning (an object regarded with awe as being the embodiment or habitation of a potent spirit) acquires the word, an illuminating bit of social history, and insight into human behavior.

The changes that words undergo are (1) degeneration, (2) elevation, (3) specialization, (4) generalization, and (5) transference.

Degeneration

Degeneration or pejorative change is the process whereby the meaning of a word becomes weaker, less agreeable, or less respectable. Degeneration occurs when people change their opinions for the worse or disparage what they dislike. Disparagement and the human tendency to pessimism account for the degeneration of these words:

villain	a rogue or knave: from the Old French *vilain*, a worker on a *villa* or farm.
sophist	one who reasons casuistically: from the Greek word for a class of philosophers and teachers who sank into disrepute.
boor	an uncouth person: from the Dutch word for farmer.
maudlin	excessively sentimental: from Mary Magdalene whose swollen and weeping countenance in medieval Christian art was irreverently attributed to dissipation.
hypocrite	one who pretends or dissembles: from the Greek word meaning actor.

Elevation

Elevation or amelioration, the opposite of degeneration, is the process whereby the meaning of a word grows stronger, more agreeable, or more respectable. As classes of people and things grow more useful or respectable, the names for them undergo elevation. Some examples of words that have been elevated are listed below:

lady	a well-bred, genteel woman; in England, a member of the aristocracy: from the Old English *hlāēfdige*, literally a loaf kneader, a maker of bread.
nice	exact, precise: from the Latin *nescire*, to be ignorant
constable	an officer of the peace: from the Latin *comes* + *stabuli*, a stable attendant.
steward	a manager or administrator of an establishment: from the Old English *stigweard*, a sty-keeper, a keeper of the pigs.
dean	the administrative head of a college; a cultural leader, as "the dean of American letters": from the Latin *decanus*, a leader of ten (soldiers or monks).

Specialization

Specialization is the process whereby a broad, general meaning contracts to a narrower, more limited one. Specialization indicates the tendency of a group of people to restrict the meaning of a word to their own experiences and interests. The following words illustrate the process of specialization:

pastor   a religious leader: from the Latin *pastor, shepherd.*

starve   to die from lack of food: from the Old English *steorfan,* to die.

girl   a female child: from the Middle English *gurle,* a child of either sex.

cortege   a funeral procession: from the French *cortège,* a procession.

Bible   the Holy Scriptures: from the Greek *biblios,* book.

Generalization

Generalization, the opposite of specialization, is the process whereby a word loses its limited meaning and becomes broadened, generalized, and diffused in meaning. No doubt generalization occurs because many people tend to think vaguely and thus to blur meaning, as the following words indicate:

larder   a pantry: from the Old French *lardier,* a storehouse for bacon.

discard   to cast aside, reject: originally to throw aside a card from one's hand.

manuscript   an author's copy of his work: from Latin *manu + script,* "written by hand"; now applied to a typewritten copy as well.

orientation   the act of turning or facing in any direction: ultimately derived from the Latin stem *oriens,* the east; originally limited to the east only.

unkempt   untidy, neglected: originally "uncombed," from the Middle English *kembe,* comb.

Transference

Transference is the process whereby words that originally expressed one meaning are used to express entirely different meanings, some of which may even be the direct opposite of the original meaning. The following words have undergone transference:

toe   a digit of the foot: now also used as a verb, meaning to touch with the toe as in "to toe the mark."

galaxy   usually the Milky Way; any system of heavenly bodies: now applied to any brilliant or splendid assemblage, as of motion picture stars.

fast   moving quickly: now also used to mean firmly fixed in place; securely closed, as a door; firm in adherence, as a fast friend.

charm   a power to please and attract; a quality or feature that exerts fascination: the original meaning of *charm* is an amulet possessing magical power; or a magic verse or formula that was chanted.

11. SYNONYMS AND ANTONYMS

One reason why English is among the most expressive, varied, and subtle of modern languages is that it abounds in synonyms. A synonym is a word that has the same meaning as another word, or nearly the same. The verbs *suspect, mistrust, distrust,* and *question* are synonyms; so are the adjectives *peaceful, serene, tranquil,* and *placid.*

It must be understood that a synonym does not always mean exactly the same thing as the word with which it is synonymous. As a matter of fact, no word ever means exactly the same as another; there is always a difference in emphasis, suggestion, or use. Words that a dictionary lists as synonyms cannot always be interchanged in the same context; therefore, good dictionaries include synonym studies that explain the differences between synonymous words.

The adjectives *main, chief, primary,* and *principal* are synonyms. In the following sentence they have about the same meaning and may therefore be used interchangeably:

Laziness was the *main* (*chief, principal, primary*) reason for Steve's failure.

Note, however, the following sentences in which this group of synonyms cannot be interchanged:

Ilene is a teacher in the *primary* grades. [Neither *main, chief,* nor *principal* may be substituted here.]

Leslie saw his *main* chance and seized it. [Idiomatic use precludes the substitution of *chief, principal,* and *primary* in this sentence.]

Peter has to list the *chief* exports of Peru. [*Principal* may be used here, but *main* is not idiomatic, and *primary* expresses the wrong meaning.]

Since synonyms are frequently not interchangeable, care must be exercised to select the word that exactly expresses the thought and that fits the context. The synonym studies in the dictionary should be consulted, for they explain how synonyms differ in use, emphasis, and suggestion. However, even in unabridged dictionaries the synonym is limited by reason of space. The best reference to consult for a listing of synonyms and a study of their meaning is the Merriam-Webster *Dictionary of Synonyms.* In the main, however, one must develop a knowledge of synonyms and the ability to discriminate among them by reading widely in the works of good writers and speakers.

The Advantages of Knowing Synonyms

The following are the chief reasons why it is helpful to have a command of synonyms:

1. *To express ideas exactly*

The selected word should express a fact or thought with preciseness. For example, an article may contain *libel,* but not *slander. Slander* is oral defamation; *libel* is written. A building in ruins may be described as *dilapidated,* but not an automobile, because *dilapidated* refers specifically to buildings and especially to stone buildings. A writer states that smallpox is an *infectious* disease, but is it? Obviously the writer does not know the difference between *infectious* and *contagious.*

2. *To avoid monotony of expression*

A common fault of ineffective writing is the monotonous and unnecessary repetition of words. The fault can be avoided by the use of appropriate synonyms. For example, an object may be *big, large, huge, colossal,* or *gigantic.* A book may be *interesting* or *absorbing;* it may *excite, stimulate, provoke, inspire,* or *fascinate* us. Something may be made bigger by being *increased, enlarged, augmented, extended, multiplied, dilated,* or *expanded.* With an adequate stock of words it is unnecessary to write, "I took a *chance* and bought a *chance* on the *chance* that I would win the automobile." Instead, the sentence can be written, "I took a *chance* and bought a *raffle* on the *possibility* that I would win the automobile."

3. *To express ideas in words that are readily understandable*

Synonyms may be used to avoid the use of rare, scholarly, and technical words that are not generally understood. To a fellow physician a doctor may speak of the *astralagus* or of an *analeptic* effect, but to a layman he should say *anklebone* and *restorative* effect respectively. Among themselves the learned may have reason to use *obsecrate, obturate,* and *anthrophagus,* but in addressing a wider audience they should substitute *beseech, close,* and *cannibal* if they wish to be understood.

4. *To impress ideas favorably upon the minds of others*

Since synonyms differ in suggestion, the synonym with a favorable suggestion should be used to recommend ideas and things to others. A wallet of *simulated* leather sounds better than one of *artificial* leather. An *elderly* man seems to be more dignified than an *old* man, and an *untruth* sounds less reprehensible than a *lie.*

5. *To avoid incongruity*

In discourse words should be in harmony with each other and with the occasion. It is incongruous to write: "The prime minister tried to avoid the queen because she was *pestering* him to press for unpopular changes in the civil disobedience bill." The synonyms *urging* or *insisting* would be more appropriate in this sentence. Liquor may be *sipped* by a lady, *imbibed* by a dandy, *drunk* by a clerk, and *swilled* or *guzzled* by a vulgarian.

The Advantages of Knowing Antonyms

An antonym is a word that means the opposite or nearly the opposite of another word. *Brave* is an antonym of *cowardly,* and *dull* is an antonym of *sharp.*

Knowing the antonym of a word increases one's ability to understand and retain the word itself. Note how the meaning of each of the following words is indicated by its antonym:

Word	Antonym
celibate	married
penurious	generous
abortive	productive
denigrate	praise
impalpable	tangible

Exercise 29

Selecting the Appropriate Synonym

Each of the following sentences contains a number of synonyms in parentheses, only one of which is appropriate. Write the appropriate synonym in the space to the right.

1. Blindness is a terrible (misfortune, affliction, adversity). _____

2. The cause of illness is frequently mental (agitation, excitement, disturbance). _____

3. The river was a (bar, barricade, barrier) between them and the enemy. _____

4. Harry's (behavior, conduct, manners, demeanor, deportment) at the dance was shocking. _____

5. We (blame, censure, condemn) Rose for the poor attendance because she mailed the notices late. _____

6. While ironing, I (seared, scorched, burned, singed) my best blouse. _____

7. The members of the committee were (called, summoned, invited) to a special meeting. _____

8. If you can (erase, delete, obliterate) the error neatly, you need not retype the letter. _____

9. Parents must teach their children to be (careful, cautious, watchful, wary) of friendly strangers on the street. _____

10. You can always depend on Jerry to (cheer, enliven, gladden) any festive occasion. _____

11. A vivid and pleasing (character, personality, individuality) is an asset to a performing artist. _____

12. Gail decided not to exercise her (alternative, option, choice) to buy either of the houses. _____

13. Many men have lost their lives in the attempt to (climb, scale, mount, ascend) that peak. _____

14. Almost everyone likes the president's (informal, colloquial, conversational) manner of speaking. _____

15. Tyson, Vermont is a (hamlet, community, village, town) of fewer than a dozen people. _____

16. Organized labor refused to support Jones in the last election because they believed that he had become (venal, corrupt, dishonest). _____

17. His persistence made him (odious, offensive, hateful, obnoxious) to the other members of the panel.

_____

18. An assistant to the mayor (suggested, intimated, insinuated) that he could get the contract for us.

_____

19. At an early age he achieved (distinction, consideration, respect) as a composer.

_____

20. Mark Twain wrote a (humorous, facetious, waggish, comical) story about a jumping frog.

_____

EXERCISE 30

FINDING ANTONYMS

For each numbered word in Column 1, find the word in Column 2 that is most nearly its antonym. Write this word in the space provided.

COLUMN 1	COLUMN 2	
1. obfuscate	plain	_____
2. good	impracticable	_____
3. possible	destroy	_____
4. rehabilitate	clarify	_____
5. simple	complex	_____
6. skillful	clumsy	_____
7. beneficent	malignant	_____
8. benign	monogamy	_____
9. bigamy	assemble	_____
10. disperse	malevolent	_____
11. bumptious	oppose	_____
12. calumnious	honesty	_____
13. deceit	birth	_____
14. demise	meek	_____
15. espouse	eulogistic	_____
16. depraved	hopeful	_____
17. derivative	dejection	_____
18. despondent	harsh	_____
19. ecstasy	virtuous	_____
20. efficacious	original	_____

EXERCISE 31

MORE ANTONYMS

For each numbered word in Column 1, find the word in Column 2 that is most nearly its antonym. Write this word in the space provided.

COLUMN 1	COLUMN 2	
1. emancipate	obscurity	_____
2. eminence	inappropriate	_____
3. felicitous	enslave	_____
4. florid	pale	_____
5. genial	antisocial	_____
6. gregarious	morose	_____
7. haphazard	planned	_____
8. harmonious	cacophonous	_____
9. heretical	remote	_____
10. ideal	real	_____
11. imminent	unwise	_____
12. judicious	rejoice	_____
13. lament	orthodox	_____
14. lavish	hasten	_____
15. legend	mute	_____
16. loiter	limited	_____
17. loquacious	history	_____
18. figurative	literal	_____
19. miraculous	normal	_____
20. mystical	rational	_____

12. JONATHAN SWIFT'S VOCABULARY

One of the great masters of English prose, Jonathan Swift is a marvelous model for serious students of English. His satirical pamphlets (such as *A Modest Proposal*) and social satires (*Gulliver's Travels*) are classics of their kind. Pay special attention to the way he uses the thirty selected vocabulary words that are printed in bold type.

A MODEST PROPOSAL
—JONATHAN SWIFT (1667–1745)

It is a melancholy object to those who walk through this great town or travel in the country, when they see the streets, the roads, and cabin doors crowded with beggars of the female sex, followed by three, four, or six children, all in rags and **importuning** every passenger for an alms. These mothers, instead of being able to work for their honest livelihood, are forced to employ all their time in strolling to beg **sustenance** for their helpless infants, who as they grow up either turn thieves for want of work, or leave their dear native country to fight for the Pretender in Spain, or sell themselves to the Barbadoes.

I think it is agreed by all parties that this **prodigious** number of children in the arms, or on the backs, or at the heels of their mothers, and frequently of their fathers, is in the present **deplorable** state of the kingdom a very great additional grievance; and, therefore, whoever could find out a fair, cheap, and easy method of making these children sound, useful members of the commonwealth would deserve so well of the public as to have his statue set up for a preserver of the nation.

But my intention is very far from being confined to provide for the children of **professed** beggars; it is of a much greater extent, and shall take in the whole number of infants at a certain age who are born of parents in effect as little able to support them as those who demand our charity in the streets.

As to my own part, having turned my thoughts for many years upon this important subject, and maturely weighed the several schemes of other projectors, I have always found them **grossly** mistaken in the **computation**. It is true, a child just dropped from its dam may be supported by her milk for a solar year, with little other nourishment; at most not above the value of 2s., which the mother may certainly get, or the value in scraps, by her lawful occupation of begging; and it is exactly at one year old that I propose to provide for them in such a manner as instead of being a charge upon their parents or the parish, or wanting food and **raiment** for the rest of their lives, they shall on the contrary contribute to the feeding, and partly to the clothing, of many thousands.

There is likewise another great advantage in my scheme, that it will prevent those voluntary abortions, and that horrid practice of women murdering their bastard children, alas! too frequent among us! sacrificing the poor innocent babes I doubt more to avoid the expense than the shame, which would move tears and pity in the most savage and inhuman breast.

The number of souls in this kingdom being usually reckoned one million and a half, of these I calculate there may be about two hundred thousand couples whose wives are breeders; from which number I subtract thirty thousand couples who are able to maintain their own children, although I apprehend there cannot be so many, under the present distresses of the kingdom; but this being granted, there will remain an hundred and seventy thousand breeders. I again subtract fifty thousand for those women who miscarry, or whose children die by accident or disease within the year. There only remain one hundred and twenty thousand children of poor parents annually born. The question therefore is, how this number shall be reared and provided for, which, as I have already said, under the present situation of affairs, is utterly impossible by all the methods hitherto proposed. For we can neither employ them in handicraft or agriculture; we neither build houses (I mean in the country) nor cultivate land; they can very seldom pick up a livelihood by stealing till they arrive at six years old, except where they are of towardly parts, although I confess they learn the rudiments much earlier, during which time they can, however, he properly looked upon only as probationers, as I have been informed by a principal gentleman in the county of Cavan, who protested to me that he never knew above one or two instances under the age of six, even in a part of the kingdom so renowned for the quickest **proficiency** in that art.

I am assured by our merchants that a boy or a girl before twelve years old is no salable commodity; and even when they come to this age they will not yield above three pounds, or three pounds and a half-a-crown at most on the exchange, which cannot turn to account either to the parents or kingdom, the charge of nutriment and rags having been at least four times that value.

I shall now therefore humbly propose my own thoughts, which I hope will not be liable to the least objection.

I have been assured by a very knowing American of my acquaintance in London that a young healthy child well nursed is at a year old a most delicious, nourishing, and wholesome food, whether stewed, roasted, baked, or boiled; and I make no doubt that it will equally serve in a fricassee or a ragout.

I do therefore humbly offer it to public consideration that of the hundred and twenty thousand children already computed, twenty thousand may be reserved for breed, whereof only one-fourth part to be males; which is more than we allow to sheep, black cattle, or swine; and my reason is that these children are seldom the fruits of marriage, a circumstance not much regarded by our savages; therefore one male will be sufficient to serve four females. That the remaining hundred thousand may, at a year old, be offered in the sale to the persons of quality and fortune through the kingdom; always advising the mother to let them suck plentifully in the last month, so as to render them plump and fat for a good table. A child will make two dishes at an entertainment for friends; and when the family dines alone, the fore or hind quarter will make a reasonable dish, and seasoned with a little pepper or salt will be very good boiled on the fourth day, especially in winter.

I have reckoned upon a medium that a child just born will weigh 12 pounds, and in a solar year, if tolerably nursed, increaseth to 28 pounds.

I grant this food will be somewhat dear, and therefore very proper for landlords, who, as they have already devoured most of the parents, seem to have the best title to the children.

Infants' flesh will be in season throughout the year, but more plentiful in March, and a little before and after; for we are told by a grave author, an **eminent** French physician, that fish being a **prolific** diet, there are more children born in Roman Catholic countries about nine months after Lent than at any other season; therefore, reckoning a year after Lent, the markets will be more **glutted** than usual, because the number of popish infants is at least three to one in this kingdom; and therefore it will have one other **collateral** advantage, by lessening the number of papists among us.

I have already computed the charge of nursing a beggar's child (in which list I reckon all cottagers, laborers, and four-fifths of the farmers) to be about two shillings per annum, rags included; and I believe no gentleman would **repine** to give ten shillings for the carcass of a good fat child, which, as I have said, will make four dishes of excellent nutritive meat, when he hath only some particular friend or his own family to dine with him. Thus the squire will learn to be a good landlord, and grow popular among his tenants; the mother will have eight shillings net profit, and be fit for work till she produces another child.

Those who are more thrifty (as I must confess the times require) may **flay** the carcass, the skin of which artificially dressed will make admirable gloves for ladies, and summer boots for fine gentlemen.

As to our city of Dublin, shambles may be appointed for this purpose in the most convenient parts of it, and butchers we may be assured will not be wanting; although I rather recommend buying the children alive than dressing them hot from the knife as we do roasting pigs.

A very worthy person, a true lover of his country, and whose virtues I highly esteem, was lately pleased in discoursing on this matter to offer a refinement upon my scheme. He said that many gentlemen of this kingdom, having of late destroyed their deer, he conceived that the want of venison might be well supplied by the bodies of young lads and maidens, not exceeding fourteen years of age nor under twelve; so great a number of both sexes in every country being now ready to starve for want of work and service; and these be disposed of by their parents, if alive, or otherwise by their nearest relations. But with due **deference** to so excellent a friend and so deserving a patriot, I cannot be altogether in his sentiments; for as to the males, my American acquaintance assured me, from frequent experience, that their flesh was generally tough and lean, like that of our schoolboys by continual exercise, and their taste disagreeable; and to fatten them would not answer the charge. Then as to the females, it would, I think, with humble submission be a loss to the public, because they soon would become breeders themselves; and besides, it is not improbable that some **scrupulous** people might be apt to **censure** such a practice (although indeed very unjustly), as a little bordering upon cruelty; which I confess, hath always been with me the strongest objection against any project, however so well intended.

But in order to justify my friend, he confessed that this **expedient** was put in his head by the famous Psalmanazar, a native of the island of Formosa, who came from thence to London above twenty years ago, and in conversation told my friend that in his country, when any young person happened to be put to death, the executioner sold the carcass to persons of quality as a prime dainty; and that in his time the body of a plump girl of fifteen, who was crucified for an attempt to poison the emperor, was sold to his imperial majesty's prime minister of state, and other great mandarins of the court, in joints from the gibbet, at four hundred crowns. Neither indeed can I deny that if the same use were made of several plump young girls in this town, who without one single groat to their fortunes cannot stir abroad without a chair, and appear at playhouse and assemblies in foreign fineries which they never will pay for, the kingdom would not be the worse.

Some persons of a desponding spirit are in great concern about that vast number of poor people who are aged, diseased, or maimed, and I have been desired to employ my thoughts what course may be taken to ease the nation of so grievous an **encumbrance**. But I am not in the least pain upon that matter, because it is very well known that they are every day dying and rotting by cold and famine, and filth and vermin, as fast as can be reasonably expected. And as to the young laborers, they are now in as hopeful a condition; they cannot get work, and consequently pine away for want of nourishment, to a degree that if at any time they are accidentally hired to common labor, they have not strength to perform it, and thus the country and themselves are happily delivered from the evils to come.

I have too long **digressed**, and therefore shall return to my subject. I think the advantages of the proposal which I have made are obvious and many, as well as of the highest importance.

For first, as I have already observed, it would greatly lessen the number of papists, with whom we are yearly overrun, being the principal breeders of the nation as well as our most dangerous enemies; and who stay at home on purpose with a design to deliver the kingdom to the Pretender, hoping to take their advantage, by the absence of so many good Protestants, who have chosen rather to leave their country than to stay at home and pay tithes against their conscience to an episcopal curate.

Second, the poorer tenants will have something valuable of their own, which by law may be made liable to distress and help to pay their landlord's rent, their corn and cattle being already seized, and money a thing unknown.

Thirdly, whereas the maintenance of an hundred thousand children, from two years old and upward, cannot be computed at less than ten shillings apiece per annum, the nation's stock will be thereby increased fifty thousand pounds per annum, beside the profit of a new dish introduced to the tables of all gentlemen of fortune in the kingdom who have any refinement in taste. And the money will circulate among ourselves, the goods being entirely of our own growth and manufacture.

Fourthly, the constant breeders, besides the gain of eight shillings sterling per annum by the sale of their children, will be rid of the charge of maintaining them after the first year.

Fifthly, this food would likewise bring great customs to taverns, where the vintners will certainly be so **prudent** as to **procure** the best receipts for dressing it to perfection, and consequently have their houses frequented by all the fine gentlemen who justly value themselves upon their knowledge in good eating; and a skillful cook, who understands how to oblige his guests, will contrive to make it as expensive as they please.

Sixthly, this would be a great inducement to marriage, which all wise nations have either encouraged by rewards or enforced by laws and penalties. It would increase the care and the tenderness of mothers toward their children, when they were sure of settlement for life to the poor babes, provided in some sort by the public, to their annual profit instead of expense. We should see an honest **emulation** among the married women, which of them could bring the fattest child to the market. Men would become as fond of their wives during the time of their pregnancy as they are now of their mares in foal, their cows in calf, their sows when they are ready to farrow; nor offer to beat or kick them (as is too frequent a practice) for fear of a miscarriage.

Many other advantages might be enumerated. For instance, the addition of some thousand carcasses in our exportation of barreled beef, the **propagation** of swine's flesh, and improvement in the art of making good bacon, so much wanted among us by the great destruction of pigs, too frequent at our tables; which are no way comparable in taste or magnificence to a wellgrown, fat, yearling child, which roasted whole will make a considerable figure at a lord mayor's feast or any other public entertainment. But this and many others I omit, being studious of **brevity**.

Supposing that one thousand families in this city would be constant customers for infants' flesh, besides others who might have it at merry-meetings, particularly weddings and christenings, I compute that Dublin would take off annually about twenty thousand carcasses; and the rest of the kingdom (where probably they will be sold somewhat cheaper) the remaining eighty thousand.

I can think of no one objection that will possibly be raised against the proposal, unless it should be urged that the number of people will be thereby much lessened in the kingdom. This I freely own, and was indeed one principal design in offering it to the world. I desire the reader will observe that I calculate my remedy for this one individual kingdom of Ireland and for no other that ever was, is, or I think ever can be upon earth. Therefore let no man talk to me of other expedients: of taxing our absentees at five shillings a pound; of using neither clothes nor household furniture except what is of our own growth and manufacture; of utterly rejecting the materials and instruments that promote foreign luxury; of curing the expensiveness of pride, vanity, idleness, and gaming in our women; of introducing a vein of **parsimony**, prudence, and temperance; of learning to love our country, wherein we differ even from Laplanders and inhabitants of Topinamboo; of quitting our **animosities** and factions, nor act any longer like the Jews, who were murdering one another at the very moment their city was taken; of being a little cautious not to sell our country and conscience for nothing; of teaching landlords to have at least one degree of mercy toward their tenants; lastly, of putting a spirit of honesty, industry, and skill into our shopkeepers; who, if a resolution could now be taken to buy only our native goods, would immediately unite to cheat and exact upon the price, the measure, and the goodness, nor could ever yet be brought to make one fair proposal of just dealing, though often and earnestly invited to it.

Therefore, I repeat, let no man talk to me of these and the like expedients, till he hath at least some glimpse of hope that there will be ever some hearty and sincere attempt to put them in practice.

But as to myself, having been wearied out for many years with offering vain, idle, visionary thoughts, and at length utterly despairing of success, I fortunately fell upon this proposal, which, as it is wholly new, so it hath something solid and real, of no expense and little trouble, full in our own power, and whereby we can incur no danger in disobliging England. For this kind of commodity will not bear exportation, the flesh being of too tender a consistency to admit a long continuance in salt, although perhaps I could name a country which would be glad to eat up our whole nation without it.

After all, I am not so violently bent upon my own opinion as to reject any offer proposed by wise men, which shall be found equally innocent, cheap, easy, and effectual. But before something of that kind shall be advanced in contradiction to my scheme, and offering a better, I desire the author or authors will be pleased maturely to consider two points. First, as things now stand, how they will be able to find food and raiment for an hundred thousand useless mouths and backs. And secondly, there being a round million of creatures in human figure throughout this kingdom, whose whole subsistence put into a common stock would have them in debt two millions of pounds sterling, adding those who are beggars by profession to the bulk of farmers, cottagers, and laborers, with their wives and children, who are beggars in effect: I desire those politicians who dislike my overture, and may perhaps be so bold as to attempt an answer, that they will first ask the parents of these mortals whether they would not at this day think it a great happiness to have been sold for food at a year old in the manner I prescribe, and thereby have avoided such a **perpetual** scene of misfortunes as they have since gone through by the oppression of landlords, the impossibility of paying rent without money or trade, the want of common sustenance with neither house nor clothes to cover them from the **inclemencies** of the weather, and the most inevitable prospect of entailing the like or greater miseries upon their breed for ever.

I profess, in the sincerity of my heart, that I have not the least personal interest in endeavoring to promote this necessary work, having no other motive than the public good of my country, by advancing our trade, providing for infants, relieving the poor, and giving some pleasure to the rich. I have no children by which I can propose to get a single penny; the youngest being nine years old, and my wife past child-bearing.

EXERCISE 32

SWIFT'S WORDS

The words and expressions in this exercise are bold in the essay you have just read. After carefully studying each word in context and looking it up in the dictionary, write the part of speech and the definition of the word in the space provided.

1. importuning

   Part of speech _____ Definition _____

2. sustenance

   Part of speech _____ Definition _____

3. prodigious

   Part of speech _____ Definition _____

4. deplorable

   Part of speech _____ Definition _____

5. professed

   Part of speech _____ Definition _____

6. grossly

   Part of speech _____ Definition _____

7. computation

   Part of speech _____ Definition _____

8. raiment

   Part of speech _____ Definition _____

9. proficiency

   Part of speech _____ Definition _____

10. eminent

    Part of speech _____ Definition _____

11. prolific

    Part of speech _____ Definition _____

12. glutted

    Part of speech _____ Definition _____

13. collateral

Part of speech _____ Definition _____

14. repine

Part of speech _____ Definition _____

15. flay

Part of speech _____ Definition _____

EXERCISE 33

MORE OF SWIFT

Just as in Exercise 32, carefully study each word in context in the essay. Look it up in the dictionary and write the part of speech and the definition in the space provided.

1. deference

   Part of speech _____ Definition _____

2. scrupulous

   Part of speech _____ Definition _____

3. censure

   Part of speech _____ Definition _____

4. expedient

   Part of speech _____ Definition _____

5. encumbrance

   Part of speech _____ Definition _____

6. digressed

   Part of speech _____ Definition _____

7. prudent

   Part of speech _____ Definition _____

8. procure

   Part of speech _____ Definition _____

9. emulation

   Part of speech _____ Definition _____

10. propagation

    Part of speech _____ Definition _____

11. brevity

    Part of speech _____ Definition _____

12. parsimony

Part of speech _____ Definition _____

13. animosities

Part of speech _____ Definition _____

14. perpetual

Part of speech _____ Definition _____

15. inclemencies

Part of speech _____ Definition _____

EXERCISE 34

TO THE SWIFT...

The vocabulary words from Exercises 32 and 33 appear in the box below. Select the proper words to ft into the blanks in these sentences.

importuning	grossly	prolific	deference	digressed	brevity
sustenance	computation	glutted	scrupulous	prudent	parsimony
prodigious	raiment	collateral	censure	procure	animosities
deplorable	proficiency	repine	expedient	emulation	perpetual
professed	eminent	flay	encumbrance	propagation	inclemencies

1. The football player had a _____ appetite, wolfing down six hero sandwiches in an hour.

2. We thought that their feud had ended, but the old _____ broke out anew at the dance.

3. Our professor frequently _____ from the subject to tell about his boyhood in Indiana.

4. The members of the House voted to _____ the congressman for the lies he had told.

5. Isaac Asimov was a _____ author, having written over 200 books.

6. My Uncle Sid _____ to being a Democrat but on Election Day he secretly voted for the Republicans.

7. On the streets of Bangkok you can see monks in orange robes _____ for food and contributions.

8. My sister's _____ investment in six-month certificates brought her 5.5% interest.

9. Since Polonius was so long-winded, it was ironic to hear him say that "_____ is the soul of wit."

10. Some people praised the old miser for his _____; most condemned him for being cheap and stingy, however.

11. A character in *The Water Engine* invented a _____ motion machine, or so he claimed.

12. When the angels appeared in Sloan's dream they were wearing glorious _____ ornamented with gold and silver.

13. It took Mr. Safran twenty years to develop his great _____ in stenography.

14. When the judge saw the _____ condition of the apartment house, he immediately ordered that the tenants be moved elsewhere at the landlord's expense.

15. Although Ellis was _____ underpaid, he stayed on because of his happiness with his coworkers.

EXERCISE 35

SWIFT, CONTINUED

Using the vocabulary contained in "A Modest Proposal," answer the following questions by selecting the correct words from the box below.

importuning	deplorable	computation	eminent	collateral
sustenance	professed	raiment	prolific	repine
prodigious	grossly	proficiency	glutted	flay

1. Which word describes a market where the supply is greater than the demand? _____

2. Which word means the same as to express discontent? _____

3. Which word is closely associated with the work of a mathematician? _____

4. Which word means to scold or to rip the skin off? _____

5. Which word is a banker likely to be interested in? _____

6. Which word is a synonym for support or means of livelihood? _____

7. Which adjective describes someone who is outstanding in his field? _____

8. Which adjective tells us the most about an elephant's size? _____

9. Which word is a synonym for fruitful? _____

10. Which word describes an unfortunate or lamentable situation? _____

EXERCISE 36

SWIFT, CONCLUDED

Do the same as you did in Exercise 35. Select the correct word from the box below.

deference	expedient	prudent	propagation	animosities
scrupulous	encumbrance	procure	brevity	perpetual
censure	digressed	emulation	parsimony	inclemencies

1. Which word describes careful or precise attention to detail? _____

2. Which word is a synonym for obstruction or hindrance? _____

3. With which word is a meteorologist most likely to be involved? _____

4. Which word means to get or obtain? _____

5. Which adjective describes good judgment in financial matters? _____

6. Which word is a synonym for continual? _____

7. Which word describes a device used in an emergency? _____

8. Which word signifies honor or respect for one's position? _____

9. With which word is a biologist most likely to be involved? _____

10. Which word can be used as both a noun and a verb? _____

VOCABULARY TEST 6

FINDING SYNONYMS

We have already studied the following words. How many of them do you know? For each of the boldface words select the word or expression that means most nearly the same and write the letter in the space to the right.

1. The waters **recede**.
   a. grow turbulent   b. draw back   c. flow smoothly
   d. become oily

2. A **credulous** mother....
   a. scolding   b. doting   c. overanxious   d. ready to believe

3. The punishment for those who **transgress**...
   a. break the law b. steal   c. riot   d. rebel

4. A **stringent** rule...
   a. wordy   b. lenient   c. severe   d. vague

5. A **chronic** disease...
   a. bronchial   b. disabling   c. continuing   d. incurable

6. A course in **anthropology**...
   a. the science of man and his works   b. marital problems
   c. the lower animals   d. ancient documents

7. A **panacea** for social ills...
   a. explanation   b. partial remedy   c. breeding ground   d. cure-all

8. The **panorama** from the window of the train...
   a. rocky knoll   b. passing scene   c. view of the horizon
   d. round house

9. A failure due to **apathy**...
   a. excessive enthusiasm   b. insufficient effort
   c. insufficient experience   d. lack of interest

10. The teacher of a **homogeneous** class...
    a. essentially alike   b. mentally superior   c. emotionally disturbed
    d. rapid-advance

11. An act of **malevolence**...
    a. evil deed   b. charisma   c. ineptitude   d. excessive emotion

12. The **protagonist** of the novel...
    a. subplot   b. villain   c. principal character   d. ghost writer

13. A **posthumous** play...
    a. tragicomic   b. delayed in production
    c. after the author's death   d. censured

14. The search for the **malefactor**...
a. accessory to a crime   b. cause of a disease
c. a mistake in calculation   d. an evildoer

_____

15. The refusal to **intercede** in the dispute...
a. take part in   b. referee   c. give testimony
d. act in one's behalf

_____

16. To **retract** a statement...
a. withdraw   b. rephrase   c. explain   d. augment

_____

17. To go in order of **precedence**...
a. age   b. rank   c. arrival   d. size

_____

18. A **pandemic** disease...
a. localized   b. contagious   c. fatal   d. widespread

_____

19. A maker of **epigrams**...
a. double-line charts   b. ornamental insignia
c. quotable inscriptions   d. verbal puzzles

_____

20. The author of an autobiographical **trilogy**...
a. long narrative poem   b. poetic lament   c. marriage hymn
d. three related literary works

_____

21. There was **pandemonium** in the forum...
a. a wild tumult   b. solemn procession   c. open hearing
d. a patriotic rally

_____

22. A **desolate** stretch of land...
a. flat   b. verdant   c. devastated   d. overpopulated

_____

23. She was called a **wanton**...
a. witch   b. lascivious person   c. habitual liar   d. cruel mother

_____

24. To make a **fetish** of something...
a. excuse for failure   b. an object of blind reverence
c. a prerequisite   d. a horrible example

_____

25. A **maudlin** complaint...
a. excessively bitter   b. unfounded   c. excessively sentimental
d. overwrought and confused

_____

26. An **unkempt** appearance...
a. gaudy   b. sudden   c. scheduled   d. untidy

_____

27. To **malign** a person...
a. to slander   b. to delay   c. to disturb   d. to drive to madness

_____

28. He thinks he has a **mandate** from the people...
a. grudging acquiescence   b. order or command
c. implied support   d. vote of confidence

_____

29. A heavy **projectile**...
a. body propelled through the air   b. abnormal child
c. wrought iron gate   d. concentrated mass

_____

30. An army of **mercenaries**...
a. hireling soldiers   b. untrained infantrymen   c. youthful soldiers
d. pillaging soldiers   _____

31. An **implacable** foe...
a. unconquerable   b. relentless   c. unknown   d. malevolent _____

32. A practitioner of **necromancy**...
a. sorcery   b. faith healing   c. prodigious feats of strength
d. embalming   _____

33. An **odious** remark...
a. unexpected   b. silly   c. strange   d. hateful   _____

34. **Facetious** explanations...
a. false   b. superficial   c. pompous   d. playful   _____

35. Sued for **libel**...
a. written defamation   b. physical assault   c. oral defamation
d. nonpayment of a debt   _____

36. **Animosities** developed between the former friends.
a. contracts   b. misunderstandings   c. hostilities   d. new rules _____

37. An **eminent** critic examined the painting.
a. biased   b. candid   c. famous   d. harsh   _____

38. He **digressed** from the topic.
a. strayed   b. backed away   c. moved ahead
d. jumped to a conclusion   _____

39. In **emulation** of his idol...
a. imitation   b. rejection   c. study   d. worship   _____

40. A vote of **censure**...
a. agreement   b. protest   c. criticism   d. restriction _____

41. The **brevity** of his argument...
a. inconsistency   b. foolishness   c. wit   d. conciseness _____

42. To **subvert** the government...
a. overthrow   b. reform   c. defend   d. defraud   _____

43. To read a **proscribed** book...
a. revised and augmented   b. condemned and banned
c. abridged   d. ghostwritten   _____

44. He delivered the **eulogy**...
a. opening prayer   b. principal speech
c. a speech in praise of someone   d. a funeral oration _____

45. We applauded Judge Helen Roth's **prudent** decision.
a. vindictive   b. wise   c. harsh   d. perfect   _____

VOCABULARY TEST 7

USING WORDS IN ILLUSTRATIVE SENTENCES

The following words and expressions have been used in the text and exercises. How many of them do you know? Use each in an illustrative sentence that throws some light on the meaning of the expression.

WORD	SENTENCE
1. scrupulous	_____
2. perpetual	_____
3. deference	_____
4. expedient	_____
5. infer	_____
6. flay	_____
7. deplorable	_____
8. convene	_____
9. symmetry	_____
10. sophisticated	_____
11. adhesive	_____
12. complement	_____
13. misanthrope	_____
14. synchronize	_____
15. automaton	_____
16. genealogy	_____
17. pathology	_____
18. didactic	_____
19. decimate	_____
20. pentagon	_____

VOCABULARY TEST 8

USING WORDS IN ILLUSTRATIVE SENTENCES

The following words have appeared in the text and exercises. How many of them do you know? Use each of the words in an illustrative sentence that throws some light on the meaning of the word.

WORD	SENTENCE
1. conflagration	_____
2. cortege	_____
3. galaxy	_____
4. orientation	_____
5. mandate	_____
6. boor	_____
7. doom	_____
8. pernicious	_____
9. abortive	_____
10. denigrate	_____
11. jovial	_____
12. prodigal	_____
13. rancor	_____
14. perceive	_____
15. coterie	_____
16. obnoxious	_____
17. obfuscate	_____
18. benign	_____
19. demise	_____
20. sobriety	_____

13. WORDS COMMONLY CONFUSED AND MISUSED

This chapter discusses a number of words and other expressions that are commonly misused. For convenience the terms are listed alphabetically. Terms frequently confused are treated together and distinguished one from the other. The discussion explains how each term is used in a faulty manner and how it is used correctly. The discussion is limited to essentials for the purpose of distinguishing between correct and incorrect use. For a fuller explanation of the terms, for unusual uses and exceptions, one should consult an unabridged dictionary.

accept, except

Accept (*v.*) means to receive with a consenting mind: He *accepted* the reward with becoming grace.

Except (*v.*) means to leave out; to exclude: We will sign the resolution if you will *except* paragraph three.

Except (*prep.*) means with the exclusion of; leaving or left out: No president, *except* Franklin Delano Roosevelt, was elected to more than two terms.

adapt, adopt

Adapt (*v.*) means to adjust; to make suitable: It is difficult to see how Joyce's novel *Ulysses* can be satisfactorily *adapted* for motion pictures.

Adopt (*v.*) means to take or receive as one's own; to select and approve: We shall *adopt* the slogan proposed at the last meeting.

adverse, averse

Adverse (*adj.*) means acting against; contrary to one's interests: The committee submitted an *adverse* report on the operation of the new traffic regulations.

Averse (*adj.*) means having an aversion to something; disliking; reluctant: The medical profession is *averse* to any health law that smacks of socialization.

advice, advise

Advice (*n.*) means recommendation regarding a decision or course of action; information or notice given. Note that *advice* is a noun and is spelled with a *c*: The older I grow the more reluctant I am to offer *advice* to younger people.

Advise (*v.*) means to counsel or to take counsel; to warn; to recommend a course of action. Notice that *advise* is a verb and is spelled with an *s*: The lawyer *advised* me to write a letter of complaint.

affect, effect

Affect (*v.*) means to act upon; to influence: It is impossible to tell how this ruling will *affect* our production schedule.

Effect (*v.*) means to bring about a result; to accomplish: How to *effect* the desired result is a problem we have not yet solved.

Effect (*n.*) means result; consequence: The *effect* of the new drug is temporary.

aggravate, irritate

Aggravate (*v.*) means to make heavy; to increase; to make worse or more severe: The dog *aggravated* the wound by scratching it. In formal discourse *aggravate* should not be used to mean provoke, exasperate, or irritate.

Irritate (*v.*) means to excite impatience, anger, or displeasure; to provoke, exasperate, annoy: The little boy *irritated* his mother by pulling on her skirt.

aggravation

Aggravation (*n.*) means an act or circumstance that increases the gravity or seriousness of a thing: The boycott was the additional *aggravation* that caused the bankruptcy. In formal discourse do not use *aggravation* to mean *irritation* or *provocation*.

WRONG:　His general disrespect for all authority is sufficient *aggravation* to discharge him.
RIGHT:　His general disrespect for all authority is sufficient *provocation* to discharge him.
WRONG:　He attributed his *aggravation* to the noise in the office.
RIGHT:　He attributed his *irritation* to the noise in the office.

all ready, already

All ready is a colloquial phrase used as an adjective to mean completely prepared or prepared in every way: The troops are *all ready* to be transported to Guam.

Already (*adv.*) means previously; prior to some specified time: The governor has *already* thrown his hat into the presidential ring.

all right, alright

All right is a colloquial phrase. As an adjective it means satisfactory: We will proceed if you think that the arrangements are *all right*. As an adverb *all right* means satisfactorily: His heart is now functioning *all right*.

Alright is considered incorrect and should not be used.

all together, altogether

All together is an adjective phrase meaning the whole in one company, place, or mass: Those books are shelved *all together* in the history reading room.

Altogether (*adv.*) means wholly; thoroughly; on the whole: The proposed program is *altogether* too expensive for our little community.

allusion, delusion, illusion

Allusion (*n.*) means a hint; an indirect reference to something generally familiar: No one here will understand an *allusion* to the Dreyfus case.

Delusion (*n.*) means a false belief; customary or fixed misconception. Note that delusion is an error of the mind or affecting the mind: The belief that we can dominate the world with nuclear weapons is a terrible *delusion*.

Illusion (*n.*) means an unreal or misleading image presented to the vision: The perspective in Turner's seascapes is managed to create the *illusion* of great distance.

alternative, choice

Alternative (*n.*) means a choice between two things, courses, or propositions, one of which must be taken: "Give me liberty or give me death" was the alternative demanded by Patrick Henry.

Choice (*n.*) means the opportunity of selecting, without compulsion, from two or more things; no selection has to be made: We had the *choice* of any suite on the twentieth floor.

among, between

Among (*prep.*) applies to *more than* two things: The excess produce was distributed *among* the poor.

Between (*prep.*) applies to only *two* things: The prize will be divided equally *between* the contestants who place first and second in the competition.

EXCEPTION: *Between* is used when a number of objects are brought together in a common relation: The church was torn by a quarrel *between* the vestry, the parishioners, and the ministers. (2) The EEC is an establishment by agreement *between* several western European nations.

amount, number

Amount (n.) is used to indicate quantity, bulk, mass: We have a large *amount* of credit in African countries.

Number (n.) is used to indicate units: (1) A *number* of people witnessed the crime. (2) The firm purchased a large *number* of tons of sugar. [But the firm purchased a large *amount* of sugar.]

any one, anyone

Any one is a phrase meaning every single thing or person of a group. *Any one* is usually followed by *of*: *Any one of* the surgeons on the panel is competent to perform the operation.

Anyone is an indefinite pronoun meaning anybody. It is not followed by *of*: *Anyone* can see the error in this line of reasoning.

appraise, apprise

Appraise (v.) means to estimate the quality, size, or weight of anything; to value in current money: (1) Whoever *appraised* the situation in the Middle East made some serious errors. (2) You must have the ring *appraised* before you insure it.

Apprise (v.) means to give notice; to inform; to advise: Thomas Mann was *apprised* by letter that he had been stricken from the honorary roll of doctors at the University of Bonn.

apt, liable, likely

In formal discourse these words are not interchangeable.

Apt (adj.) means the following: (1) fit or suitable: The point is illustrated by an *apt* quotation. (2) *habitually tending to*: In this area the dogwood is *apt* to flower late. (3) inclined or customarily disposed: We are *apt* to think of our grandparents with pity and contempt. (4) quick to learn; dexterous: He is an *apt* statistician.

Liable (adj.) means subject, exposed, or open to something possible or likely, especially something undesirable: If one parks at a fire hydrant, one is *liable* to a $50.00 fine. Children who play with fire are *liable* to burn themselves.

Likely (adj.) means probable or suitable: In this class John is the most *likely* to succeed. I have found a *likely* spot for our summer home.

as...as, so...as

As...as is used for affirmative statements: Business is *as* good *as* we can expect.

So...as is used for negative statements: Business is not *so* good *as* we expected.

as, like

As (conj.) is used when a verb follows or is understood: Do *as* we do. [NOT Do *like* we do.] It is fifty miles *as* the crow flies. [NOT *like* the crow flies.]

Like (adj.), meaning similar to or resembling, is used as follows: The painting looks *like* a Gauguin. [Note that *like* is not followed by a verb.]

Like (adv.), meaning in a similar manner, is used as follows: He struts *like* a peacock.

beside, besides

Beside (prep.) means by or at the side of: During the entire ceremony he stood *beside* me.

Besides means in addition to; over and above. *Besides* may be used as a preposition: *Besides* being a nuisance, the cleaning establishment below us is a fire hazard. *Besides* may also be used as an adverb: We signed a three-year contract and had to post a thousand dollars in security *besides*.

bring, take, fetch, carry

Bring (v.) means to come with (something): When she returns from Paris, she always *brings* me perfume.

Take (v.) means to bear or carry (something) away from the speaker: *Take* the rent to the office and get a receipt.

Fetch (v.) means to go and get (something) and bring it back: Throw the stick into the water, and the dog will *fetch* it.

Carry (v.) means to convey from one place to another regardless of direction: We need a station wagon to *carry* all our equipment.

can, may

Can (v.) means power or ability: I *can* lift two hundred pounds. You *can* (are able to) play Chopin études.

May (v.) means permission to do something: *May* I (will you allow me to) go to the beach? You *may* (have my permission to) play Chopin's études because you *can* (have the ability to) play them.

claim, assert

Claim (v.) means to demand as right or due; to assert one's right to: After the bank robber had been convicted, the informer *claimed* the reward.

Assert (v.) means to state as true; declare; affirm; to put (oneself) forward boldly: Throughout their trial for espionage they vehemently *asserted* their innocence.

compare to, compare with

Compare to is used to represent one thing as similar or analogous to another; to liken: He *compared* the nets in *A Portrait of the Artist as a Young Man* to the bondages in *Of Human Bondage*.

Compare with is used to note similarities and dissimilarities: If you want to appraise the relative stature of Galsworthy and Mann as novelists, compare *The Forsyte Saga* with *Buddenbrooks*.

complement, compliment

Complement (v.) means to complete: These two discussions *complement* each other. Two of the common meanings of the *noun* complement are: (1) something that completes or perfects another thing and (2) a full quantity or amount: (1) These serving spoons will be a *complement* to your silver service. (2) The *complement* of this ship, crew, and officers, is sixty-five.

Compliment (n.) means an expression of admiration, praise, or congratulation: Edith Wharton accepted Lewis' dedication of *Babbitt* to her as a *compliment.*

common, mutual

Common (adj.), as distinguished from *mutual,* means belonging to or shared by two or more individuals or things: This is the *common* beach for the bungalow colony. Since they have many things in *common,* their marriage should be a happy one.

Mutual (adj.) means reciprocal, interchangeable: Although they are political opponents, they hold each other in *mutual* esteem. For protection from their more powerful enemies, they signed a treaty of *mutual* aid.

consul, council, counsel

A *consul* (n.) is a government agent appointed to reside in a foreign state to protect the interests of the citizens of the appointing government: In *Buddenbrooks,* Thomas Buddenbrook serves as *consul* to the Netherlands.

A *council* (n.) is an advisory assembly: The Trade Union *Council* of New York has called upon all of labor to support the demands of the transit workers.

Counsel (n.) means (1) a lawyer or lawyers and (2) advice: (1) The *counsel* for the defense moved for an adjournment. (2) The *counsel* (advice) that parents give, the children ignore.

Counsel (v.) means to give advice: Parents must *counsel* their children and expect to be ignored.

contemptuous, contemptible

Contemptuous (adj.) means manifesting disdain; scornful: He was *contemptuous* of the efforts to unionize the workers.

Contemptible (adj.) means despicable: It is *contemptible* to mock anybody because of a physical handicap.

continual, continuous

Continual (adj.) means proceeding without interruption or cessation; of regular or frequent recurrence: Their marriage was marred by *continual* quarreling.

Continuous (adj.) emphasizes the idea that the succession is unbroken: The *continuous* life of man is now threatened by nuclear explosives.

138

credible, creditable, credulous

Credible (*adj.*) means capable or worthy of belief: In the extortion trial he was a *credible* witness for the defense. The story is astounding, but *credible*.

Creditable (*adj.*) means meritorious, praiseworthy: As Joan, Miss Cruikshank gave a *creditable* performance. NOTE: At present to call anything *creditable* is to damn it with faint praise.

Credulous (*adj.*) means ready or disposed to believe, especially on weak or insufficient evidence: She is a *credulous* mother; she believes everything her children tell her.

different from

Different from is the correct form to express contrast: The last proposal by China is no *different from* its previous proposals. *Different than* and *different to* are incorrect and should not be used.

differ from, differ with

Differ from expresses dissimilarity between persons, things, and opinions: The second edition *differs from* the first by the removal of numerous typographical errors and the addition of an index.

Differ with is used to state that one person's beliefs are at variance with another's: It was during his lean years in Vienna that Hitler began to *differ with* the Social Democrats.

dominate, domineer

Dominate (*v.*) means to rule over, control; to occupy a commanding position: The president could *dominate* a meeting with his oratory.

Domineer (*v.*) means to rule arbitrarily or despotically; to tyrannize: He is a strong and selfish father who *domineers* his family.

due to

Due to is an adjective phrase meaning attributable to or ascribable to. As an adjective it must directly modify a noun or pronoun: The rise in the price index is *due to* a sharp increase in the price of services. [*Due to* modifies the noun *rise*.] In standard discourse *due to* should *not* be used to mean *because*: The price index rose *due to* a sharp increase in the cost of services. [*Due to* does not modify any noun or pronoun in this sentence.]

WRONG: *Due to* the unrest in Iran, we have changed our plans.

RIGHT: *Because* of the unrest in Iran, we have changed our plans.

OR: Our change of plans was *due to* the unrest in Iran. [*Due to* now modifies the noun *change*.]

elicit, illicit

Elicit (*v.*) means to draw or bring out or forth; to evoke: After hours of questioning, they finally *elicited* the truth from David.

Illicit (*adj.*) means not permitted or authorized; unlawful: Traffic in drugs is *illicit*.

fewer, less

Fewer, the comparative form of the adjective *few*, is used with units and numbers of things: The advertisement brought *fewer* responses than we had expected.

Less is used with quantity, mass, and bulk: They sent us *less* sugar than we ordered [but *fewer* pounds]. There was *less* objection than we had anticipated. But there were *fewer* (individual) objections.

flaunt, flout

Flaunt (*v.*) means to display ostentatiously: She *flaunted* her mink coat before her friends.

Flout (*v.*) means to treat with contempt: The postal workers do not dare to *flout* the law by striking.

forcible, forceful

Forcible (*adj.*) means effected by force; characterized by the use of force or violence: The police made a *forcible* entry by battering down the doors.

Forceful (*adj.*) means powerful; vigorous; effective: The attorney made a *forceful* appeal for clemency.

former and latter, first and last

Former and *latter* (adj.) are used to designate one of *two* persons or things: Of the two propositions I favor the *former,* but my partner favors the *latter.*

First and *last* (adj.) are used to designate one of three or more persons or things: Of the steak, roast, fish, and fowl, I prefer the *first* and the *last.*

hanged, hung

Hanged (p.p. of *hang*) is used in reference to execution: He was *hanged* by the neck until he died.

Hung (p.p. of *hang*) is used to mean the suspension of any object: We have *hung* the mobile in our foyer.

healthful, healthy, wholesome

Healthful (adj.) means promoting health or conducive and beneficial to it: For asthmatics the climate of Arizona is *healthful.*

Healthy (adj.) means possessing health; of sound condition: What *healthy* children she has!

Wholesome (adj.) means conducive to moral or general well-being; conducive to bodily health: Dr. Spock's books on infant care are popular because they are full of *wholesome* advice. Children eat too many sweets and not enough *wholesome* food.

imply, infer

Imply (v.) means virtually to include or mean: The president's remark seems to *imply* that he will reject the proposal for a summit conference. Their week of silence *implies* that they are angry with us.

Infer (v.) means to draw a conclusion from; to deduce: I *infer* from that remark that he will reject the proposal.

indict, indite

Indict (v.) means to charge with an offense; to bring a formal accusation against, as a means of bringing to trial: The gangster was *indicted* for evasion of income tax.

Indite (v.) means to compose or write a speech, poem, etc.: William Carlos Williams has *indited* a number of poems about his city, Paterson.

ingenious, ingenuous

Ingenious (adj.) means showing cleverness of invention or construction; having intuitive faculty: This *ingenious* device is a high chair, a stroller, and a car bed. Mother was an *ingenious* cook who could make a delicious meal from almost nothing.

Ingenuous (adj.) means frank and candid; naive: He made an *ingenuous* confession of his neglect and promised to be more attentive in the future. He was *ingenuous* enough to believe that his coworkers would rejoice in his promotion

its, it's

Its is a possessive pronoun: The dog bared *its* teeth and growled.

It's is the contraction of it is: *It's* never too late to mend.

kind, sort, type

Kind, sort, and *type* (n.) are singular in number and must be used with the singular demonstratives *this* and *that: this kind, sort, type; that kind, sort, type.* The plural forms are *these kinds, sorts, types; those kinds, sorts, types.*

kind of, sort of, type of

Kind of, sort of, and *type of* should not be followed by the definite articles *a* and *an:* This is the *kind of* noise that sets my teeth on edge. Musical chairs is the *sort of* game that young children like. I am looking for some *type of* air conditioner that does not require its own power line.

lay, lie

Lay is a transitive verb that means to put or place an object in position: I will *lay* the matter before the grievance committee. The principal parts of *lay* are *lay, laid, laid*: I *lay* the rug. I *laid* the rug. I *have laid* the rug.

Lie is an intransitive verb meaning to recline. As an intransitive verb *lie* does not take an object: He *lies* down for a nap every afternoon. Your jacket is *lying* on the steps where you dropped it this morning. The principal parts of *lie* are *lie, lay, lain*: I *lie* down. I *lay* down. I *have lain* down.

majority, plurality

In voting, *majority* (n.) means a number of votes or voters constituting more than half of the total number cast: Since sixty-seven of the ninety members present voted for James, he was elected by a *majority*.

Plurality (n.) is used when there are three or more candidates. It means the excess of votes received by the leading candidate over those received by the next candidate: The results of the ballot are as follows: Jones, 201; Knight, 147; Downs, 132. Therefore, Jones wins by a *plurality* of 54. *Plurality* is also used to mean the largest number of votes cast for a single candidate: In the results posted above, Jones received a *plurality*, but not a *majority*.

militate, mitigate

Militate (v.) means to operate (against or in favor of); to have effect or influence: Every factor *militated* against our changes of success. The discrepancies in the evidence will *militate* for a dismissal of the charges.

Mitigate (v.) means to lessen in force or intensity; to moderate the severity of anything: Nothing could *mitigate* his guilt or his regret.

officially, officiously

Officially (adv.) means authoritatively: I have not yet been *officially* notified of the appointment.

Officiously (adv.) means forward in tendering or obtruding one's services upon others: If she interferes *officiously* once again, she will be discharged.

practicable, practical

Practicable (adj.) means capable of being put into practice; done, or effected; capable of being used or traversed, or admitting of passage: Scientists have not yet discovered a *practicable* method of converting sea water to fresh water. Space shuttles are not yet *practicable* for general travel.

Practical (adj.) means sensible and businesslike when applied to persons: Because he is a *practical* man, Mr. Berry is a good general manager. When applied to a thing *practical* means valuable in practice; gained by experience; useful (as opposed to theoretical). It takes two years of experience to be licensed as a *practical* nurse.

principal, principle

Principal (n.) means (1) a leader or chief, (2) a sum of money that accrues interest, (3) one who employs another to act for him or her: (1) The *principals* who negotiated the merger of the two banks were Mr. Simms and Mr. Slater. (2) She tried to live within her income so that she could leave the *principal* to her blind daughter. (3) Howland, the *principal*, has appointed me as his agent with power of attorney to act for him in all matters pertaining to this transaction.

Principal (adj.) means first or highest in rank, value, etc.: The *principal* cause of the accident was carelessness.

Principle (n.) has many meanings. Those in most common use are (1) a fundamental truth or law and (2) a governing law of conduct: (1) In these two problems, the *principle* is the same. (2) He made it a *principle* never to accept a gift from a client.

prone, supine

In reference to position *prone* and *supine* are often confused.

Prone (*adj.*) means reclining with the face downward: In basic training we learned to shoot a rifle from a *prone* position.

Supine (*adj.*) means reclining with the face upward: For two months he lay *supine* in bed with his arms and legs in traction.

recommend, refer

Recommend (*v.*) means to commend; to present as worthy of confidence, acceptance, etc.: You should ask your dentist to *recommend* an orthodontist.

Refer (*v.*) means to direct the attention or thought to something; to direct (someone) for information or anything required: Our general practitioner *referred* me to Dr. Jones

NOTE: The patient is *referred*; the specialist is *recommended* for his skill.

terse, trite

Terse (*adj.*) means concise, pithy: Hemingway was the master of a *terse* literary style.

Trite (*adj.*) means hackneyed, stale, outworn: Throughout the dinner Lisa bored me with her *trite* observations on life and love.

therefor, therefore

Therefor (*adj.*) means for that or this; for it. Note that this word is spelled without a final e: He found and returned a large sum of money and was rewarded *therefor*.

Therefore (*adv.*) means in consequence of that; as a result: Note that this word ends in e: We have little money; *therefore* we shall have to tax each member two dollars.

transpire

Transpire (*v.*) meaning to occur, happen, or to take place is regarded as incorrect or vulgar by many. The following use is therefore questionable: Since I was not present at the board meeting, I do not know what *transpired*.

Transpire is correctly used to mean to give off or emit waste matter through the surface; to escape through pores; to escape from secrecy, as to leak out and become known: A heated body *transpires* moisture in the form of sweat. What happened at Yalta *transpired* years later, bit by bit.

unique

Unique (*adj.*) means the only one of its kind extant: Since I can find no coin like this listed in any of the catalogues, I believe it to be *unique*.

Unique should not be used to mean *unusual* or *rare*.

WRONG: These are the most *unique* roses I have ever seen.
RIGHT: These are the most *unusual* roses I have ever seen.

verbal, oral

Verbal (*adj.*) means of or pertaining to words; expressed in words, either written or spoken. Since *verbal* is ambiguous in meaning, it should be used only if the expression referred to is both written and oral: Only humans are capable of *verbal* (both spoken and written) communication.

Oral (*adj.*) means uttered by mouth; spoken: I finally consented to present an *oral* (spoken) report on conditions in the Fifth Ward. [A *verbal* report could be spoken or written.]

EXERCISE 37

USING THE CORRECT WORD

If the boldface word in each of the following phrases is correct, write **C** *in the space to the right. If the word is incorrect, write the correct word in the space.*

1. To **except** the invitation

2. **Averse** criticism of the novel

3. To give **advice**

4. To **aggravate** the teacher

5. To **affect** a change in the situation

6. To **dominate** the discussion

7. **All ready** to go

8. With **delusions** of wealth and grandeur

9. To give a **delusion** of height

10. **Between** the three of us

11. **Appraised** of his sudden death

12. **Liable** to imprisonment

13. **Liable** to succeed

14. The house **besides** the stream

15. To pay the artist a **complement**

16. The American **consul** in Lisbon

17. To do a **contemptible** deed

18. To hold a **council** of war

19. To **illicit** all of the facts

20. To eat **healthy,** wholesome food

EXERCISE 38

USING THE CORRECT WORD

If the boldface word in each of the following phrases is correct, write **C** *in the space to the right. If the word is incorrect, write the correct word in the space.*

1. An interesting **kind of a** business _____
2. To hire a **practicable** nurse _____
3. To adhere to the **principle** of truth _____
4. The **principal** of the academy _____
5. The **principle** reason for the disturbance _____
6. The **most unique** book in the library _____
7. To report the news as it **transpires** _____
8. To **recommend** him for promotion _____
9. Lying **prone** on his back _____
10. Attempt to **mitigate** his wrath _____
11. To **infer** by a gesture _____
12. To **imply** by your silence _____
13. To **flaunt** the order of the court _____
14. To use **less** gallons of gasoline _____
15. An **apt** student of mathematics _____
16. A large **amount** of pens and pencils _____
17. A remark **all together** unworthy of him _____
18. **Mutual** love and understanding between the two _____
19. To **lay** down and die _____
20. To **counsel** the parents of difficult children _____

Exercise 39

Finding the Right Word

In the following sentences find the exact word for each of the expressions in parentheses and write the word in the space to the right.

1. Edith can (make suitable) her report to meet the magazine's format. _____

2. In meting out the punishments you should (leave out) those who freely confessed. _____

3. The engineers are trying to (turn aside) the course of the river. _____

4. Ernie merely shrugged off the (contrary to his interests) report on his activities. _____

5. He (stated as true) the truth of his evidence over and over again. _____

6. Only a doting parent could think that story (worthy of being believed). _____

7. I (hold opinions at variance with) you about the fundamental causes of broken homes. _____

8. The bully (rules tyrannically) the class because of his physical strength. _____

9. Ellen has a (characterized by power) personality. _____

10. He proposed an (showing cleverness of mind) scheme to defraud the widow of her inheritance. _____

11. I have read the document carefully, but I do not (draw a conclusion) anything dishonorable. _____

12. The Republican won by a small (number of votes more than the next candidate). _____

13. In this struggle time (has effective influence for) us. _____

14. He is not noted for writing (concise and pithy) communications. _____

15. At the auction we bought six lots or bundles and paid $319 (for those things mentioned). _____

16. No matter what precautions we take, our agreements will eventually (leak out and become known). _____

17. He refused to put his (spoken by mouth) objections in writing. _____

18. While living in Japan, Linda (took as her own) the native dress. _____

19. Throughout the rest of his life he never once (turned his mind) to that incident.

_____

20. After we have treated the fur, rain will not (act upon) it.

_____

21. The senator's (indirect reference) to possible corruption aroused the ire of his fellow legislators.

_____

22. The seeming difference in length of these lines is an (misleading image presented to the eye).

_____

23. The (two propositions, one of which must be taken) was to make a public apology or be horsewhipped.

_____

24. Michael enjoyed throwing the ball so that the dog would (go and get it and bring it back) it.

_____

25. A belief in witches was (shared by most) to the people of Salem.

_____

EXERCISE 40

FINDING THE RIGHT WORD

In the following sentences find the exact word for each of the expressions in parentheses and write the word in the space to the right.

1. No one knows (contraction of *who is*) responsible for this condition. _____

2. Maxine made several (sensible and businesslike) suggestions. _____

3. Automatic dry-cleaning machines are (capable of being put into operation). _____

4. We dislike the personnel director because she is (forward in obtruding services). _____

5. Tell the guests to (put or place) their coats on the bench. _____

6. Mentally retarded children can (acquire knowledge or skill) to do simple work in a sheltered environment. _____

7. Every dog has (third person singular possessive neuter pronoun) day. _____

8. Urban dwellers sometimes tend to think that country people are (candid and naive). _____

9. The mayor's statement to the press (virtually means) that he will resign. _____

10. The teacher believed in filling her pupils with what she called (conducive to their general well-being) fear. _____

11. She also made them do (conducive to health) exercises fifteen minutes every day. _____

12. The mothers have decided to continue the car pool because it is (reciprocally and interchangeably) beneficial to them. _____

13. They were huddled (as a whole group) under the shed to keep dry. _____

14. Houses in this area (are allowed) be converted for single-room occupancy. _____

15. The merchandise has (sometime in the past) been shipped. _____

16. They (authoritatively) passed the qualifying test. _____

17. Some of the new miracle drugs produce injurious side (results or consequences). _____

18. The Japanese are quick to (take as their own) many Western customs. _____

19. Many parents consult a child psychologist for (recommendation of a course of action) about how to manage their children. _____

20. Many psychiatrists listen to their patients and discuss their problems, but refuse to (recommend a course of action) them. _____

21. The mobster's (unlawful) business was broken up by the F.B.I. _____

22. They think that the (evaluation of worth in money) is high and have appealed it to the tax board. _____

23. The rebellious players were (manifesting disdain) of their weak coach. _____

24. No one is (of a believing mind) enough to believe that story. _____

25. You dare not (treat with contempt) the judge's ruling. _____

147

EXERCISE 41

FINDING THE RIGHT WORD

In the following sentences find the exact word for each of the expressions in parentheses and write the word in the space to the right.

1. The company's financial difficulties were (made worse or more severe) by the recession. _____

2. (The greatest number) were destroyed in the war. _____

3. If we pull (the whole of us in one effort), we can move the rock. _____

4. In this model you have your (selection without compulsion) of six beautiful colors. _____

5. I found my earrings (preposition applying to more than two things) your jewelry. _____

6. The (advisory assembly) has adjourned. _____

7. Bootlegging is an (not permitted or authorized) practice. _____

8. Marie's playing is (vigorous and effective). _____

9. We dropped several clues, each one (directing the attention) to another. _____

10. The victim was lying (face downward) in the gutter. _____

11. She asked me to (inform) her of any change in our plans. _____

12. I am sending you written confirmation of our (uttered by mouth) agreement. _____

13. Our friends ask us to (come with) them maple syrup from Vermont. _____

14. The editor reduced the rambling directions to a few (concise, pithy) sentences. _____

15. To enjoy camp, children must be (capable of adjusting). _____

16. The space flight was postponed several times because of (contrary to favorable) weather. _____

17. Please (direct the attention of) all applicants to the Marriage Bureau. _____

18. Rheumatic fever was a (shared by many) disease of childhood. _____

19. The victim (asserted his right) to compensation. _____

20. (Put or place) the bundles down. _____

Exercise 42

DISCRIMINATING BETWEEN WORDS FREQUENTLY CONFUSED

The following pairs of words are frequently confused. Look up each word in the dictionary, indicate its part of speech, write its meaning, and use the word in an illustrative sentence of your own. Be sure to use the word as you define it.

1. deprecate   Part of speech _____ Definition _____

   Sentence _____

2. depreciate   Part of speech _____ Definition _____

   Sentence _____

3. precedents   Part of speech _____ Definition _____

   Sentence _____

4. precedence   Part of speech _____ Definition _____

   Sentence _____

5. abduct   Part of speech _____ Definition _____

   Sentence _____

6. kidnap   Part of speech _____ Definition _____

   Sentence _____

7. alias   Part of speech _____ Definition _____

   Sentence _____

8. pseudonym   Part of speech _____ Definition _____

   Sentence _____

9. complement   Part of speech _____ Definition _____

   Sentence _____

10. compliment   Part of speech _____ Definition _____

    Sentence _____

EXERCISE 43

DISCRIMINATING BETWEEN WORDS FREQUENTLY CONFUSED

The following pairs of words are frequently confused. Look up each word in the dictionary, indicate its part of speech, write its meaning, and use the word in an illustrative sentence of your own. Be sure to use the word as you define it.

1. illegible   Part of speech _____ Definition _____

   Sentence _____

2. ineligible   Part of speech _____ Definition _____

   Sentence _____

3. lead   Part of speech _____ Definition _____

   Sentence _____

4. led   Part of speech _____ Definition _____

   Sentence _____

5. bibliography   Part of speech _____ Definition _____

   Sentence _____

6. biography   Part of speech _____ Definition _____

   Sentence _____

7. farther (as distinguished from further)

       Part of speech _____ Definition _____

   Sentence _____

8. further   Part of speech _____ Definition _____

   Sentence _____

9. prodigy   Part of speech _____ Definition _____

   Sentence _____

10. progeny   Part of speech _____ Definition _____

   Sentence _____

14. JAMES THURBER'S VOCABULARY

IDIOMS

An idiom is an expression that is illogical or ungrammatical and that means something other than its literal statement. For example, the literal meaning of *cannot help* is *cannot aid or assist*: I *cannot help* you harvest the wheat. But *cannot help*, usually followed by the present participle, is an idiom meaning *obliged* to or *cannot refrain from*: I *cannot help* feeling sorry for him. Similarly, the expression *look out* may be used literally or as an idiom.

LITERAL: Go to the window and *look out*. (Peer outside.)
IDIOM: *Look out*, or you will fall! (Beware, be cautious.)

Idioms are often the most suggestive and picturesque expressions in the language. Many are colloquial and salty; others contain social and literary allusions that enrich meaning. Idioms are most readily acquired by listening and reading. In these ways we have all learned many idioms, but there are many more that are worth knowing. Since idioms do not follow rules, the only way to accelerate the learning of them is to memorize them.

IDIOMATIC USE

Idioms should not be confused with idiomatic use. Idiomatic use is a term that refers (1) to standard combinations of words peculiar to the language or (2) to a word specifically limited in meaning and application. For example, consider the expressions *compare to* and *compare with*. *Compare to* indicates a definite resemblance: He *compared* Chopin's ability as a pianist *to* Liszt's. But *compare with* indicates an examination of similarities and dissimilarities: He *compared* William Carlos Williams *with* Walt Whitman. Note that, unlike idioms, idiomatic use does not involve a change in meaning.

The use of *fewer* and *less*, *number* and *amount* is also idiomatic. *Fewer* and *number* refer to units: I have a large *number* of pencils, but *fewer* pens than I thought. *Less* and *amount* refer to quantity or bulk: There is a large *amount* of flour on hand, but *less* sugar than we need. Note however, that *fewer* and *number* are used for units of measurement: We have a *number of pounds* of sugar, but *fewer pounds* of flour.

Idiomatic use is customary, accepted use and phrasing. In English, idiomatic use is so arbitrary, capricious, and dense, that it can be learned only by years of attentive listening and reading, by developing an ear and a "feel" for language. Idioms, on the other hand, are stereotyped expressions. Although they, too, are most readily acquired as the by-product of listening and reading, they can be memorized from lists. Below is a selected list of useful idioms employed by educated speakers and writers.

A Selected List of Useful Idioms

a moot point	a point subject to discussion: His degree of guilt is *a moot point* that the court must decide.
to hold a brief for	to advocate or defend: I *hold no brief for* bigotry no matter what guise it takes.
to cast the first stone	to be the first to find fault: He said, "I *will not cast the first stone* at the secretary."
the wages of sin	the result of wrongdoing: *The wages of sin* is death.
a labor of love	work done without payment: He conducts the orchestra as *a labor of love*.
salad days	one's youth or prime: When Mohammed Ali was in his *salad days*, he was unbeatable.
to eat humble pie	to be submissive: If Louis *will eat humble pie*, he may get his job back.
to give free rein (to)	to give complete freedom: He took the job with the understanding that he *would be given free rein*.
to give the lie to	to charge (someone) with falsehood: She *gave the lie to* the testimony of the witness for the defense.
to hold forth (on a subject)	to speak at length: I would like to hear him *hold forth on* the subject of civil rights.
to pinch pennies	to economize: No one ever got rich by *pinching pennies*.
to make amends	to compensate: A parent can never *make amends* for neglecting a child.
to make a mountain out of a molehill	to treat a trifle with importance: The analyst convinced his patient that he was *making a mountain out of a molehill*.
to make bricks without straw	to do something without the necessary material: Congress must pass the appropriation bill, for it cannot expect us to *make bricks without straw*.
to stir up a hornet's nest	to cause serious trouble: The president's remark about the Mexican War *stirred up a hornet's nest* in Texas.
to pay the piper	to bear the effects or results of doing something: He who dances must *pay the piper*.
a house of cards	something insubstantial: In the Great Depression the Insull empire fell apart like *a house of cards*.
to kick over the traces	to be riotous; declare one's independence; rebel: It is not unusual for a minister's son *to kick over the traces*.

to lie fallow	to do nothing; to be unused: Although Marcos was tired, he was afraid *to lie fallow* for fear that his talent would dissipate.
the lion's share	the largest amount: The boxer earned a large amount of money, but his manager took *the lion's share*.
the low ebb	the lowest point of fortune, honor, or strength: Even during *the low ebb* of his career when he was blacklisted, he sold a number of scenarios under an assumed name.
(something is) not worth the candle	not worth the effort or price: When Betty finally achieved fame, she did not enjoy it and realized that it was *not worth the candle*.
to the manor born	accustomed to good things or genteel living: When she wanted to attract a man or charm a wealthy woman, Becky Sharp could behave as if she were *to the manor born*.
a red herring	a distraction; an attempt to divert the attention: The author keeps her readers baffled to the very end by *drawing several red herrings* across the murderer's trail.
to wear sackcloth and ashes	to be in low spirits; repentant: If he had expressed remorse and *worn sackcloth and ashes*, the community might have forgiven him.
to sow wild oats	to lead a wild life; to dissipate: In youth he *sowed his wild oats*; in senility he memorialized them.
to strain at a gnat	to labor on trifles, or to be deterred by trifles: John's big opportunity passed him by while he was, as usual, *straining at a gnat*.
at the top of one's bent	at the height of form or ability: For about five years Liz worked *at the top of her bent*, and then she quickly disintegrated.
to ride a high horse	to assume a haughty, demanding manner: If Mrs. Wilson *rides a high horse* with the servants, they will pack up and leave.
sour grapes	to disparage something that you cannot have: Eddie said he didn't want the job anyway, but we knew it was *sour grapes*.
to pass muster	to satisfy requirements: My report is rather slight, but it will undoubtedly *pass muster* in Mr. Fry's class.
to stick to one's guns	to refuse to yield; to maintain that one is right: The witness was interrogated for hours, but he *stuck to his guns* through it all.

to be caught on the horns of a dilemma	to be caught in an undesirable situation: Any man who is engaged to two women at the same time is *caught on the horns of a dilemma*.
to curry favor	to make a servile attempt to please: Alan's frequent trips to the front office are an attempt *to curry favor* with the bosses.
with tongue in cheek	insincerely or facetiously: He reproached her *with tongue in cheek*, but she took him seriously and began to cry.
a bird of passage	a transient: The queerest *bird of passage* in our town when I was a boy was the old basket woman who came out of the mountains every spring.
to cap the climax	to astonish; to surpass an established high point of achievement: The president's absconding with the company's funds really *capped the climax* of the financial scandal.
to put the cart before the horse	to reverse the logical order; to put the wrong end first: Writing the report before making an outline is *putting the cart before the horse*.
caviar to the general	above the average person or too difficult for him: Stefan Wolpe is a talented and original composer, but I am afraid that his music is *caviar to the general*.
to come a cropper	to fail: If Walter continues to invest his money so haphazardly, he will soon *come a cropper*.
(to shed) crocodile tears	insincerity; feigned sorrow: In one of Hardy's poems a widow wears mourning and *sheds crocodile tears* for her husband, who is not yet dead.
to draw in one's horns	to reduce demands or expectations: After two unsuccessful attempts to dominate the organization, he *drew in his horns*.
to throw dust in one's eyes	to deceive: For years Sam *has been throwing dust in* his wife's eyes, but he is becoming so brazen that she will soon find him out.
to gild the lily	to brighten something already brilliant; to carry something to excess: Adding sequins to that gorgeous dinner gown is really *gilding the lily*.
to give a horse his head	to give one his way; to refrain from curbing a person: Since Louis is so certain, let us *give the horse his head* and see what he can accomplish.
to go to the wall	to fail; to give up a struggle: Mr. Cooper *went to the wall* during the early days of the Great Depression.

to haul (one) over the coals	to rebuke or reproach one severely: For his persistent lateness to class, the instructor was *hauled over the coals* by the dean.
to make common cause	to join others: In the recent strike, the cutters' union refused *to make common cause* with the other unions in the industry.
to make free with	to take liberties: Odysseus and his men entered Polyphemus' cave and *made free with* his food and wine.
to put a good face on	to make the best of a situation: Jackie's father opposed the marriage, but he *put a good face on* it and gave the bride away.
to cast pearls before swine	to waste things of value on the stupid or unappreciative: She thought that reading her verses to them was like *casting pearls before swine*.
to live in a fool's paradise	to be in dubious safety; to be in an uncertain position: Susan is *living in a fool's paradise* because the effects of the drug are only temporary.
to run the gauntlet	to suffer severe criticism or ill treatment: At the sales meeting the new representative was *made to run the gauntlet*.
to wear one's heart on one's sleeve	to make an open and excessive display of one's emotions: If he had not *worn his heart on his sleeve*, no one would know about his rebuff.
to swap horses in midstream	to vote against a candidate running for reelection: The governor said it would be a mistake for us to *swap horses in midstream*.
to cool one's heels	to be kept waiting: We were forced to *cool our heels* in the outer office.
a wolf in sheep's clothing	a knave in the guise of a friend: Smith came to us like *a wolf in sheep's clothing* and wrecked our organization.
to hold a candle to (something)	to qualify; to compare to: As a diva the new soprano cannot *hold a candle to* the great stars of the past.
to hold one's peace	to withhold adverse criticism: Despite severe provocation, he *held his peace* and refused to be drawn by his opponents on the right.
to look a gift horse in the mouth	to criticize a gift: It may not be as much as you expected to receive from your aunt, but don't *look a gift horse in the mouth*.

a horse of a different color	an entirely different kind of person or situation: Tom will never get through medical school, but his cousin Eduardo is *a horse of a different color*.
to run amuck	to rush about in a murderous frenzy: Escaping from the cell block, the prisoner *ran amuck* and slew two guards.
to be at cross purposes	to be in conflict: Ever since he was a little boy, Justin has *been at cross purposes* with his father
to beg the question	to assume the very point raised in a question: In blaming comic strips for the increase in juvenile delinquency, the psychoanalyst was *begging the question*.
to raise a hue and cry	to make a clamor or outcry: When Simpson learned that he was to be dismissed quietly, he *raised such a hue and cry* that the effort to get rid of him was abandoned.
to make a scene	to create a disturbance: Paula thought that by *making a scene* she could force the store to refund her money.
a month of Sundays	a long time: It has been *a month of Sundays* since I heard a pianist the equal of Gilels.
to go scot-free	to escape without punishment: He received a six-month sentence, but his accomplice *got off scot-free*.
to spare the rod	to refrain from punishment: *Spare the rod* and spoil the child.
to have (keep) one's ear to the ground	to be on the alert for something: I don't know of any opening for your daughter at present, but I'll *keep my ear to the ground*.
an eye to the main chance	attention centered on the main point: Beware of him because he is an ambitious man who has his *eye to the main chance*.
to keep (have) one's eye peeled	to be on the lookout for something: I *have my eye peeled* for a jacket like the one I saw in Macy's last month.
out of hand	beyond control: If the situation in Panama gets *out of hand*, we may have to send in the Marines.
to hold water	to be sound and consistent: If the plan *holds water*, we will implement it immediately.
to put one's hands on	to find: I know that I have the book you asked for, but I can't *put my hands on* it now.

FUN WITH IDIOMS

Readers of the *New Yorker* magazine enjoyed James Thurber's cartoons and off-beat humor for three decades. As a satirist who concentrated on the foibles of contemporary society, he used a lighter touch than Jonathan Swift, preferring whimsy to the stinging lash. In works of fiction (*The Secret Life of Walter Mitty*), plays (*The Male Animal*), and prose sketches (*Fables for Our Time*), Thurber showed an uncommon interest in language and our modern idiom.

MY SECRET WORLD OF IDIOM
—JAMES THURBER (1894–1961)

Two years ago my wife and I, looking for a home to buy, called on a firm of real estate agents in New Milford. One of the members of the firm, scrabbling through a metal box containing many keys, looked up to say, "The key to the Roxbury house isn't here." His partner replied "It's a common lock. A skeleton will let you in." I was suddenly once again five years old, with wide eyes and open mouth. I pictured the Roxbury house as I would have pictured it as a small boy, a house of such dark and nameless horrors as have never crossed the mind of our little bat-biter.

It was of sentences like that, **nonchalantly** tossed off by real-estate dealers, great-aunts, clergymen, and other such **prosaic** persons that the enchanted private world of my early boyhood was made. In this world, businessmen who phoned their wives to say that they were tied up at the office sat roped to their swivel chairs, and probably gagged, unable to move or speak, except somehow, miraculously, to telephone; hundreds of thousands of businessmen tied to their chairs in hundreds of thousands of offices in every city of my fantastic **cosmos**. An especially fine note about the binding of all the businessmen in all the cities was that whoever did it always did it around five o'clock in the afternoon.

Then there was the man who left town under a cloud. Sometimes I saw him all wrapped up in the cloud, and invisible, like a cat in a burlap sack. At other times it floated, about the size of a sofa, three or four feet above his head, following him wherever he went. One could think about the man under the cloud before going to sleep; the image of him wandering around from town to town was a sure **soporific**.

Not so the mental picture of a certain Mrs. Huston, who had been terribly cut up when her daughter died on the operating table. I could see the doctors too vividly, just before they set upon Mrs. Huston with their knives, and I could hear them. "Now, Mrs. Huston, will we get up on the table like a good girl, or will we have to be put there?" I could usually fight off Mrs. Huston before I went to sleep, but she frequently got into my dreams, and sometimes she still does.

I remember the **grotesque** creature that came to haunt my **meditations** when one evening my father said to my mother, "What did Mrs. Johnson say when you told her about Betty?" and my mother replied, "Oh, she was all ears." There were many other wonderful figures in the secret, **surrealist** landscapes of my youth: the old lady who was always up in the air, the husband who did not seem to be able to put his foot down, the man who lost his head during a fire but was still able to run out of the house yelling, the young lady who was, in reality, a soiled dove. It was a world that, of necessity, one had to keep to oneself and **brood** over in silence because it would fall to pieces at the touch of words. If you brought it out into the light of actual day and put it to the test of questions, your parents would try to laugh the miracles away, or they would take your temperature and put you to bed.

Such a world as the world of my childhood, is, alas, not yearproof. It is a ghost that gleams, flickers, vanishes away. I think it must have been the time my little Cousin Frances came to visit us that it began surely and forever to dissolve. I came into the house one rainy dusk and asked where Frances was. "She is," said our cook, "up in the front room crying her heart out." The fact that a person could cry so hard that his heart would come out of his body, as perfectly shaped and glossy as a red velvet pincushion was news to me. For some reason I had never heard the expression, so common in American families whose hopes and dreams run so often counter to **attainment**. I went upstairs and opened the door of the front room. Frances, who was three years older than I, jumped up off the bed and ran past me, sobbing, and down the stairs.

My search for her heart took some fifteen minutes. I tore the bed apart and kicked up the rugs and even looked in the bureau drawers. It was no good. I looked out the window at the rain and the darkening sky. My cherished mental image of the man under the cloud began to grow dim and fade away. I discovered that, all alone in a room, I could face the thought of Mrs. Huston with cold **equanimity**. Downstairs in the living room, Frances was still crying. I began to laugh.

EXERCISE 44

THURBER'S WORDS

The words and expressions in this exercise are bold in the essay you have just read. After carefully studying each word in context and looking it up in the dictionary, write the part of speech and the definition of the word in the space provided.

1. nonchalantly

   Part of speech _____ Definition _____

2. prosaic

   Part of speech _____ Definition _____

3. cosmos

   Part of speech _____ Definition _____

4. soporific

   Part of speech _____ Definition _____

5. grotesque

   Part of speech _____ Definition _____

6. meditations

   Part of speech _____ Definition _____

7. surrealist

   Part of speech _____ Definition _____

8. brood

   Part of speech _____ Definition _____

9. attainment

   Part of speech _____ Definition _____

10. equanimity

    Part of speech _____ Definition _____

EXERCISE 45

MORE OF THURBER

The vocabulary words from Exercise 44 appear in the box below. Select the proper words to fit in the blanks in these ten sentences.

nonchalantly	cosmos	grotesque	surrealist	attainment
prosaic	soporific	meditations	brood	equanimity

1. My favorite _____ is a warm glass of milk and a quiet lullaby.

2. The movie makeup department prepared a _____ mask with which the villain was to terrify the little boy.

3. Mom used to _____ about our financial problems, but she is much happier today.

4. The art dealers sponsored an auction of Salvador Dali's _____ paintings.

5. With the _____ of their objective, the invading troops withdrew.

6. Curt's _____ in the face of impending disaster was admirable.

7. Most of that director's films are exciting but I found his latest to be _____ and dull.

8. With the bank robber's gun trained on him, the bank manager _____ sauntered into the vault.

9. Uncle Howard maintained that anyone who studied the _____ could not remain an atheist.

10. The bell interrupted my _____ and brought me back to reality.

EXERCISE 46

LEARNING AND USING IDIOMS

Each of the following sentences contcins a literal expression in parentheses. In the space provided write the idiom for each of the literal expressions.

1. With the help of a good lawyer, the guilty man (escaped without punishment). _____

2. He (spoke at length) on Shakespeare's imagery. _____

3. How can I (compensate) for the harm I have done? _____

4. You must learn not to (give complete freedom to) your anger. _____

5. I will not (be submissive) to get a promotion. _____

6. I will (join with) any organization that struggles for peace. _____

7. The babysitter (takes liberties with) our candy. _____

8. Producing Shakespeare is for him (work done without compensation). _____

9. In my (youth) I walked five miles every day. _____

10. His partner takes the (largest amount) of the profit. _____

11. After years of submission he finally (declared his independence). _____

12. A young man is expected to (lead a wild life). _____

13. His music is (too difflcult and austere for most people). _____

14. Don't (feign sorrow) for my misfortunes. _____

15. The supervisor (rebuked her severely). _____

16. The inmate escaped from his cell and (ran about in a frenzy). _____

17. When the city closed the park, the parents (cried out). _____

18. If you question her, you will (cause serious trouble). _____

19. Every other year the land (is not cultivated). _____

20. His business empire collapsed (like something insubstantial). _____

EXERCISE 47

LEARNING AND USING IDIOMS

Each of the following sentences contains a literal expression in parentheses. In the space provided write the idiom for each of the literal expressions.

1. I can see now that I have been (treating a trifling thing as important).

2. That issue is raised at this crucial moment as a (distraction).

3. For weeks he worked (at the height of his ability).

4. In our childhood Uncle John was a (transient visitor).

5. Do you think that our dress will (be suitable)?

6. Someday, despite his assurance, he will (fail).

7. To do that first is to (work in the wrong order).

8. Susan told the story (as a joke).

9. When they challenged his figures Herb (insisted that he was right).

10. We will wait until he (reduces his demands).

11. He is an independent man who refuses to (attempt to please those in power).

12. It takes a very clever man to (deceive her).

13. Ellen made such excellent proposals that we have decided to (give her her way completely).

14. If I don't get the appointment, I will (make the best of it) anyway.

15. When their aunt died, they learned that they had been (living in dubious safety).

16. The salesmen (were kept waiting) in the boss' outer offlce.

17. As a singer she cannot (compare to) Whitney Houston.

18. Passing the scrutiny of my husband's family was like (being subjected to severe and cruel criticism).

19. In lecturing to women's clubs Vic behaved as if he were (wasting his remarks on the stupid and unappreciative).

20. Chuck was a foolish man who wasted his time (laboring on trifles).

EXERCISE 48

EXPLAINING THE MEANING OF IDIOMS

Each of the following sentences contains an idiomatic expression in parentheses. In the space to the right explain the meaning of each idiomatic expression.

1. I am tired of living (from hand to mouth). _____

2. Tell Gene to (hold his tongue). _____

3. The atcused (made a clean breast of) the crime. _____

4. When I meet Olivia I will (give her a piece of my mind). _____

5. Try as we might, we could not (give him the slip). _____

6. Everything in the shop (got out of hand) today. _____

7. Do not (make a practice of) reporting late to work. _____

8. Now that you are an adult, you must (put away) childish things. _____

9. If everyone (pulls his weight), the job will be done in a week. _____

10. I cannot (make head or tail of) these directions. _____

11. I refuse (to make light of) the argument. _____

12. Quote me exactly and don't (put words in my mouth). _____

13. The pianist (has taken Moscow by storm). _____

14. I (took to heart) my pastor's advice. _____

15. While there is hope, don't (throw in the sponge). _____

16. By this time all the presidential aspirants (have thrown their hats in the ring). _____

17. I refuse to (turn my back on) my old friend Carlos. _____

18. He tried in vain to (call off) the engagement. _____

19. We must all (get behind) the president. _____

20. One cabinet member regularly (puts his foot in his mouth). _____

15. JAMES FENIMORE COOPER'S VOCABULARY

James Fenimore Cooper, the author of *The Last of the Mohicans* (1826), was the first major American novelist. In addition to his celebrated *Leatherstocking Tales*, Cooper was an astute social critic of the young American society. In this essay, Cooper comments on inexactness in language and pompous, overblown styles of expression.

ON LANGUAGE
—JAMES FENIMORE COOPER (1789–1851)

Language being the medium of thought, its use enters into our most familiar practices. A just, clear and simple expression of our ideas is a necessary accomplishment for all who **aspire** to be classed with gentlemen and ladies. It renders all more respectable, besides making **intercourse** more intelligible, safer and more agreeable.

The common faults of American language are an ambition of effect, a want of simplicity, and a **turgid** abuse of terms. To these may be added **ambiguity** of expression. Many **perversions** of significations also exist, and a formality of speech, which, while it renders conversation ungraceful and destroys its playfulness, seriously weakens the power of the language, by applying to ordinary ideas, words that are suited only to themes of **gravity** and dignity.

While it is true that the great body of the American people use their language more correctly than the mass of any other considerable nation, it is equally true that a smaller proportion than common attain to elegance in this accomplishment, especially in speech. Contrary to the general law in such matters, the women of the country have a less agreeable utterance than the men, a defect that great care should be taken to remedy, as the nursery is the birthplace of so many of our habits.

The limits of this work will not permit an **enumeration** of the popular abuses of significations but a few shall be mentioned, in order that the student may possess a general clue to the faults. "Creek," a word that signifies an *inlet* of the sea or of a lake is misapplied to running streams, and frequently to the *outlets* of lakes. A "square" is called a "park," "lakes" are often called "ponds," and "arms of the sea" are sometimes termed "rivers."

In pronunciation, the faults are still more numerous, partaking decidedly of **provincialisms**. The letter *u*, sounded like double *o*, or *oo*, or like *i*, as in vir*too*, for*tin*, for*tinate*; and *ew*, pronounced also like *oo*, are common errors. This is an exceedingly vicious pronunciation, rendering the language mean and **vulgar**. "New," pronounced as "*noo*," is an example, and "few," as "*foo*"; the true sounds are "*nu*" and "*fu*," the *u* retaining its proper soft sound, and not that of "*oo*."

The attempt to reduce the pronunciation of the English language to a common rule, produces much confusion, and taking the usages of polite life as the standard, many **uncouth innovations**. All know the pronunciation of plough; but it will scarcely do to take this sound as the only power of the same combination of final letters, for we should be compelled to call though, thou; through, throu; and tough, tou.

False accentuation is a common American fault. Ensign (insin,) is called *ensyne*, and engine (injin,) *engyne*. Indeed, it is a common fault of narrow associations, to suppose that words are to pronounced as they are spelled.

Many words are in a state of **mutation**, the pronunciation being unsettled even in the best society, a result that must often arise where language is as variable and undetermined as the English. To this class belong "clerk," "cucumber," and "gold," which are often pronounced as spelled, though it were better and more in conformity with polite usage to say "clark," *coucumber*," (not cow*cumber*,) and "goold." For *lootenant* (lieutenant) there is not sufficient authority, the true pronunciation being "*levtenant*." By making a familiar compound of this word, we see the uselessness of attempting to reduce the language to any other laws than those of the usages of polite life, for they who affect to say *lootenant*, do not say "*lootenant-co-lo-nel*," but "*lootenant-kurnel*."

The polite pronunciation of "either" and "neither," is "i-ther" and "ni-ther," and not "eether" and "neether." This is a case in which the better usage of the language has respected **derivations**, for "*ei*" in German are pronounced as in "height" and "sleight," "*ie*" making the sound of "ee." We see the **arbitrary** usages of the English, however, by comparing these legitimate sounds with those of the words "lieutenant colonel," which are derived from the French, in which language the latter word is called "*co-lo-nel*."

Some changes of the language are to be regretted, as they lead to false **inferences**, and society is always a loser by mistaking names for things. Life is a fact, and it is seldom any good arises from a **misapprehension** of the real circumstances under which we exist. The word "gentleman" has a positive and limited signification. It means one elevated above the mass of society by his birth, manners, **attainments**, character and social condition. As no civilized society can exist without these social differences, nothing is gained by denying the use of the term. If **blackguards** were to be *called* "gentlemen," and gentlemen, "blackguards," the difference between them would be as obvious as it is today.

The word "gentleman," is derived from the French gentilhomme, which originally signified one of noble birth. This was at a time when the characteristics of the condition were never found beyond a **caste**. As society advanced, ordinary men attained the qualifications of nobility, without that of birth, and the meaning of the word was extended. It is now possible to be a gentleman without birth, though, even in America, where such distinctions are purely conditional, they who have birth, except in extraordinary instances, are classed with gentlemen. To call a laborer one who has neither education, manners, accomplishments, tastes, associations, nor any one of the ordinary **requisites**, a gentleman, is just as absurd as to call one who is thus qualified, a fellow. The word must have some especial signification, or it would be synonymous with man. One may have gentlemanlike feelings, principles and appearance, without possessing the liberal attainments that distinguish the gentleman. Least of all does money alone make a gentleman, though as it becomes a means of obtaining the other requisites, it is usual to give it a place in the claims of the class. Men may be, and often are very rich, without having the smallest title to be deemed gentlemen. A man may be a distinguished gentleman and not possess as much money as his own footman.

This word, however, is sometimes used instead of the old terms, "sirs," "my masters," &c.&c., as in addressing bodies of men. Thus we say "gentlemen," in addressing a public meeting, in **complaisance**, and as, by possibility, some gentlemen may be present. This is a license that may be tolerated, though he who should insist that all present were, as individuals, gentlemen, would hardly escape ridicule.

What has just been said of the word gentleman is equally true with that of lady. The standard of these two classes rises as society becomes more civilized and refined; the man who might pass for a gentleman in one nation, or community not being able to maintain the same position in another.

The inefficiency of the effort to **subvert** things by names is shown in the fact that, in all civilized communities, there is a class of men, who silently and quietly recognize each other as gentlemen; who associate together freely and without reserve, and who admit each other's claims without scruple or distrust. This class may be limited by prejudice and arbitrary enactments, as in

Europe, or it may have no other rules than those of taste, sentiment and the silent laws of usage, as in America.

The same observations may be made in relation to the words master and servant. He who employs laborers, with the right to command, is a master, and he who lets himself to work, with an obligation to obey, a servant. Thus there are house, or domestic servants, farm servants, shop servants, and various other servants; the term master being in all these cases the **correlative**.

In consequence of the domestic servants of America having once been negro-slaves, a prejudice has arisen among the laboring classes of the whites, who not only dislike the term servant, but have also rejected that of master. So far has this prejudice gone, that in lieu of the latter, they have resorted to the use of the word *boss,* which has precisely the same meaning in Dutch! How far a **subterfuge** of this nature is worthy of a manly and common sense people, will admit of question.

A similar objection may be made to the use of the word "help," which is not only an innovation on a just and established term, but which does not properly convey the meaning intended. They who aid their masters in the toil may be deemed "helps," but they who perform all the labor do not assist, or help to do the thing, but they do it themselves. A man does not usually hire his cook to *help* him cook his dinner, but to cook it herself. Nothing is therefore gained, while something is lost in simplicity and clearness by the substitution of new and imperfect terms, for the long established words of the language. In all cases in which the people of America have retained the *things* of their ancestors, they should not be ashamed to keep the *names*.

The love of turgid expressions is gaining ground, and ought to be corrected. One of the most certain evidences of a man of high breeding is his simplicity of speech; a simplicity that is equally removed from vulgarity and exaggeration. He calls a spade, a "spade." His enunciation, while clear, deliberate and dignified, is totally without strut, showing his familiarity with the world, and in some degree, reflecting the qualities of his mind, which is polished without being addicted to sentimentalism, or any other **bloated** feeling. He never calls his wife, "his lady," but "his wife," and he is not afraid of lessening the dignity of the human race, by styling the most elevated and refined of his fellow creatures, "men and women." He does not say, in speaking of a dance, that "the attire of the ladies was exceedingly elegant and peculiarly becoming at the late assembly," but that "the women were well dressed at the last ball"; nor is he apt to remark, "that the Rev. Mr. G ____ gave us an elegant and searching **discourse** the past sabbath," but that "the parson preached a good sermon last Sunday."

The utterance of a gentleman ought to be deliberate and clear, without being measured. All idea of effort should be banished, though nothing lost for want of distinctness. His emphasis ought to be almost **imperceptible**; never halting, or abrupt; and least of all, so placed as to give an idea of his own sense of cleverness; but regulated by those slight intonations that give point to wit, and force to reason. His language should rise with the subject, and, as he must be an educated and accomplished man, he cannot but know that the highest quality of eloquence, and all **sublimity**, is in the thought, rather than in the words, though there must be an *adaptation* of the one to the other.

This is still more true of women than of men, since the former are the natural agents in maintaining the refinement of a people.

All cannot reach the highest standard in such matters, for it depends on early habit, and particularly on early associations. The children of gentlemen are as readily distinguished from other children by these peculiarities as by the greater delicacy of their minds, and higher tact in breeding. But we are not to abandon all improvement, because perfection is reached but by few. Simplicity should be the first aim, after one is removed from vulgarity, and let the finer shades of accomplishment be acquired as they can be attained. In no case, however, can one who aims at **turgid** language, exaggerated sentiment, or **pedantic** utterance, lay claim to be either a man or a woman of the world.

EXERCISE 49

COOPER'S WORDS

The words in this exercise are printed in bold type in the essay you have just read. After carefully studying each word in context and looking it up in the dictionary, write the part of speech and the definition of the word in the space provided.

1. aspire

   Part of speech _____ Definition _____

2. turgid

   Part of speech _____ Definition _____

3. ambiguity

   Part of speech _____ Definition _____

4. gravity

   Part of speech _____ Definition _____

5. provincialisms

   Part of speech _____ Definition _____

6. uncouth

   Part of speech _____ Definition _____

7. innovations

   Part of speech _____ Definition _____

8. mutation

   Part of speech _____ Definition _____

9. derivations

   Part of speech _____ Definition _____

10. arbitrary

    Part of speech _____ Definition _____

Exercise 50

More of Cooper

Just as in Exercise 49, carefully study each word in context in the essay. Look it up in a dictionary and write the part of speech and the definition in the space provided.

1. attainments

   Part of speech _____ Definition _____

2. caste

   Part of speech _____ Definition _____

3. requisites

   Part of speech _____ Definition _____

4. subvert

   Part of speech _____ Definition _____

5. subterfuge

   Part of speech _____ Definition _____

6. bloated

   Part of speech _____ Definition _____

7. imperceptible

   Part of speech _____ Definition _____

8. sublimity

   Part of speech _____ Definition _____

9. adaptation

   Part of speech _____ Definition _____

10. pedantic

    Part of speech _____ Definition _____

16. THE EFFECTIVE USE OF WORDS

Persuasive speaking and writing depends upon the effective use of words. To be effective words should be selected according to the following principles:

EXACT WORDS

Choose the word that expresses a thought with exactness and preciseness according to the fact.

Do not confuse words that are similar in sound and appearance: for example, *avert* and *advert*; *receipt* and *recipe*.

> *avert* means to ward off, turn aside: Her quick thinking *averted* an accident.
> *advert* means to refer to: Not once during the evening did he *advert* to our army days.
> *Receipt* is a written acknowledgment of having received goods, money, etc.: When you return the shirts to the store, be sure to get a *receipt*.
> *Recipe* means a formula for preparing a dish in cookery: I followed your *recipe*, and the pot roast was delicious.

Do not confuse words that are related in meaning: for example, *oral* and *verbal*; *alias* and *pseudonym*.

> *Oral* means spoken: Without witnesses, no *oral* contract is binding.
> *Verbal* means in words, whether spoken or written: I want deeds rather than *verbal* expressions of affection.
> *Alias* means a name assumed for illegitimate reasons: The gangster is known to the police by four *aliases*.
> *Pseudonym* means a name assumed for respectable reasons: He writes under two *pseudonyms*.

APPROPRIATE WORDS

Choose words that your audience will find appropriate and understandable.

In addressing children and the intellectually immature, use simple, popular words. Of the following sentences use the second rather than the first:

> The *nomenclature* and *terminology* of this subject are readily *comprehensible*.
> The *names* and *terms* of this subject are easy to *understand*.

In addressing the generally educated public, use general rather than technical words. Instead of the following terms, known to biologists, botanists, and bacteriologists respectively, use the explanation of each:

> *syndesmosis,* the connection of bones by ligaments, etc., rather than in a joint.
> *synoicous,* pertaining to the presence of male and female flowers on one head.
> *monotricha,* bacteria having the organs of locomotion at one pole.

VIVID WORDS

Choose words that express thought vividly and exactly.

Use concrete words to visualize a thought. Concrete words refer to tangible objects that we can see and hence can picture in the mind's eye: *apple, desk, hoe, smoke*. A verb is said to be concrete when it suggests a sense image to the mind: *limped, staggered, trudged, flapped, waved*.

Use specific words that express limited, definite, precise meanings rather than vague, general ones.

SPECIFIC: *Ten people* stood on the shore of Barger's Pond and watched the boy drown.

VAGUE: *A few people* stood on the shore of the pond and watched the fatal accident.

NOTE: Abstract words are indispensable and must be used to express ideas and concepts: *death, mercy, honesty, connection, equality*. Sometimes it is possible to concretize an abstraction by using a figure of speech. For example, Shakespeare concretizes *concealment* by calling it "a worm i' the bud [that feeds] on her damask cheek." Two other abstract words that Shakespeare concretizes are *mercy* that "droppeth as the gentle rain from heaven" and *sleep* "that knits up the ravell'd sleave of care."

General words are also indispensable. It is not always possible or desirable to be specific. We may know, for example, that a *man* knocked on the door without knowing who he was or what he looked like. Sometimes, also, vague and general statements are advantageous. If thirty people were present at a meeting, the attendance may seem small and our cause unattractive. If we call the attendance *moderate*, however, others may assume that we attract a larger attendance and more support.

USE OF SYNONYMS TO AVOID MONOTONY

Use synonyms to avoid the unneccessary and monotonous repetition of words at too frequent intervals. [See *Synonyms and Antonyms*, page 33.]

MONOTONOUS: The principal *character* in the play is unconvincing because he is *characterized* by *characteristics* that are unreal and *uncharacteristic*.

IMPROVED: The *protagonist* of the play is unconvincing because he is *portrayed* with *traits of personality* that are unreal and *uncharacteristic*.

PERSUASIVE WORDS

Choose words that will help to persuade others to your point of view.

To recommend a thing, act, or belief use terms with favorable associations or connotations. In each pair of terms listed below the second is likely to make the more favorable impression.

a *real* diamond	a *genuine* diamond
the *first* Bon Soir Shoppe	the *original* Bon Soir Shoppe
artificial leather	*simulated* leather
domestic products	*American* products
a *useful* knowledge of French	a *practical* knowledge of French
an *old* man	an *elderly* man
a *truant* officer	an *attendance* officer
the *janitor* of the building	the *custodian* of the building
a *cheap* purse	an *inexpensive* purse

To discredit a person, thing, act, or belief use terms with unfavorable associations. In each pair of terms listed below, the second is likely to make the more unfavorable impression.

a political *leader*	a political *boss*
an *alcoholic*	a *drunkard*
a *fearful* man	a *cowardly* man
a *falsehood*	a *lie*
parsimonious	*miserly*

MIXED FIGURES OF SPEECH

Do not mix figures of speech.

A mixed figure of speech is an incongruous and ludicrous blend of two or more figures of speech.

He was caught like a snake in the grass. [A blend of *caught like a rat in a trap* and *to creep like a snake in the grass.*]

He was led like a sheep to the slaughter. [A blend of *like a lamb to the slaughter* and *like a wolf in sheep's clothing.*]

He is an early bird who makes hay while the sun shines. [The early bird *catches the worm* and *make hay while the sun shines* both mean to take advantage of a situation.]

Climbing stairs made her pant like a fish out of water. [A blend of *pant like a dog* and *gasp like a fish out of water.*]

On our ship of state, the keystone of democratic liberties is the Bill of Rights. [A keystone is part of an arch, not of a ship.]

TRITE EXPRESSIONS

Try to avoid the use of trite expressions.

English abounds with set or stereotyped expressions that have become commonplace and ineffectual. Their original impact has been dulled by overuse and familiarity. They roll off the listener and reader *like water off a duck's back.* They encourage the lazy to rely on stale words instead of seeking fresh words and insights. They spring so readily to tongue and pen, they cover ideas so easily that they preclude originality and preciseness of expression. Many clichés are merely dull and feeble; but many are so banal that they excite laughter.

It must be admitted, however, that it is impossible to avoid the occasional use of a cliché. They are so numerous, they spring from so many sources, they are so packed with wisdom, so apt, so rich in allusions, both folk and literary, that they are indispensable. Banning clichés would effectively stop most communication. Moreover, there are occasions when the cliché *fills the bill to a "T,"* when no other expression would be so apposite.

EXERCISE 51

DETECTING MIXED FIGURES OF SPEECH

Each of the following sentences contains a figure of speech. If the figure is correctly used, write "Correct" in the space provided. If the figure is mixed, explain why.

EXAMPLE

She is a lovely girl, but she is as homely as a sinner.   <u>as homely as sin</u>

---

1. The charming but unscrupulous son is the fatted calf of the family.   _____

2. They were warned to beware of Greeks bearing gift horses.   _____

3. Bringing up that touchy topic was like opening a Pandora's box.   _____

4. Like Caesar, we must beware the tides of March.   _____

5. In the financial world, poor George is like a babe in arms.   _____

6. Straws in the wind indicate a Democratic landslide in the coming election.   _____

7. In the automobile accident his wife was killed, but he escaped by a hair's breadth.   _____

8. When the doctor approached him with the hypodermic needle, the child began to squeal like a pig in the poke.   _____

9. At the stockholder's meeting he won a Pyrrhic victory, although it immensely increased his power in the financial world.   _____

10. Unable to find her opponent's Achilles heel, she withdrew from the chess match.   _____

11. She established her fame as a hostess with the Barmecide feasts that were prepared by her French chef.   _____

12. By the time he was brought before the judge, he was as meek as a church mouse.   _____

13. The president is the captain of our ship of state.   _____

14. The thieves were caught redhanded as they were rifling the safe.   _____

15. He is not a boastful man, but neither does he hide his talents under a bushel.   _____

VOCABULARY TEST 9

SEARCHING FOR DEFINITIONS

We have already studied the following words. How many of them do you know? For each of the boldface words select the word or expression that means most nearly the same and write the letter in the space to the right.

1. Sheila **dominates** the committee.
   a. tyrannizes   b. directs   c. controls   d. advises   _____

2. Bootlegging is **illicit**.
   a. unlawful   b. extinct   c. difficult   d. tedious   _____

3. Don't **flout** my authority.
   a. doubt   b. treat with contempt   c. undermine   d. question   _____

4. Jeff was ejected **forcibly**.
   a. vigorously   b. rapidly   c. violently   d. emphatically   _____

5. What do you **infer** from this letter?
   a. believe   b. mean   c. expect   d. deduce   _____

6. The grand jury refused to **indict** him.
   a. accuse   b. arrest   c. investigate   d. release   _____

7. Country people are not necessarily **ingenuous**.
   a. clever   b. suspicious   c. naive   d. generous   _____

8. He was elected by a **majority** of votes.
   a. the largest number cast   b. more than the number received by
   others   c. more than half the number cast   d. a large number   _____

9. Any delay will **militate** against the acceptance of our proposal.
   a. mobilize   b. arrange   c. moderate   d. influence   _____

10. The candidate's speech was **terse** and effective.
    a. concise   b. hackneyed   c. earthy   d. florid   _____

11. Nancy owns a **unique** etching by Picasso.
    a. unusual   b. rare   c. one of the first impressions
    d. the only one of its kind   _____

12. **Oral** arguments are futile.
    a. overheard   b. written   c. spoken   d. indefinite   _____

13. When you ask for contributions, do not **except** Mr. Molina.
    a. exclude   b. overlook   c. solicit   d. approach   _____

14. Who **adapted** this story for the stage?
    a. approved   b. transcribed   c. purchased   d. adjusted   _____

15. I am **averse** to putting women in public office.
a. enthusiastic about   b. reluctant to   c. giving consideration to
d. hopeful about _____

16. There is still hope of **averting** the strike.
a. calling   b. preventing   c. ending   d. prolonging _____

17. Your idea that I am wealthy is a **delusion**.
a. joke   b. false belief   c. unreal image   d. pretense _____

18. They stoutly **asserted** their innocence.
a. proved   b. repeated   c. declared   d. intoned _____

19. The countries signed a treaty of **mutual** aid.
a. financial   b. limited   c. economic   d. reciprocal _____

20. It is **contemptible** to tease an inferior.
a. despicable   b. gratifying   c. creditable   d. dexterous _____

21. To believe that story one must indeed be **credulous**.
a. worthy of belief   b. charitable   c. plausible
d. disposed to believe _____

22. No one thought that the name was a **pseudonym**.
a. name assumed for illegitimate reasons
b. name assumed by actors   c. anagram of a name
d. name assumed for legitimate reasons _____

23. The editor overlooked the **malapropism**.
a. colophon   b. vulgarism   c. broken type
d. incorrect use of a word _____

24. He lacked the courage to **perpetrate** such an outrage.
a. plan   b. commit (something bad)   c. defend (something bad)
d. conceal (something bad) _____

25. Les was proud of his **progeny**.
a. necromancy   b. orison   c. offspring   d. genius _____

26. His **alternative** was a fine or imprisonment.
a. sentence   b. free choice   c. dilemma
d. compulsory choice between two things _____

27. You should have the ring **appraised**.
a. insured   b. enlarged   c. reproduced   d. valued _____

28. Robert tried to **elicit** the truth from his son.
a. extract   b. conceal   c. provoke   d. acknowledge _____

29. You will be **officially** notified by the clerk.
a. arrogantly   b. legally   c. authoritatively   d. properly _____

30. He lay **prone** upon the floor.
a. moribund   b. motionless   c. reclining with face down   d. unconscious _____

31. What happened there will **transpire** sooner or later.
   a. become known b. expire c. recede d. vanish _____

32. Jim's **uncouth** behavior upset his tennis fans.
   a. crude b. unusual c. shrill d. mild _____

33. Gordon's **ingenious** plan was adopted.
   a. simple b. jovial c. subtle d. clever _____

34. The play is full of **trite** situations.
   a. stale b. melodramatic c. experimental d. obscene _____

35. The resolution was **adopted** unanimously.
   a. modified b. reviewed c. accepted d. tabled _____

36. Don't interfere so long as their fighting is merely **verbal**.
   a. in writing b. in threats c. in words d. in speech _____

37. No one understood Tony's **allusion** to the affair.
   a. reference b. objection c. hint d. relation _____

38. Small furniture will give the room the **illusion** of size.
   a. misleading appearance b. suggestion c. dimension d. aura _____

39. We had not been **apprised** of James' failure.
   a. warned b. informed c. fearful d. dejected _____

40. The American **consul** was recalled.
   a. attorney b. espionage agent c. advisory assembly
   d. government agent _____

41. The teacher was **contemptuous** of Sarah's excuses.
   a. incredulous b. scornful c. abashed d. foiled _____

42. There will be a **continual** showing of the motion picture from
   ten A.M. to eleven P.M.
   a. occasional b. intermittent c. spasmodic d. of regular occurrence _____

43. Despite our fears Michelle did **creditable** work.
   a. excellent b. meritorious c. acceptable d. average _____

44. He likes to play with young children because he can **domineer** them.
   a. control b. direct c. tyrannize d. protect _____

45. She did not mean to **imply** anything disrespectful.
   a. suggest b. assert c. infer d. name _____

VOCABULARY TEST 10

USING WORDS IN ILLUSTRATIVE SENTENCES

The following idioms have already been presented. Show that you know them by using each in an illustrative sentence that shows how the idiom is used and suggests its meaning.

IDIOM	SENTENCE
1. to make bricks without straw	_____
2. salad days	_____
3. to cast the first stone	_____
4. to give the lie to	_____
5. to beg the question	_____
6. out of hand	_____
7. to go scot-free	_____
8. to cast pearls before swine	_____
9. to pinch pennies	_____
10. to hold a candle to	_____
11. a horse of a different color	_____
12. caviar to the general	_____
13. to put a good face on it	_____
14. to go to the wall	_____
15. to throw dust in (one's) eyes	_____
16. to strain at a gnat	_____
17. to curry favor	_____
18. to be caught on the horns of a dilemma	_____
19. to sow (one's) wild oats	_____
20. to wear sackcloth and ashes	_____

APPENDIX

Supplementary List of Latin Word Elements Used in English Word Building

Root	Meaning	Examples of Use
acr	sharp, acute	acrimonious, acrid
aer, air	air	aerial, airplane
ag, act	to do, to drive	agitate, action
agri, agra	field	agriculture, agrarian
ali	another	alias, alibi
alien	foreign	alien, alienate
alter	another	alter, alternative
amat	to love	amatory, amateur
anim	mind, passion, soul	animal, animate
ann	year	annual, anniversary
apt	to fit, to adjust	adapt, aptitude
aqu	water	aqueduct, aquarium
arm	to arm	army, armor
art	art, skill	artist, artisan
aud, audit	to hear	audible, audition
avi	bird	aviary, aviation
bell	war	belligerent, rebellion
been	good, well	benediction, benefactor
brev	short	brevity, abbreviate
cad, cas	to fall	cadence, casual
cap, capit	head	captain, capital, precipice
cap, caps, cep	to take	captive, recapitulate, reception
cent	one hundred	centipede, century
cid, cis	to cut, to kill	suicide, incision
cit, citat	to summon, to put into motion	incite, recitation
civi, civili	city, citizen	civil, civilization
clam, clamat	to cry out	exclaim, clamor, exclamation
cognosc, cognit	to become acquainted with	recognize, cognizant, cognoscenti
compl, complet	to fill	comply, completion
cor, cord, cour	heart	core, cordial, encourage
corp, corpor	body	corpse, corporeal, incorporate
cresc	to grow	crescent, excrescence
cret	grown	concrete, accrete
curr, curs	to run	current, excursion
da, don	to give	data, mandate, donate
doe, doct	to teach, to prove	docile, doctrine
dom	home	domain, domicile
domin	to rule	domineer, dominate
er	to wander, go	err, errand
equ	equal	equation, adequate

ROOT	MEANING	EXAMPLES OF USE
ev	an age	coeval, medieval
fall, fals	to deceive	fallacy, falsify
fam	report	famous, infamy
fin	end	final, finite
fix	to fasten	aflfix, fixture
flat	blown	inflate, deflate
flect, flex	to bend, bending	deflect, reflexive
flu	to flow	fluency, confluent
fund, fus	to pour	refund, profuse, effusion
gen, gener	race, origin, class	progeny, genesis, generation
ger, gest	to carry, to carry on	gesture, suggest, belligerent
grad, gress	to step, to walk	graduate, degrade, progress
greg	flock, herd	gregarious, aggregate
junct	a joining	junction, adjunct
labor	to work	laboratory, elaborate
lapid	stone	lapidary, dilapidated
leg, lect	to choose, to read	legible, select
loqu, locus	to speak	elocution, loquacious
luc	light	lucid, elucidate
mal	bad	malady, malefactor
man	hand	manual, manicure
mar	sea	marine, maritime
mon, monit	to warn, to remind	monitor, admonish
mor, mort	to die	mortal, moribund
mov, mot	to move	movable, motion
omni	all	omnipotent, omnivorous
oper	a work	opera, operation
pac	peace	pacific, pacify
pel, puls	to drive	repel, compulsion
pend	to hang	pendant, depend
plen	full	replenish, plenary
pon, posit	to place	position, proponent
rat, ratio	reason, plan	ratio, rational
rid, ris	to laugh	deride, risible
rog, rogat	to ask	arrogant, interrogate
rupt	broken	rupture, bankrupt
scien	knowing	science, prescience
sea, sess	to sit, to remain seated	sedentary, session
sent, sens	to feel, to think	sensible, sentiment
serv	to serve	servant, servile
sol, solut	to loose	dissolve, solution
sum, sumpt	to take	resume, consumption
surg, surrect	to rise	surge, insurrection
tang, tact	to touch	tangible, contact
tempor	time	temporary, extemporize
terr	land, earth	territory, terrace
urb	city	urban, urbanity
vag	to wander	vagabond, vagary
val	to be strong, to have worth	valor, valuable
vine, vict	to conquer	convince, victory
volv, volut	to roll	revolve, convolution

SUPPLEMENTARY LIST OF GREEK WORD ELEMENTS USED IN ENGLISH WORD BUILDING

ROOT	MEANING	EXAMPLES OF USE
agogue	leader	demagogue, pedagogue
agon	contest	agony, protagonist
angel	messenger	evangel, archangel
arch	first, chief, commander	archaic, patriarch, monarch
aster, astron	star	disaster, astronomy
bar, baro	heavy weight	barometer, baritone
bibl, biblio	book	Bible, bibliophile
chiro	hand	chiropodist, chiropractor
dem, demo	people	democracy, endemic
dendr, dendro	tree	philodendron, dendrite
derm	skin	epidermis, dermatology
dox	opinion	orthodox, paradox
dyna	power	dynamic, dynasty
eu	well, good	euphony, eugenics
gamy	marriage	monogamy, polygamy
gram	written	diagram, epigram
grapho, graphy	to write	graphology, telegraphy
helio	sun	heliograph, heliocentric
melo	song	melody, melodrama
micr, micro	small	microscope, microcosm
mono	one	monologue, monograph
morph	body, form	amorphous, morphology
neo	new	neophyte, neologism
nomy	law, order	astronomy, economy
ortho	straight	orthodox, orthopedic
pan, panto	all	panacea, Pan-Slavic, pantomime
ped, pedi	child	pedagogue, pediatrician
phos, photo	light	photograph, phosphorous
phys, physic	nature	physical, physiology
polis, polit	city, citizen	metropolis, cosmopolite
pseudo	false	pseudo, pseudonym
psych, psycho	breath, soul, mind	psychic, psychologist
pus, pod	foot	octopus, tripod
scope	see, look at	microscope, telescope
spher, sphere	sphere	spherical, atmosphere
tech, techno	skill, art	technology, technical
tel, tele	far	telescope, telepath, telephone
thei, theo	God	pantheism, theology
trop, trope	turning	heliotrope, tropic
typ, type	print, image	typical, prototype

SUPPLEMENTARY LIST OF PREFIXES

PREFIX	MEANING	EXAMPLES OF USE
a, an	without, not	amoral, anarchy
amb, ambi	both	ambidextrous, ambiguity
amphi	around, on both sides	amphitheater, amphibious
anti	against	antidote, antipathy
apo	from, away from, off	apology, apostate
bi	two	bisect, bicycle
cata, cath	down, against	catastrophe, cataract, cathode
contra	against, opposed	contradict, controversial
die	across, through	diagram, diameter
epi, eph	upon, on the outside	epilogue, ephemeral
extra	beyond, outside	extraordinary, extrovert
hemi	half	hemisphere, hemistich
hetero	different	heterogeneous, heterodox
hyper	over, above	hyperbole, hypercritical
hypo	under	hypodermic, hypostatic
infra	lower, less than	infrahuman, inframarginal
intra	within	intramural, intracellular
juxta	near, nearby	juxtaposition, juxtatropical
mete	after, beyond	metaphysical, metamorphosis
multi	many, much	multitude, multiply
ob	to, toward, opposite, facing	obstacle, obverse
para, par	by the side of, near	parallel, parable
peri	around	periscope, perimeter
preter	past, before, exceeding	preternatural, preterit
proto	first, earliest form of	protoplasm, prototype
retro	back	retrograde, retrospection
semi	half, almost, twice in a given period	semitropical, semiannual
subter	below, underneath, less than	subterfuge, subterranean
super	over, above	superman, supercilious
supra	above	supraterrestrial, supramolecular
ultra	outside, excessive	ultramarine, ultramodern
vice	one who takes the place of	viceroy, vice-president

SUPPLEMENTARY LIST OF SUFFIXES

SUFFIX	MEANING	EXAMPLES OF USE

Noun Suffixes

age	relating to, relationship	adage, homage
an, ian	belonging to, concerned with	American, agrarian, electrician
ant, ent	agency or instrumentality	irritant, servant, agent
ate	office or function	mandate, consulate
ation, ition	act or state of	education, recognition
ese	of, relating to	Chinese, journalese
ine	action, procedure, art, place	medicine, discipline
ite	native or citizen of, member of a party	urbanite, Brooklynite
ity	state of being	paucity, sagacity
oid	something like	anthropoid, alkaloid
or	state or quality, agent or doer	ardor, candor, aviator, auditor
ory	a place of, serving for	dormitory, ambulatory
sign, tion	act or state of	persuasion, recognition
tude	that which is	certitude, beatitude
ure	process, act, being, state, rank	creature, literature, brochure, fracture, procedure

Adjective Suffixes

aceous, acious	of the nature of, like, pertaining to	mendacious, pugnacious, herbaceous
ant	participial ending	ascendant, pleasant
ate, ite	possessing or being	desolate, delicate, favorite
cle, cule	little	corpuscle, molecule, animalcule
escent	growing, in a state of	obsolescent, adolescent
fic	doing, causing, making	soporific, terrific
id	relating to groups, families	acid, humid
il, ile	pertaining to, suited for, capable of	utensile, servile, civil
ine	like, characterized by	feline, feminine
ive	having the nature or quality of, giving or tending to	positive, negative, active, productive

Verb Suffixes

ate	to make	tolerate, venerate
esce	to increase, grow, become	effervesce, coalesce
fy	to make, to render	electrify, deify
ize	to render or make subject to	colonize, satirize

Supplementary List of Foreign Terms Used in English

Latin

a fortiori (ā fōr´shĭ ōr´ī) For a still stronger reason; all the more.
EX. Peace must be maintained *a fortiori*; the next war will literally destroy the world.

alter ego (al´tər ē´gō; ĕg´ō) Another self; a bosom friend.
EX. Throughout his life D. H. Lawrence searched for a man who would be his *alter ego*.

amicus curiae (əmī´kəs kyoŏr´īē) "A friend of the court"; a person or group who gives advice or presents a brief in a legal case in which he is not involved.
EX. As *amicus curiae* the American Civil Liberties Union presented a brief in the Larsen case.

annus mirabilis (ăn´əs mə răb´ə līs) "A wonderful year"; a year in which great events occur.
EX. His *annus mirabilis* was 1922, the year he completed the *Quartet in G Minor*, the *Symphony in D Minor*, and his opera *The Tocsin*.

argumentum ad hominem (är gū mĕn´təm ăd hŏm´ĭnĕm) "An argument against a person"; an argument based on a person's morality; an appeal to emotion and prejudice rather than to facts.
EX. Rather than discussing the issues, my opponent's speech is entirely *argumentum ad hominem*.

casus belli (kās´əs bĕl´ī) A pretext or cause of war.
EX. Hitler seldom bothered to find a *casus belli* before attacking a nation.

corpus delicti (kôr´pəs dē lĭk´tī) "The body of the crime"; a legal phrase meaning evidence that a crime has been committed. Sometimes the expression is mistaken to mean the body of the victim.
EX. Without a *corpus delicti* the district attorney cannot seek an indictment.

ex cathedra (ĕks kə thē´drə, kăth´ə drə) "From the chair"; by the authority of one's position.
EX. The pronouncement was made *ex cathedra* and must be obeyed.

flagrante delicto (flə grän´tə də lĭk´tō) "While the crime is blazing"; in the very act; red-handed.
EX. Since the cashier was caught *flagrante delicto*, his attorney could not present a defense and was forced to enter a plea for mercy.

hic jacet (hĭk jās´ət) "Here lies"; an epitaph.
EX. *Hic jacet* my wife Amanda.
Stranger, do not sigh.
At last she knows peace
And so do I.

Homo sapiens (hō´mō sā´pĭ ĕnz´) Man as a rational being; the genus of mankind as distinct from other animals.
EX. A misanthrope is a person who is contemptuous of *Homo sapiens*.

in extremis (ĭn ĭks strēē´mĭs) Near death; in the last extremity.
EX. Hearing that the king was *in extremis*, the priest rushed to the palace to administer the last rites.

in loco parentis (ĭn lō´kō pə rĕn´tĭs) "In the place of a parent"; acting as one's guardian.
EX. During his brother's long illness, he acted *in loco parentis* for his nieces and nephews.

in re *or* **re** (ĭn rē´) In reference to; concerning.
EX. *In re* the Casson affair, a firm of actuaries has been hired to audit the books for the last five years.

ipse dixit (ĭp´sĭ dĭk´sĭt) "He himself has said it"; an assertion without proof.
EX. He talks incessantly, and his every statement is delivered as an *ipse dixit*.

mirabile dictu (mĭ răb´əlē dĭk´tu) Strange to say; marvelous to relate.
EX. The mechanic jiggled a lever, and, *mirabile dictu*, the motor started without a cough or a groan.

modus operandi (mō´dəs ōp´ə răn´dĭ) Mode of operating or working; a working agreement.
EX. The Long River Bridge Authority is seeking a *modus operandi* with the Long River Township.

modus vivendi (mō´dəs vĭ věn´dĭ) "Manner of living"; temporary agreement; a way of coexisting with a person or nation despite fundamental disagreement.
EX. Both ambassadors agreed on a *modus vivendi* that allowed free trade to continue.

ne plus ultra (nē´ plŭs ŭl´trə) Nothing more beyond; perfection.
EX. The Rolls Royce is the *ne plus ultra* of cars.

obiter dictum (ŏb´ə tər dĭk´təm) The plural is *obiter dicta*. An incidental opinion by a judge or critic; not binding; a digression or an aside.
EX. This book of *obiter dicta* is a delightful supplement to his critiques.

pax vobiscum (păks vō bĭs´kəm) Peace; peace be with you.
EX. Murmuring *pax vobiscum* the anchorite genuflected before the queen.

persona non grata (pər sō´nə nŏn grā´tə) An unacceptable person; an acceptable person is *persona grata*. These terms are frequently applied to official representatives of a country.
EX. The American consul is *persona non grata* in Peru and will have to be recalled.

prima facie (prī´mə fā´shĭē´) On the face of or on the surface; at first view; on first appearance.
EX. Possession of drugs is *prima facie* evidence of participation in the illegal drug traffic.

pro bono publico (prō bō´nō pŭb´lĭ kō) "For the public good"; a favorite signature of those who write letters to editors of newspapers and magazines.

pro tempore (prō těm´p ərē´) Often shortened to *pro tem*; temporarily; for the time being.
EX. He is chairman *pro tem* of the Committee on Good and Welfare.

quid nunc (kwĭ d´ nŭngk´) "What now"; one who is curious to know everything that passes; a gossip.
EX. For years, old Jones was the *quid nunc* on the faculty.

quondam (kwŏn´dăm) Former.
EX. Hurricane Goetz, a *quondam* ballet dancer, he says, is a contender for the heavyweight championship in wrestling.

rara avis (rā´rə ā´v ĭs) A rare bird; an unusual specimen; an extraordinary person.
EX. Among politicians he is regarded as a *rara avis* because of his bluntly honest opinions.

reductio ad absurdum (rĭ dŭk´shĭ ō´ ăd ăb sər´dəm) A reduction to an absurdity; carrying an argument or action to logical extremes.
EX. Many conditions in Huxley's *Brave New World* are a *reductio ad absurdum* of conditions and tendencies already present in the world.

sanctum sanctorum (săngk´təm səngktōr´əm) "Holy of holies"; the office of an awesome person.
EX. It was five years before Mr. Bartle invited me into his *sanctum sanctorum* and implied that, if I worked hard, I might be made a member of the firm.

sine qua non (sĭ´nĭ kwā nŏn´) "Without which there is nothing"; a prerequisite; an indispensable condition.
EX. Mutual respect, if not love, is the *sine qua non* of a successful marriage.

sub rosa (sŭb rō´zə) "Under the rose"; privately; confidentially.
EX. I have been told *sub rosa* that the Joneses are on the verge of separation.

sui generis (soo´ī jĕn´ərĭs) Of his, her, its own kind; in a class by itself; unique.
EX. This book is *sui generis* a masterpiece, but it will not appeal to many.

vade mecum (vā´dĭ mē´kəm) "Go with me"; a manual or handbook; a book carried as a constant companion.
EX. The Bible is the *vade mecum* of many Christians.

vox populi (vŏks pŏp´yoo li) "The voice of the people"; shortened to *vox pop*. This expression is one half of the expression, "Vox populi, vox Dei"; "The voice of the people is the voice of God." *Vox pop* is a favorite signature of letters in newspapers.

French

agent provocateur (ä zhän′ prô vô kə tər′)
A person who incites another person or an
organization like a political party or trade
union to commit an illegal act for which they
can be punished.
EX. The union soon suspected him of being
an *agent provocateur* and expelled him.

amour-propre (ä mōōr′ prō′pr) Self-esteem;
self-love; vanity.
EX. If you are lacking in *amour-propre*, no one
will take you seriously.

au courant (ō kōō rän′) Up-to-date; well up
in or informed in.
EX. To be *au courant* one must read several
newspapers daily.

bête noir (bet′ nwär′) "A black beast"; a pet
aversion; a detested person.
EX. Knowing that Thomas à Becket was the
King's *bete noir*, a group of loyal knights
murdered him in the cathedral.

bon vivant (bôn′ vē vän′) An epicure; a lover
of good living; a man about town.
EX. Beau Brummel was a famous *bon vivant* of
the eighteenth century.

chef-d'oeuvre (chĕf′dûv′r) Chief work; a
masterpiece.
EX. *War and Peace* is Tolstoy's *chef-d'oeuvre*.

comme il faut (kô mēl fō′) As it ought to be;
in good form; proper.
EX. It was not *comme il faut* for a man to dine
without a jacket.

contretemps (kôn trə tän′) Embarrassing
moment.
EX. The groom's dropping the ring was the
first in a series of *contretemps* that made a
shambles of the wedding.

coup de grâce (kōō′ də gräs′) "A blow of
mercy"; the death blow; a final, decisive stroke.
EX. We had won a series of naval victories,
but the atomic bombing of Hiroshima and
Nagasaki was Japan's *coup de grâce*.

de rigeur (də rē gûr′) In good form or taste;
according to strict etiquette.
EX. In American courtship today, a chaperon
is no longer *de rigueur*.

dernier cri (dĕr nyĕ krē′) The last word; the
latest fashion.
EX. This gown by Dior is the *dernier cri* from
Paris.

deshabille (dĕz′ə bē′ə) Undressed or partly
undressed; in negligee. The expression also
appears as *dishabille* and *en deshabille*.
EX. For her to be seen in the garden *en
deshabille* was definitely compromising.

enfant terrible (än fän tĕ rē′bl) "A bad child";
a child whose behavior is embarrassing; a
person who embarrasses his party or organization by blunt remarks.
EX. Charles Wilson's inopportune remarks
made him the *enfant terrible* of the
Eisenhower cabinet.

en rapport (än räpôr′) In harmony; mutual
understanding and sympathy.
EX. For a satisfactory song recital the singer
and the accompanist must be *en rapport*.

femme fatale (făm′ fə tăl′) A woman who
lures men to destruction; a female spy.
EX. In former times the "vamp" was the
motion picture conception of the *femme fatale*.

fin de siècle (fän′ də syĕ′kl) End of the century;
a period free from social and moral traditions;
decadent.
EX. He belongs with the French *fin de siècle*
school of writers.

hors de combat (ôr′ də kôm bä′) "Out of
the combat"; incapacitated, disabled.
EX. Glenway strained a ligament in his first
race and was *hors de combat* for the rest of
the season.

idée fixe (ē dā′ fēks′) A fixed idea; an obsession.
EX. Communism is an *idée fixe* with him; he
sees communism as the cause of all his
troubles.

ingénue (ăn zhĕ nū′) The part of an ingenuous
girl, esp. as represented on the stage; the
actress who plays such a part.
EX. She is too old to play an *ingenue*, but no
one can equal her in such a role.

insouciance (ĭn sōō′sĭ əns) Lack of concern;
indifference.
EX. His is the *insouciance* of the rich who
have never known hardship and deprivation.

maître d'hôtel (mĕ´tr dō tĕl´) A steward or butler; a headwaiter.
EX. To get a desirable table in that restaurant one must give the *maître d'hôtel* a large tip.

mélange (mĕ länzh´) A mixture; a medley.
EX. This room is furnished in a *mélange* of Chippendale, Hepplewhite, and Grand Rapids pieces.

ménage (mā näzh´) Household; family.
EX. The expenses of the king's *ménage* amounted to over a million pounds a year.

mise en scène (mē´ zän sĕn´) Stage setting or equipment; the surroundings in which anything is seen.
EX. He is a fascinating raconteur because of the way he describes the *mise en scène* of a story.

montage (mŏn täzh´) Arrangement in one composition of pictorial elements borrowed from several sources; a picture made in this way.
EX. The director of the picture has attempted to achieve effects by the use of *montage*, but the elements do not blend, and the film lacks artistic unity.

noblesse oblige (nô blĕs´ ô blēzh´) "Nobility obligates"; a code of behavior of the aristocracy; the graciousness of the nobility.
EX. The Rockefeller family's gift to the school is an excellent example of *noblesse oblige*.

nouveau riche (noō vō rēsh´) The newly rich; upstart.
EX. It took little time for the *nouveau riche* to force his way into society.

pièce de résistance (pyĕs´de rə zēs täns´) The main course or dish; the most valuable object in a collection.
EX. Of all these paintings, the Goya is the *pièce de résistance*, the one most widely admired and coveted.

potpourri (pŏt poŏr´ ĭ *or* pō poō rē´) Mixture; medley; miscellany.
EX. This stage piece is a boring *potpourri* of song, dance, spectacle, miming, and skits.

qui vive (kē´ vēv´) "Who goes there"; an alert.
EX. The security police are on the *qui vive* for any muttering or complaints that may develop into resistance.

raison d'être (rĕ zôn´dĕ´tr) "Reason for being"; justification.
EX. Many acute and tolerant critics can find no *raison d'être* for Henry Miller's *Tropic of Cancer*.

rapprochement (rä prôsh män´) Developing mutual understanding; a term in diplomacy for the establishment of friendly relations between countries.
EX. Aunt Martha helped to bring about a *rapprochement* between her feuding brothers.

rendezvous (rän´ də voō) An appointment or engagement of two or more people to meet at a fixed time or place; a place for such a meeting.
EX. Their midnight *rendezvous* was a small restaurant in the Loop.

riposte (rĭpōst´) A term in fencing meaning a quick thrust after a parry; a quick answer; repartee.
EX. In time she learned to curb her tongue and withhold the sharp *riposte*.

sang froid (sän frwä´) "Cold blood"; self-possession; composure.
EX. With the utmost *sang froid* the housing inspector admitted that he had accepted favors from the Red Star Construction Company.

soupçon (soōp sôn´) "Suspicion"; a bit; a small portion.
EX. The ragout needs a *soupçon* of cooking sherry.

tour de force (toōr´ də fôrs´) A feat of skill or strength; a trick in music, drama, or literature; an exhibition of great technical or mechanical skill.
EX. The series of literary parodies in *Ulysses* is a dazzling display, a *tour de force* that shows Joyce's mastery of language and his intimate knowledge of English literature.

vis-à-vis (vēz ə vē´) A person or thing that is face to face with another; opposite; in reference to; opposed to.
EX. When he stands *vis-à-vis* his accusers, I am sure that his bravado will disappear.

volte-face (vŏlt´ fäs´) An about-face; a complete reversal of policy, opinion, or attitude.
EX. It is unlikely that the boxing commissioners will execute a *volte-face* and allow the rogue boxer to fight again.

Italian

a cappella (ä´ kəp pĕl´ə) Unaccompanied singing, especially choral music.
EX. Since the last half of the recital will be sung *a cappella*, the instrumentalists will be able to fill another engagement on the same evening.

bravura (brĕ vyoŏr´ə *or* brä voōr´ rä) "Bravery"; a display of spirit and dash.
EX. The truth is that young Mr. Bixon is incapable of the kind of *bravura* pianism required by the showier compositions of Liszt.

con amore (kôn ä mô´rĕ) "With love and devotion"; tenderly.
EX. You will be able to play this passage *con amore* if you retard slightly.

presto (prĕs´tō) Rapidly; quickly; a direction in music calling for a fast tempo.
EX. In the traditional sonata the second movement is usually a *presto* movement.

punctilio (pŭngk tĭl´ĭ ō) A fine point; a nice point of behavior or etiquette; fastidiousness; meticulousness.
EX. The duel was fought with the utmost *punctilio*; neither contestant was injured, and their honor was satisfied.

vendetta (vĕn dĕt´ə) A blood feud; from the feuding families of Corsica who avenged the death of relatives.
EX. The rivalry between the gangs has developed into a *vendetta* in which three youths have already been slain.

Supplementary List of Words Frequently Mispronounced

Word	Correct Pronunciation	
accuracy	(ăk′yə rə sĭ)	AK yuh ra sy
across	(ə krôs′)	a KROSS
actual	(ăk′chōō əl)	AK choo el
acumen	(ə kū′mən)	a KU men
agenda	(ə jĕn′də)	a JEN da
antipodes	(ăn tĭp′ə dēz′)	an TIP o dez
apropos	(ăp′rə pō′)	Ap ra PO
archipelago	(är′kə pĕl′ə gō)	Ar ki PEL a go
august	(ô gŭst′)	aw GUST
automaton	(ô tŏm′ə tŏn′)	aw TOM a ton
autopsy	(ô′tŏp sĭ)	AW top si
awry	(ə rī′)	a RYE
bestial	(bĕs′chəl	BESS chal
	bĕst′yəl)	BEST yal
blackguard	(blăg′ärd)	BLAG ard
breadth	(brĕdth)	BREDTH
breeches	(brĭch′ĭz)	BRITCH ez
calculate	(kăl′kyə lāt′)	CAL kyuh late
cello	(chĕl′ō)	CHEL o
chasm	(kăz′əm)	KAZ m
clandestine	(klăn dĕs′ĭn)	clan DES tin
comely	(kŭm′lĭ)	KUM li
comptroller	(kən trō′lər)	kon TROLL er
coup	(kōō)	KOO
covert	(kŭv′ərt)	KUV ert
credence	(krē′dəns)	CREE dence
crevasse	(krə văs′)	cre VASS
cruel	(krōō′el)	CROO el
culinary	(kū′lə nə rī)	CUE li na ri
deleterious	(dĕl′ə tĭr′i əs)	del e TEER i us
depth	(dĕpth)	DEPTH
despicable	(dĕs′pĭ kə bəl)	DES pi ca b'l
desultory	(dĕs′əl tōr′ĭ)	DES ul to ri
diphtheria	(dĭf thĭr′ĭə)	dif THEER i a
diphthong	(dĭf′thông)	DIF thong
dirigible	(dĭr′ə jə bəl)	DIR i ji b'l
disastrous	(dĭ zăs′trəs)	di ZAS trous
drowned	(dround)	DROWND
epistle	(ĭ pĭs′əl)	e PIS'l
epitome	(ĭ pĭt′ə mĭ)	e PIT o me
equitable	(ĕk′wə tə bəl)	EK wi ta b'l
exigency	(ĕk′sə jən sĭ)	EK si jen si
exponent	(ĕk spō′nənt)	ek SPO nent
formally	(fôr′mə lĭ′)	FOR ma li
formidable	(fôr′mĭ də bəl)	FOR mi da b'l

geography	(jĭ ŏg´rə fĭ)	ji OG ra fi
grievous	(grē´vəs)	GREE vus
grimace	(grĭ mās´)	gri MACE
heinous	(hā´nəs)	HAY nus
hygiene	(hī´jēn)	HIGH jeen
impotent	(ĭm´pə tənt)	IM po tent
irrelevant	(ĭrĕl´ə vənt)	ir REL e vent
irrevocable	(ĭrĕv´ə kə bəl)	ir REV o ka b'l
lamentable	(lăm´ən tə bəl)	LAM en ta b'l
longevity	(lŏn jĕv´ə tĭ)	lon JEV i ti
machination	(măk´ə nā´shən)	mak i NA shun
maniacal	(mə nī´ə kəl)	ma NI a k'l
naive	(nä ēv´)	nah EEV
onerous	(ŏn´ər əs)	ON erus
orgy	(ôr´ jĭ)	OR jee
partner	(pärt´nər)	PART ner
perform	(pər fôrm´)	per FORM
perhaps	(pər hăps´)	per HAPS
plebeian	(plĭ bē´ən)	ple BEE an
plethora	(plĕth´ə rə)	PLETH o ra
popular	(pŏp´yə lər)	POP u lar
positively	(pŏz´ə tĭv lĭ)	POZ i tiv li
posthumous	(pŏs´chōō məs)	POS choo mus
prelate	(prĕl´ĭt)	PREL it
quiet	(kwī´ət)	KWI it
recognize	(rĕk´əg nīz´)	RECK og nize
respite	(rĕs´pĭt)	RES pit
ribald	(rĭb´əld)	RIB ald
schism	(sĭz´əm)	SIZ'm
scion	(sī´ən)	SIGH un
superfluous	(sŭ pər´flōō əs)	su PER floo us
travail	(trăv´āl, trăv´əl)	TRAV ail, TRAV'l
ultimatum	(ŭl´tə mā´təm)	ul ti MAY tum
vagary	(və gār´ĭ)	va GAIR I
violence	(vī´ə ləns)	VI o lence
violet	(vī´ə lĭt)	VI o lit
width	(wĭdth)	WIDTH
zoology	(zō ŏl´ə jĭ)	zo OL o ji

1,400 Words That Bright People Ought to Know

A

abate
aberration
abeyance
abhor
abject
ablution
abnegation
abrade
abscond
absolution
absolve
abstemious
abstract
abstruse
abut
abysmal
acclimate
accolade
accoutrement
accretion
acerbity
acme
acquiescence
acrimonious
acumen
adage
adamant
adjunct
adroit
adulation
adventitious
advert
aegis
affable
affectation
affidavit
affinity
affluent
agenda
agglomeration
aggrandizement
agnostic
agrarian
alacrity
alias
allegory
alleviate
alliteration

allusion
altercation
altruist
amazon
ambergris
ambiguous
ameliorate
amenable
amenities
amoral
amorphous
amortization
amplifier
amulet
anachronism
anagram
analgesic
analogy
analysis
anathema
ancillary
animosity
animus
anodyne
anneal
annotate
anomalous
antediluvian
anthology
anthropology
anthropomorphic
anticlimax
antimony
antipathy
antithesis
antonym
apathetic
aphasia
aphorism
apiary
apocalyptic
apocryphal
apogee
apotheosis
appellation
appendage
apportion
apposite
apprise

appurtenance
apropos
apt
arable
arbiter
archaic
archetype
archives
arduous
arraign
arrant
arrears
arrogate
arroyo
articulation
artifact
artifice
ascetic
aseptic
askance
asperity
aspersion
assiduous
assimilate
assuage
asterisk
asteroid
astral
astringent
astronaut
atavism
atelier
atheist
atom
atrophy
attenuate
attrition
augury
aureole
auspicious
austerity
automaton
autonomous
avaricious
avatar
avid
avocation
avuncular
awry
axiom

B

bagatelle
bale
ballistics
banal
baroque
bastion
bathos
batten
bayou
beatific
bedizen
beldam
beleaguered
belles-lettres
bellicose
belligerent
bemused
benevolent
benign
bereavement
bestial
bibliography
biennial
billingsgate
bizarre
blasé
blasphemy
blatant
bonanza
boorish
booster
bowdlerize
brackish
breviary
broach
bucolic
buffet
bumptious
buoyant
bureaucracy
burgeon
burnoose
buskin

C

cabal
cache
cadaver
caesura
caitiff
cajole
calligraphy
calumny
candor
capillary
capital
capitulate
capricious
carnivorous
carrion
cartographer
caryatid
casuistry
cataclysm
catalyst
catapult
catechism
categorical
catharsis
cathartic
cathode
caucus
caustic
cavil
celestial
celibate
censure
centaur
centrifugal
ceramics
cerebral
chameleon
charlatan
chauvinism
chimera
chiromancy
choler
chronological
circuitous
circumlocution
circumspect
circumvent
clandestine

cleavage
cliché
clique
coadjutor
codicil
coercion
cogent
cogitate
cognate
cognizant
cognomen
coherent
colander
collate
colloquial
colloquy
collusion
comatose
comely
comestibles
comity
commensurate
commiserate
compendium
complacent
complaisant
complicity
compunction
computer
concatenated
concave
concentric
conch
concomitant
concordat
concrete
concupiscence
concurrence
condone
conduit
confrere
congenial
congenital
conglomeration
conjecture
connive
connotation
constraint
construe
context
contiguous

contingency
contravene
contumacious
convivial
convoluted
copious
corollary
corporeal
corpulent
correlation
corroborate
coruscate
cosmonaut
coterie
countdown
covert
cozen
crass
credence
credible
creditable
creditor
credo
credulity
credulous
crepuscular
crescent
criterion
crotchety
crux
cryptic
cubicle
culpable
culvert
cupidity
curator
curmudgeon
cursive
cursory
cyclotron
cynic
cynosure

D

debacle
debauch
debenture
debilitating
debut
decadent
deciduous

decimate
décolleté
décor
decorum
decrepitude
deductive
defection
deference
definitive
deleterious
deliquescent
demagogue
demesne
demonic
demotic
demur
denigrate
denotation
denouement
depilate
deprecate
depredation
deracinate
derogatory
descant
desideratum
desuetude
desultory
devious
dexterous
dialectics
diatribe
diction
dictum
didactic
diffidence
diffuse
digital
digress
dilatory
dilettante
dipsomaniac
discomfiture
discursive
dishabille
disparage
disparity
dispassionate
disputation
disquisition
dissemble

dissimulation
dissonant
distaff
distrait
doggerel
dolorous
dormant
doxology
dross
duenna
duplicity
duress

E

ebullient
ecclesiastical
eclat
eclecticism
effete
effigy
effluvium
effulgent
egotist
egregious
electrode
electron
electrostatic
elegiacal
elicit
elusive
emanate
emblazon
embryonic
emendation
emeritus
emollient
emolument
empirical
empyreal
emulate
encomium
endemic
enervate
engender
enigmatic
enjoin
enmity
ennui
enormity
entomology
entrepreneur

eolithic
ephemeral
epicurean
epigram
epithet
epitome
equanimity
equine
equitable
equity
equivocal
equivocation
erose
errant
erudition
escarpment
eschatology
escheat
esculent
esoteric
espousal
esthetic
ethics
ethnic
etymology
eugenics
eulogy
euphemism
euthenics
evanescent
evince
eviscerate
exacerbate
excision
excoriate
execrable
execrate
exegesis
exhort
exhume
exigency
ex officio
exorcise
exordium
exotic
expatiate
expatriate
expedite
expostulation
extant
extenuating

extirpation
extradite
extraneous
extrinsic
extrovert

F

façade
facet
facetious
facile
fallacious
fallible
fane
farrier
fastidious
fatuous
feasible
febrile
feckless
fecund
felicitous
feral
fester
fetid
fetish
fetters
fiduciary
figment
figurative
fiscal
fission
flaccid
floe
fluted
foible
foment
foray
foreclosure
formidable
forte
fortuitous
fracas
frieze
frond
fruition
fulcrum
funereal
furtive
fustian

G

gainsay
galaxy
gambit
gamut
garnishee
garrulous
gasconade
gastronomy
genealogy
generic
genre
genuflect
germane
germinate
gestate
gesticulate
glaucoma
glossary
grandiloquent
graphic
gratuitous
gravamen
gregarious
grimace
grisly
guerdon
guile
gustatory

H

hackles
hackneyed
halcyon
harbinger
harridan
heinous
heretic
heterogeneous
hiatus
hibernal
hirsute
histrionic
holocaust
homily
homogeneous
hortatory
hoyden
humility
hummock

husbandry
hustings
hybrid
hyperbole
hyperborean
hypothecate

I

iconoclast
ideology
idiom
idiosyncratic
ignominious
illusive
imagery
imbibe
imbue
immolation
immure
immutable
impalpable
impasse
impassive
impeach
impeccable
impecunious
imperturbable
impervious
implacable
implementation
implicit
imply
imponderable
importune
impotence
impregnable
imprimatur
improvident
impugn
impunity
impute
inadvertence
incantation
incarcerate
incarnadine
incarnation
inchoate
incidence
incipient
incisive
incognito

incompatible
incongruous
incontinent
incorrigible
incredible
incredulity
incredulous
increment
incriminate
incubus
inculcate
incumbent
indict
indigenous
indigent
indolent
inductive
indulgent
ineffable
ineluctable
inept
inertia
inexorable
inexpugnable
infallible
infer
ingénue
ingenuous
ingratiate
inherent
inhibit
inimicable
iniquitous
innate
innocuous
innuendo
inorganic
insatiable
inscrutable
insensate
insidious
insipid
insolent
insolvent
insouciance
insular
intaglio
integral
integument
intelligentsia
interceptor

intergalactic
interim
interlocutory
internecine
interstellar
interstices
intestate
intimidate
intransigence
intrepid
intrinsic
introvert
inundate
inured
invalidate
invective
inveigh
inveterate
invidious
invoice
irascible
irony
irrelevant
irrevocable
isotope
itinerary

J

jargon
jejune
jeremiad
jingo
journeyman
jowl
judicious
juncture
jurisprudence
juxtapose

K

kaleidoscope
kinetic

L

lachrymose
laconic
laity
lament
larceny
largess

latent
lateral
laudable
lechery
lectern
legacy
lethargy
levity
lexicographer
lexicon
libel
libido
libretto
licentious
limbo
lissome
litany
literal
literati
litigation
livid
loquacious
lubricity
lucid
lucrative
ludicrous
lugubrious
luxuriant
lyrical

M

macadam
macerate
Mach
machination
maelstrom
magnanimous
maladroit
malapropism
malcontent
malefactor
malevolent
malign
malingerer
malleable
mammal
mandate
mandatory
mania
manifest
manumit

mastodon
maudlin
maunder
mauve
maxim
mayhem
meander
median
mediate
melee
mendacious
mentor
mercurial
meretricious
mesa
mesmerize
metaphor
metaphysical
meticulous
miasma
microcosm
microsecond
milieu
militant
millennium
minaret
minion
miniscule
misanthrope
misapprehension
miscreant
misogynist
missile
missilry
mitigate
modicum
modulation
moiety
molecule
mollify
momentum
moor
moratorium
morbid
mordant
mores
morganatic
moribund
mote
motley
mugwump

mulch
mundane
munificent
murrain
mutable
mutual
myopic
myriad
mystic

N

naive
nascent
natal
neap
nebulous
necromancy
nefarious
negotiable
nemesis
neophyte
nepotism
neutron
nirvana
nomadic
nonchalance
nosegay
nostalgia
noxious
nubile
nucleus
nugatory

O

obdurate
obeisance
objectively
objurgation
oblation
obligatory
oblivion
obloquy
obsequies
obsequious
obsidian
obsolete
obstetrician
obstreperous
obtuse
occident

occult
odalisque
odious
odium
offal
offertory
officious
olfactory
ominous
omnipotent
omnipresent
omniscient
omnivorous
onerous
onus
opaque
opportunist
opprobrium
optimism
optimum
option
opus
orbit
orgy
orison
ornithology
orotund
orthography
oscillator
ostensible
ostracize
overweening
oxidation

P

pachyderm
paddock
paeon
palatable
palliative
palpable
palpitation
panacea
pandemonium
panegyric
panoply
parable
paradigm
paradox
paragon
paramour

paranoiac
parapet
paraphrase
parasite
pariah
parity
parlous
parochial
parody
paroxysm
parsimonious
particle
parturition
passé
pastiche
pathfinder
pathological
pathos
patina
patriarch
patrimony
paucity
payload
peculation
pecuniary
pedagogue
pedant
pediment
pejorative
penchant
pendulous
penitent
pennate
pensive
penurious
perdition
peregrination
peremptory
perennial
perfidious
perfunctory
perigee
peripatetic
periphery
peristyle
perjury
pernicious
peroration
perquisite
persiflage
perspective

perspicuity
perspicuous
pertinacious
peruse
perversity
petulant
pharisaical
philology
phlegmatic
phobia
physiognomy
physiological
picaresque
piebald
pique
piscatorial
plagiarize
plangent
platitude
platonic
plausible
plebeian
plebiscite
plenary
plethora
poignant
polemic
polity
polyglot
porphyry
portentous
posthumous
postprandial
potpourri
pragmatic
precedence
precept
preciosity
precipitate
précis
preclude
precocious
predatory
predicate
predilection
preeminent
preempt
prehensible
premonitory
preponderance
prerogative

presage
prevaricate
primogeniture
primordial
privy
probes
probity
proclivity
procrastinate
prodigal
proficient
profligate
progenitor
prognosticate
projectile
proletarian
prolific
prolix
promulgate
propagate
propellants
propensity
prophylactic
propinquity
propitious
proponent
propulsion
prosaic
proscenium
proscribe
proselytize
prosody
protagonist
protégé
protocol
proton
prototype
provenance
provender
provincial
provocative
proximity
proxy
pseudonym
psyche
psychiatry
psychopathic
psychosis
pterodactyl
puerile
punctilious

pundit
pusillanimous
putative

Q

quadruped
quagmire
quandary
quarantine
queasy
querulous
quietist
quietus
quintessence
quorum

R

rabid
radar
radioactive
radium
ramification
rampart
rancor
rapacious
rapprochement
rational
rationalization
raucous
reactionary
reactor
recalcitrant
recherché
recidivism
reciprocal
recluse
recondite
recreant
recrimination
recusant
redaction
redolent
redundant
refection
refractory
refulgent
refurbish
refutation
regimen
relegate

relevant
remonstrate
renaissance
rendezvous
repartee
repertory
replete
reprehensible
reprobate
reproof
require
rescind
residue
resilient
respite
restive
resurgent
reticent
reticulated
retrospective
reverie
revile
revulsion
ribald
rime
risible
robot
rocket
rococo
rood
rostrum
rotunda
rudimentary
ruminate
rustic
rusticate

S

sacerdotal
sacrilegious
sacrosanct
sadism
salient
salubrious
salutary
salver
sanctimonious
sanguine
sapid
sapient
sarcasm

sardonic
sartorial
satellite
satiate
satire
saturnine
satyr
savant
scarify
scatological
schism
scion
scrupulous
scrutiny
scurrilous
secular
sedentary
sedulous
semantics
senescence
senile
sensory
sensual
sensuous
sententious
sentient
septic
sepulcher
sequacious
sequester
seraph
serried
servile
sibyl
simian
simile
similitude
simony
simulacrum
simulated
sinecure
sirocco
skeptic
skittles
slander
sleazy
sluice
smug
sobriety
sobriquet
sodality

solicitous
soliloquy
soluble
somnolent
sonar
sonorous
sophist
sophistication
soporific
space
spacecraft
spasmodic
spate
spatiography
specious
spectrum
splenetic
spoliation
spontaneity
spoonerism
sporadic
spurious
squalid
squeamish
staccato
staid
stamina
status
statutory
stealth
stereotyped
stigma
stilted
stipend
stoic
stolid
stratagem
strategic
stratum
stricture
strident

stultify
suave
subjective
sublimate
subliminal
subsidiary
subsidy
substantive
subterfuge
succinct
supercilious
superficial
superimpose
supernal
supernumerary
supersonics
supervene
supine
suppositious
surcease
surfeit
surname
surreptitious
surveillance
suture
sycophant
syllogism
symmetry
synonym
synthesis

T

taciturn
talisman
talon
tangible
tantamount
tarn
tautology
tawdry

telemetering
teleology
temerity
temporal
tenable
tendentious
tenebrous
tenet
tenuous
tenure
termagant
terminology
terrapin
terse
testy
therapeutic
thermonuclear
threnody
thwart
timbre
titular
tocsin
tonsure
torpid
tortuous
torturous
touchstone
toxic
tractable
traduce
transcendentalism
translucent
transpire
traumatic
trenchant
trencherman
trepidation
triolet
trite
troglodyte
trope

truckle
truculent
trumpery
truncate
tumbril
tumid
tundra
turbid
turgid
turpitude
tutelary

U

ubiquitous
ukase
umbrage
unconscionable
unctuous
undulation
unilateral
unmitigated
untenable
uranium
urbane
ursine
usurpation
usury
utopia
uxorious

V

vacillate
vagary
valedictory
valid
vampire
vapid
vehement
venal
venerable

venial
verbatim
verbose
vermicular
vernal
vertiginous
vestige
viable
vicarious
vicissitude
vindicate
vindictive
virago
virulent
viscid
vitiate
vitreous
vitriolic
vituperation
vivisection
vociferous
volatile
volition
votary
vulnerable

W

warhead
warranty
welter
whimsical
whorl
wraith

Z

zealot
zealous
zenith
zenophobe

A Sampler of Computer and Internet Terms

In the closing decades of the twentieth century, our living language has been enriched by the introduction of computer terms. Thousands of words and idioms were created to accommodate the new technology, and we are now fairly comfortable as we listen to masters of the new universe talking about *bytes, browsers, chat rooms, CD-ROM, debugging, coaxial cables, hackers, crackers, cybernetics, push technology,* and so on.

The following selection is a useful guide through the basic terms that your parents and grandparents never heard about.

WORD	MEANING
abort	to cancel a command
access provider	a company that helps in gaining entry to the Internet
acquire	to obtain a file
acronym	a word formed from the initial parts of the other words, for example, BASIC = <u>B</u>eginner's <u>A</u>ll-Purpose <u>S</u>ymbolic <u>I</u>nstruction <u>C</u>ode
afaik	e-mail abbreviation for "as far as I know"
afair	e-mail abbreviation for "as far as I remember"
algorithm	a series of instructions useful in problem solving
alpha testing	the first steps in testing a new software product
analog computer	a computer that allows representation to vary along a continuum
annotate	to add explanatory notes to text; to make textual explanations
append	to add information at the end of a file
applet	an exclusive program for a small, specific job
archive	a filing system for information to be stored for a long time
arrange	to organize the icons on the screen neatly
artificial intelligence	using computers to simulate human thinking
associate	guiding a computer so that a particular file will always be processed by a particular program
attributes	the properties of files in MS-DOS and similar operating systems
audit trails	records that show how data was entered into the computer
backtracking	a trial-and-error problem-solving method
backup copy	program copy that can be used to restore missing or damaged files
bandwidth	the speed at which a communication system can transmit data
bang	an exclamation mark ("!")
bank switching	using more than one set of memory chips at different times while assigning them the same addresses
banner	a page with a name in large letters, identifying a printout
bare metal	computer hardware
baud	a device that measures the speed with which information is transmitted
bells and whistles	fancy features added to a computer program
benchmarks	programs used in the testing of the performance of a computer or some software items
beta testing	second series of tests of a new software product
binary addition	basic arithmetic operation performed by computers
bit	stands for "binary digit." The only two possible binary digits are 0 and 1.

WORD	MEANING
bitnet	a wide-area network connecting university computer centers
black widow	a destructive computer program
board	a printed circuit for a computer
bogus	refers to anything that is phoney, incorrect, or valueless
bomb	to flop, to crash
boot	to start up a computer
bounce	to return something to its sender
brittle	operational but easily disrupted by slight changes in conditions
brownout	extended period of insufficient power line voltage
browser	computer program that allows the user to read hypertext on files or on the World Wide Web
buffer	a holding area for data
bug	a program error
byte	amount of memory space (normally eight bits) needed to store one character
cache	a storage place for data to avoid having to read it from a slower device such as a disk
CD-ROM (Compact Disk Read-Only Memory)	an optical disk holding computer data
cell	a unit of information that forms a building block for a chart or database
chat room	a simulated area in which users can communicate with each other in real time
circularity	problem that arises when a computer cannot finish a task until it has already finished it—a Catch-22 situation
clear	to make a screen go blank
clone	a computer that is an exact imitation of another; similarly with a software product
close	to exit a program and remove it from the computer's memory
coaxial cable	a cable consisting of a single conductor inside insulation and a conductive shield
COBOL (Common Business-Oriented Language)	a programming language for business data processing
compatible	able to work together (as in "My printer is compatible with my IBM")
computer	a machine capable of carrying out instructions on data
computer conferencing	the use of computer networks to enable people to communicate in real time while working together
configure	to set up a computer or program for a particular purpose
console	main keyboard and screen of a computer
cracker	a rogue who breaks into a computer via the Internet and uses it without authorization
crippleware	software distributed free as a "come-on" in an incomplete version
cryptography	the technology of encoding information to keep it from unauthorized eyes
cursor	a visual indicator on a computer terminal that shows the position of the next entry
cybernetics	the study of how electrical and mechanical systems are controlled

WORD	MEANING
cyberspace	the part of our world that exists in computer systems rather than in any specific location
daemon	a continuous background program that is activated by a particular event
daisy chain	connecting devices in sequence with cables
daisy wheel	a printer that uses a rotating wheel as a type element
database	collection of data stored on a disk for ease in retrieval
deadlock	a standstill in which each of two processes is waiting for the other to do something
debug	to make a program free from errors
decibel	a unit for expressing relative difference in power
decoder	a circuit that recognizes particular patterns
dedicated	limited to only one function
delete	to take out an unwanted item
deselect	to instruct the program that you do not want to work with a particular object
deskew	to straighten
desktop	a whole computer screen, representing one's workplace
digital computer	one that represents information in discrete form
dingbats	special characters that are neither letters nor mathematical symbols
directory	an area on a disk where the names and locations of files are stored
disk	a round, flat device coated with a magnetic substance in which computer data may be filed
document	a file that contains a text to be printed
dot	a period (.), often used in file names or Internet addresses
download	to transmit material from a central computer to a smaller one
drag	to use a mouse to move an object
dump	to transfer data from one place to another
echo	to send information back to its origin
edit	to review a file and make changes in it
e-mail	transmission of messages by a computer from one person to another
emoticon	a typewritten symbol for a facial expression, often used in e-mail; for example, :) denotes a grin, and–) = tongue in cheek
encryption	the act of converting information into a code to keep unauthorized people from reading it
envelope	the imaginary outline enclosing an object. "Pushing the envelope" means working close to, or at, the limits
environment	the display and human interface provided by software
ergonomics	the science of designing products and working environments to suit human needs
execute	to do what an instruction says to do
export	to save a file in an altered format
extension	a program that enhances the power and ability of the operating system
fencepost error	programming mistake caused by doing something one less or one more time than was necessary
fiber optics	cables that carry light rather than electrical energy

WORD	MEANING
field	some part of a record in a database that contains one piece of information
file	a block of information stored on disks, tapes, or similar media
flame	an irate e-mail message
flowchart	a schematic representation of a sequence of operations
font	a complete set of printing type of one size and face
footprint	the amount of space on a work unit that a device takes up
format	an arrangement of information that is stored or displayed
fractal	a shape that contains an infinite amount of fine detail
gateway	connection between different computer networks
gigabyte	approximately one billion bytes (10^9)
glitch	false or spurious signal that occurs inside a computer, generally caused by a brief, unwanted surge of electrical power
graphics	the use of computer output devices to produce pictures
hacker	an exceptionally skilled computer programmer; also, one who breaks into computers without authorization
handshaking	the exchange of signals between two computers to indicate that data transmission is going ahead successfully
hard copy	a printout of computer output
heuristic	a problem-solving technique that benefits from trial-and-error
hierarchical	arranged in such a way that some items are above or below others
histogram	a graphic representation of a frequency distribution in which the bars indicate how many times something occurs
hit	an occasion on which someone looks at a web page
icon	small picture on a screen that represents a particular object, group of files, or operation
information superhighway	a network of electronic and digital communication equipment linking homes/offices to the Internet
initialize	to prepare a clean tape for use
input	information that is fed to a computer
integrated circuit	an electronic device with many miniature transistors and other circuit elements
Internet	a cooperative message-forwarding system that links worldwide computer networks
keyboarding	entering data through the keyboard by typing
laptop	small, lightweight computer (under 8 lbs.) with a flip-up screen
legacy	anything remaining from a previous version of the hardware or software
load	to transfer information from a disk into a computer's memory
matrix printer	a printer that forms letters and symbols by patterns of dots
megahertz	"million hertz" or "million cycles per second," a measure of a computer's clock speed
menu	a list of choices that appears on the screen
merge	to insert data from one file into a document from another file
microprocessor	an integrated circuit that holds the entire central processing unit (CPU) of a computer, all on one silicone chip
modem	a device that encodes data for transmission over a particular medium
module	a part of a larger system

WORD	MEANING
monitor	a device like a TV set that accepts symbols from a computer and displays information on its screen
motherboard	the principal circuit board of a computer
mouse	a computer input device that a user manipulates on a pad by pressing one or more buttons
nano	a prefix meaning one billionth (10^9) of a gram
netiquette	network etiquette; doing the right thing
nibble	a group of four bits, or half of one byte
node	an individual computer in a network
notebook	a lightweight computer that resembles a looseleaf notebook
nudge	using the arrow key, not the mouse, to move an object in small increments
number crunching	arithmetical calculations to reach a bottom line
object code	a program written in machine instructions rather than in a programming language
offset	the distance, in a computer memory, betwen one location and another
on-line	connected to a computer
orphan	the last line of a paragraph if it appears by itself as the first line of a page
output	that which a computer generates as a result of its calculations
paint program	a type of program for drawing pictures on a personal computer
parsing	using a computer to analyze the structure of statements in a human or artificial language
password	a secret sequence of characters that is required to use a computer system
peripheral	a device connected to a computer; examples: terminals, disk drives
phreak	a person who tries to defraud telephone companies
piracy	the unauthorized copying of software
pixel	one of the individual dots that make up a graphical image
port	a connection where a computer can be linked to an external device
primitive	a basic element or concept leading to the formation of larger elements or concepts
profile	a file of information that shows how the user normally wants something done
programming	the process of creating instructions for a computer to carry out
prompt	a signal that appears on a computer terminal screen to show that the computer is ready to receive input
protocol	the regulation of data transmission between computers
push technology	the allowing of information providers to deliver data directly to individuals
RAM (Random Access Memory)	a device enabling any location in memory to be found
robust	trustworthy even under varying or unusual conditions
scanner	a device that allows a computer to read a printed or handwritten page
scroll	to move information across the screen as if the screen were a porthole through which you were looking

WORD	MEANING
semiconductor	a solid crystalline substance that has electrical conductivity greater than an insulator but less than a good conductor, and whose conduction properties can therefore be manipulated easily
server	a computer that provides services to another computer
shell	a program that accepts operating system commands and causes them to be executed
software	programs that give direction to a computer
SPAM	Stupid Person's AdvertiseMent (junk e-mail)
spamming	trying to reach many people on the Internet by posting the same message to all available news groups or e-mailing it to all possible addresses
spreadsheet	a table of numbers arranged in rows and columns
stochastic	involving probability or chance; random
surfing	the practice of browsing through the contents of newsgroups on the World Wide Web
synthesizer	a machine using solid-state circuits to duplicate the sounds of musical instruments or speech
telnet	a command that lets you use your computer as a terminal
thread	a series of messages in a discussion forum, each responding to the previous one
toolbox	a group of icons that represent frequently used commands
transistor	a semiconductor device that permits a small current in one place to control a larger current in another place
trojan horse	a computer program with a concealed destructive function, such as one that would erase the disks on specified date
turnkey	a computer system that is prepared to perform an assigned task with no further preparation
twiddle	to make small adjustments in settings
typeface	the size or style of the letter or character on the type
undo	a command that allows the computer user to reverse the effects of the most recent operation
user-friendly	easy to operate
vaccine	a computer program that provides protection from disruptive viruses
vaporware	nonexistent software promoted to intimidate rivals
virtual reality	the simulation of a person's entire environment by computer
virus	a computer program that automatically copies itself, thereby infecting other disks and disrupting computer operation
wait state	a short delay when a microprocessor reads data from memory, to allow extra time for a response from the memory chips
warez	pirated software
web page	a file of information made available for viewing on the World Wide Web
widow	the first line of a paragraph when it appears by itself as the last line of a page (see orphan)
word processing	using a computer to prepare written documents
work station	a powerful microcomputer used for scientific or engineering calculations
wrap	to flow text from one line or column to the next
zoom	to focus closely on a small area of a document

SELECTED LIST OF 225 TROUBLESOME SPELLING WORDS

While developing an extensive and effective vocabulary, it is also important to be able to spell those words correctly. Some people have a natural affinity for spelling while others, regardless of their intelligence, are never quite sure about *ible* or *able*, the number of "e"s in *cemetery*, how many double consonants there are in *success* or *recommendation*, and if it's "i before e except after c," why is *neighbor* an exception.

To be sure, there are many spelling rules that are helpful. But for those of you who have struggled with memorizing those rules since the primary grades and are still uncomfortable with them, the next best thing to do (outside of relying upon your computer's *Spellcheck*) is to practice writing the troublesome words over and over again. Accordingly, we have selected 225 of the "problem" words for you to review and transcribe—five times each, at least.

A

aberration
access
accommodate
acknowledgment
acquainted
acquitted
adroit
advisability
aegis
allotment
amateur
antithesis
appellation
appraisal
archaic
ascetic
atrophy
attorneys
auditor

B

banal
barrel
benefited
besmirch
bizarre
bouillon

C

cache
cacophony
calumny
canvass
catastrophe
cemetery
censor
champagne
changeable
chattel
chicanery
chiropractor
circuit
cite
clientele
collateral
colossal
colleague
commodious
complimentary
connoisseur
consummate
corollary
corroborate
coup
cryptic
culpable
cursory
cynosure

D

dearth
debacle
decorum
defendant
deferred
deign
deleterious
delinquent
demeanor
derogatory
desultory
diphtheria
disastrous
discernible
dismissal
dread
dyspeptic

E

ebullient
eccentric
ecstasy
ephemeral
equilibrium
excel
exegesis
existence

F

financier
forfeit
fracas
fulfill
fulsome
furlough

G

genealogy
glimpse
grammar
grateful
guarantee

H

heir
hemorrhage
hindrance
hosiery
hypocrisy

I

idol
imperceptible
indelible
indict
indifference
indiscreet
indispensable
ingenious
isthmus

J

jeopardize
jewelry
juvenile

K

khaki
kudos

L

labeled
larynx
legible
liaison
license
lien
lightning
liquefy
luscious

M

maintenance
maim
medieval
mediocre
mnemonics
morgue
mortgage
mournful
mucilage
municipal

N

notable
noticeable
novacaine

O

occasionally
occurred
octopus
ordinance

P

pamphlet
parallel
parliament
pastime
pavilion
peaceable
penicillin
perseverance
personnel
phlegm
picnicking
pierce
plague
plaintiff
possession
precede
prejudice
preoccupied
privilege
procedure
prosecute
psychiatrist
pursuit

Q

querulous
queue
questionnaire
quizzical

R

racist
rarefy
rationale
recede
rehabilitate
remembrance
remittance
resonance

S

sacrilegious
scimitar
scissors
seize
sergeant
siege
site
solitary
soothe
sophomore
strait jacket
subtle
sulphur
summit
superintendent
supersede
surpass
susceptible
sycophant

T

theoretical
torrent
tortoise
tourniquet
tragedy
traitor
treadle
trifle
typographical

U

unify
unique
unkempt
usherette
usurious
usurp

V

vacuum
vague
valorous
vandalism
vermin
vilify

W

wail
waive
waitress
wangle
warrant
wharf
whimsical
wince
winsome
wrath
wrest

Y

yield
yodel

Z

zealous
zephyr

ANSWER KEY

Preliminary Test

1. a 2. a 3. a 4. c 5. b 6. c 7. b 8. c 9. b 10. a 11. c 12. c 13. b 14. d 15. b
16. b. 17. d 18. a 19. a 20. c 21. b 22. c 23. a 24. c 25. b 26. c 27. c 28. c 29. c
30. b 31. b 32. d 33. a 34. a 35. a 36. d 37. a 38. c 39. b 40. a 41. d 42. a 43. b
44. a 45. c 46. a 47. c 48. b 49. b 50. c

Exercise 1

1. nuance
2. compilation
3. articulate
4. erudition
5. random
6. lexicographer
7. covet
8. verbiage
9. survive
10. exorcise
11. intractable
12. emulate
13. advocacy
14. demagogue
15. ideological
16. cajole
17. badinage
18. efficacy
19. treatises
20. inundated
21. parables
22. contamination
23. correlation
24. immortalize
25. conjure

Exercise 2 (Parts of Speech)

1. adj.
2. noun
3. adj.
4. noun
5. adj.
6. adj.
7. adv.
8. noun
9. adj.
10. verb
11. adv.
12. adv.
13. adv.
14. adv.
15. noun
16. noun
17. adj.
18. adj.
19. adj.
20. noun
21. adj.
22. adj.
23. noun
24. adj.
25. adj.

Exercise 8 (Parts of Speech)

1. noun
2. noun
3. noun
4. noun
5. noun
6. noun
7. verb
8. noun
9. noun
10. noun
11. adj.
12. verb
13. adj.
14. noun
15. adj.
16. verb
17. adj.
18. verb
19. verb
20. noun
21. adj.
22. verb
23. noun
24. verb
25. adj.

Exercise 9

1. ecclesiast
2. ecclesiastical
3. ecclesiastic
4. Ecclesiastes
5. renaissance
6. renaissance
7. 14th c. Italy
8. eminence
9. Eminence
10. prominent, distinguished
11. correspond
12. correspondent
13. a correspondent
14. corresponding
15. survivor
16. survival
17. survival of the fittest
18. emergence
19. emergency
20. emergent
21. prevailing
22. prevalent
23. prevalence
24. compiling
25. compiler

Exercise 10

1. GON
2. PLET
3. PER
4. FOR
5. IM
6. VA
7. MIS
8. NI
9. NIC
10. EX
11. AP
12. MEN
13. PRE
14. IR
15. DO
16. PREF
17. REV
18. POS
19. IN
20. BAT
21. REP
22. HOS
23. IM
24. COM
25. FAT

Exercise 11 (Pronunciation)

1. sī´ən
2. ŏn´ər əs
3. nä ēv´
4. děs´əl tôr ē
5. hā´nəs
6. ĭn kong´grōō əs
7. măk´ə nā´shəns
8. kō´vərt
9. ěk´wiət bəl
10. ŭl tə mā´təm
11. rĭb´əld
12. rěs´pĭt
13. pŏs´chə məs
14. kwäm
15. ăp rə pō´

Exercise 12 (Pronunciation)

1. är kə pěl´ə gō
2. ô gŭst´
3. kōō
4. ěk´spō nənt
5. ĭm´pə tənt
6. ĭ rěl´ə vənt
7. lə měn´tə bəl
8. sĭz´ əm
9. tə pŏg´rə fē
10. běs´chəl
11. klăn děs´tĭn
12. kăz´əm
13. děs´əl tôr ē
14. mə nī´ə kəl
15. plěth´ər ə
16. vā´gə rē
17. dĭ zăs´trəs
18. ə kyōō mən
19. ô tŏm ə tən
20. ô tŏp´sē

Vocabulary Test 1

1. c 2. b 3. a 4. b 5. c 6. b 7. d 8. d 9. b 10. b 11. d 12. a 13. c 14. c 15. a
16. c 17. c 18. a 19. a 20. d 21. a 22. b 23. a 24. b 25. a 26. d 27. b 28. a 29. c
30. b 31. b 32. a 33. d 34. c 35. d 36. b 37. b 38. c 39. b 40. a

Exercise 15

1. tour de force
2. mélange
3. al fresco
4. bona fide
5. in medias res
6. non de plume
7. petit bourgeois
8. faux pas
9. avante-garde
10. carte blanche
11. zeitgeist
12. deus ex machina
13. magnum opus
14. status quo
15. laissez-faire
16. non sequitur
17. cause célèbre
18. sotto voce
19. dilettante
20. aficionado

Exercise 16

1. chauvinist
2. gerrymander
3. sadist
4. thespian
5. boycott
6. sardonic
7. pasteurization
8. byronic
9. bowdlerize
10. malapropism
11. quixotic
12. spoonerism
13. canter
14. mecca
15. bedlam
16. jeremiad
17. lothario
18. cesarean
19. draconic
20. philippic

Exercise 17

1. skeptic
2. hedonistic
3. herculean
4. Maecenas
5. eulogy
6. Croesus
7. epicurean
8. euphemism
9. adamant
10. philippic
11. chimera
12. Eden
13. stoic
14. jovial
15. cryptic
16. Mammon
17. paucity
18. martial
19. philippic
20. Augustan

Exercise 18

1. a. rainbowlike
   b. Iris
2. a. gay
   b. Jove
3. a. warlike
   b. Mars
4. a. volatile
   b. Mercury
5. a. conceit
   b. Narcissus
6. a. surly
   b. Saturn
7. a. loud
   b. Stentor
8. a. tease
   b. Tantalus
9. a. amorous
   b. Eros
10. a. orgiastic
    b. Bacchus
11. a. distrustful
    b. Cynics
12. a. tirade
    b. Jeremiah
13. a. diabolical
    b. Satan
14. a. tyrannical
    b. Draco
15. a. denunciation
    b. Philip

Exercise 19

1. Jezebel
2. terpsichorean
3. Augustan
4. hedonism
5. lucullan
6. Maecenas
7. draconian
8. stoicism
9. solon
10. maudlin
11. calliope
12. dionysian
13. cornucopia
14. argonaut

Exercise 20 (Parts of Speech)

1. noun
2. adj.
3. noun
4. noun
5. adj.
6. noun or adj.
7. adj.
8. adj.
9. noun
10. verb

Exercise 21 (Parts of Speech)

1. noun
2. noun
3. adj.
4. adj.
5. noun
6. adj.
7. noun
8. noun
9. verb
10. verb

Exercise 22

1. multitude
2. fervent
3. lugubrious
4. fledgling
5. metaphor
6. fraternal
7. copious
8. sumptuous
9. lamentation
10. expedite

Exercise 23

1. fledgling
2. eclat
3. relevancy
4. sanctuary
5. warp
6. allegory
7. stalwart
8. lugubrious
9. expedite
10. sumptuous

Exercise 24

1. obsequies
2. copious
3. metaphor
4. inquest
5. secular
6. multitude
7. espouse
8. fraternal
9. fervent
10. lamentation

Vocabulary Test 3

1. c 2. b 3. c 4. d 5. b 6. a 7. b 8. c 9. a 10. c 11. a 12. d 13. c 14. c 15. c
16. b 17. a 18. b 19. d 20. b 21. d 22. a 23. b 24. c 25. a 26. a 27. d 28. b 29. d
30. a 31. b 32. b 33. d 34. b 35. b 36. d 37. a 38. d 39. a 40. c

Exercise 25

1. carry
2. move
3. carry
4. see
5. yield
6. believe
7. throw
8. bear
9. lead to
10. say
11. see
12. come
13. draw
14. twist
15. hold
16. write
17. believe
18. turn
19. make
20. send

Exercise 27

1. forward | go | a group moving along
2. forward | thought | introductory act
3. bad | do | evil doer
4. together | feeling | mutual understanding
5. wrong | man | one who detests humanity
6. into | say | to accuse of a crime
7. forward | go | movement toward a goal
8. back | tighten | confined
9. in | voc | appeal to a higher power
10. between | move | came between
11. under | turn | to undermine
12. after | write | additional information
13. across | carry | convey from one place to another
14. together | time | to operate in unison
15. under | bear | endure pain
16. to | tighten | be present at
17. across | send | system of gears
18. together with | turn | having a top that can be folded back
19. apart from | believe | damaged
20. out | throw | sudden exclamation
21. back | draw | cancellation
22. between | come | interference
23. in place of | write | prohibited
24. from | lead | subtractions
25. before | go | priority

Exercise 28

1. geometry
2. hydrophobia
3. logic
4. sophomore
5. anthropoids
6. monogram
7. autobiography
8. pandemic
9. geocentric
10. genocide
11. automaton
12. telephone
13. epigraph
14. genealogy
15. chronology
16. sophist
17. pathology
18. phonics
19. hydraulic
20. panegyric

Exercise 29

1. affliction
2. agitation
3. barrier
4. deportment
5. blame
6. scorched
7. called
8. erase
9. wary
10. enliven
11. personality
12. option
13. scale
14. conversational
15. hamlet
16. corrupt
17. offensive
18. intimated
19. distinction
20. waggish

Exercise 30

1. clarify
2. malevolent
3. impracticable
4. destroy
5. complex
6. clumsy
7. harsh
8. malignant
9. monogamy
10. assemble
11. meek
12. eulogistic
13. honesty
14. birth
15. oppose
16. virtuous
17. original
18. hopeful
19. dejection
20. impracticable

Exercise 31

1. enslave
2. obscurity
3. inappropriate
4. pale
5. antisocial
6. remote
7. planned
8. cacophonous
9. orthodox
10. unwise
11. remote
12. unwise
13. rejoice
14. limited
15. history
16. hasten
17. mute
18. literal
19. normal
20. rational

Exercise 32 (Parts of Speech)

1. verb
2. noun
3. adj.
4. adj.
5. verb
6. adv.
7. noun
8. noun
9. noun
10. adj.
11. adj.
12. verb
13. adj. or noun
14. verb
15. verb

Exercise 33 (Parts of Speech)

1. noun
2. adj.
3. verb or noun
4. adj. or noun
5. noun
6. verb
7. adj.
8. verb
9. noun
10. noun
11. noun
12. noun
13. noun
14. adj.
15. noun

Exercise 34

1. prodigious
2. animosities
3. digressed
4. censure
5. prolific
6. professed
7. importuning
8. prudent
9. brevity
10. parsimony
11. perpetual
12. raiment
13. proficiency
14. deplorable
15. grossly

Exercise 35

1. glutted
2. repine
3. computation
4. flay
5. collateral
6. sustenance
7. eminent
8. prodigious
9. prolific
10. deplorable

Exercise 36

1. scrupulous
2. encumbrance
3. inclemencies
4. procure
5. prudent
6. perpetual
7. expedient
8. deference
9. propagation
10. censure

Vocabulary Test 6

1. b 2. d 3. a 4. c 5. c 6. a 7. d 8. b 9. d 10. a 11. a 12. c 13. c 14. d 15. a
16. a. 17. b 18. d 19. c 20. d 21. a 22. c 23. b 24. b 25. c 26. d 27. a 28. b 29. a
30. a 31. b 32. a 33. d 34. d 35. a 36. c 37. c 38. a 39. a 40. c 41. d 42. a 43. b
44. c 45. b

Exercise 37

1. accept
2. adverse
3. C
4. C
5. effect
6. C
7. C
8. C
9. an illusion
10. Among
11. Apprised
12. C
13. Likely
14. beside
15. compliment
16. C
17. C
18. C
19. elicit
20. healthful

Exercise 38

1. kind of
2. practical
3. C
4. C
5. principal
6. unusual
7. C
8. C
9. supine
10. C
11. C
12. C
13. flout
14. fewer
15. C
16. number
17. altogether
18. C
19. lie
20. C

Exercise 39

1. adapt
2. except
3. direct
4. adverse
5. asserted
6. credible
7. differ with
8. domineers
9. forcible
10. ingenious
11. infer
12. plurality
13. affects
14. terse
15. altogether
16. transpire
17. oral
18. adopted
19. alluded
20. affect
21. allusion
22. illusion
23. alternate
24. fetch
25. common

Exercise 40

1. who's
2. practical
3. practicable
4. officious
5. lay
6. adapt
7. its
8. ingenuous
9. implies
10. healthy
11. healthful
12. mutually
13. all together
14. may
15. already
16. officially
17. effects
18. adopt
19. advice
20. counsel
21. illicit
22. appraisal
23. contemptuous
24. credulous
25. flout

Exercise 41

1. aggravated
2. majority
3. all together
4. choice
5. among
6. council
7. illicit
8. forceful
9. referring
10. prone
11. apprise
12. verbal
13. bring
14. terse
15. adaptable
16. adverse
17. refer
18. common
19. claimed
20. Lay

Exercise 42 (Parts of Speech)

1. verb
2. verb
3. noun
4. noun
5. verb
6. verb
7. noun
8. noun
9. noun
10. verb

Exercise 43 (Parts of Speech)

1. adj.
2. verb
3. noun
4. verb
5. noun
6. noun
7. adv.
8. adj. or adv.
9. noun
10. noun

Exercise 44 (Parts of Speech)

1. adv.
2. adj.
3. noun
4. adj. or noun
5. adj.
6. noun
7. adj. or noun
8. verb or noun
9. noun
10. noun

Exercise 45

1. soporific
2. grotesque
3. brood
4. surrealist
5. attainment
6. equanimity
7. prosaic
8. nonchalantly
9. cosmos
10. meditations

Exercise 46

1. went scot-free
2. held forth
3. make amends
4. give free rein
5. eat humble pie
6. make common cause
7. makes free with
8. a labor of love
9. salad days
10. lion's share
11. kicked over the traces
12. sow his wild oats
13. caviar to the general
14. cry crocodile tears
15. hauled her over the coals
16. ran amuck
17. raised a hue and cry
18. stir up a hornet's nest
19. lies fallow
20. like a house of cards

Exercise 47

1. making a mountain out of a molehill
2. red herring
3. at the top of his bent
4. bird of passage
5. pass muster
6. come a cropper
7. put the cart before the horse
8. with tongue in cheek
9. stuck to his guns
10. draws in his horns
11. curry favor
12. pull the wool over her eyes
13. give her full rein
14. put on a good face
15. living in a fool's paradise
16. cooled their heels
17. hold a candle to
18. running the gauntlet
19. casting pearls before swine
20. straining at gnats

Exercise 48

1. in poverty
2. be quiet
3. confessed to
4. reveal my anger
5. evade him
6. went wrong
7. get in the habit of
8. forget about
9. works hard
10. understand
11. trivialize
12. speak for me
13. been a huge success
14. followed
15. give up
16. have announced their candidacy
17. abandon
18. cancel
19. support
20. says the wrong thing

Exercise 49 (Parts of Speech)

1. verb
2. adj.
3. noun
4. noun
5. noun
6. adj.
7. noun
8. noun
9. noun
10. adj.

Exercise 50 (Parts of Speech)

1. noun
2. noun
3. noun
4. verb
5. noun
6. adj.
7. adj.
8. noun
9. noun
10. adj.

Exercise 51 (Parts of Speech)

1. prodigal son
2. Greeks bearing gifts
3. Correct
4. Ides of March
5. Correct
6. Correct
7. Correct
8. like a pig
9. Correct
10. Correct
11. an imaginary feast
12. as poor as a church mouse
13. Correct
14. Correct
15. Correct

Vocabulary Test 9

1. c 2. a 3. b 4. c 5. d 6. a 7. c 8. c 9. d 10. a 11. d 12. c 13. b 14. d 15. b
16. b 17. b 18. c 19. d 20. a 21. d 22. d 23. d 24. b 25. c 26. d 27. d 28. a 29. b
30. c 31. a 32. a 33. d 34. a 35. c 36. c 37. a 38. a 39. b 40. d 41. b 42. d 43. b
44. c 45. a

NOTES

NOTES

NOTES

NOTES